The Caregiving Trap

Praise for
The Caregiving Trap

A very objective, informative and heart-warming guide for adult children who find themselves caring for aging parents, many think, simply because they are the daughter or son, they know what is best for their parent and then feel guilty because they are overwhelmed by the task. Too often I have heard, "I think we made a mistake in our decision." Reading the experiences of this author will give confidence to the reader that the solutions offered are not only professional and objective, but equally as important, they are from the heart.

—**Astrid Tertel**, caregiver

"Today is the time to make connections with our parents before time passes. Time also for the conversation of care, years before care is needed." Pamela Wilson asks the reader to appreciate the fragility of life by valuing our relationships, and to take a proactive stance by realizing that how we live now will shape the future as we age. She offers a toolbox of strategies to help the caregiver move forward with foresight, knowledge, and skills to plan for the future.

—**Tina Wells, MA**, Alzheimer's Association Colorado

Pamela Wilson has provided us with an information-rich, enormously detailed and practical, very deeply personal, and even fearless exploration and understanding of the all-too-often simply overwhelming care-giving process. It will be a book—like her practice phone number—that I keep within close reach in my own office, and imagine sharing with patients and their families for years to come.

—**Jay Schneiders, PhD., ABPP**,
Clinical Neuropsychologist & Health Psychologist

There is a phrase from Pamela Wilson's new book The Caregiving Trap that says it all: "Logic is absent from many caregiving situations as emotions take over the driver's seat." Being a nurse who has been a caregiver for over 40 years, I wish I had found Pamela's book much earlier in my life. Caring for elders is a special skill. Over the last 15 years while caring for my own aging parents, I have encountered absolutely wonderful, patient souls who clearly have a gift with this population. But the trick for the rest of us is to listen to these knowledgeable folks. Pamela is an expert who has provided heartfelt, concrete advice to guide others through this challenging process.

—**Patricia A. Herlily, Ph.D., R.N.**, CEO and Founder of Rocky Mountain Research

No one is more experienced or knowledgeable in helping caregivers and care recipients than Pamela Wilson. Pamela is an educator and a professional caregiver. She knows what works and her advice is more than theory, it has been tested in practical application.

—**John J. Horan, CMSP/CFSP**, Horan & McConaty

This book is a must read not only for any health professional interacting with the elderly and disabled individuals but also for any adult who could possibly find themselves in a care giving situation or the recipient of caregiving now or in the future. Pamela's personal and professional experience, along with extensive research, offers a compassionate, perceptive and detailed resource. Familiar scenarios, probing questions, and realistic options are presented, all with the end goal of better quality of life for both the recipient of care and the caregiver.

—**Linda Warwick**, RN Hospice and Alternative Therapy Practitioner

The
Caregiving
Trap

SOLUTIONS FOR LIFE'S
UNEXPECTED CHANGES®

PAMELA D. WILSON

New York

The Caregiving Trap
SOLUTIONS FOR LIFE'S UNEXPECTED CHANGES®

© 2016 **PAMELA D. WILSON**.

Published in New York, New York, by Morgan James Publishing. Morgan James and The Entrepreneurial Publisher are trademarks of Morgan James, LLC.
www.MorganJamesPublishing.com

The Morgan James Speakers Group can bring authors to your live event. For more information or to book an event visit The Morgan James Speakers Group at www.TheMorganJamesSpeakersGroup.com.

Disclaimers: The author of this book does not dispense medical or psychological advice or prescribe the use of any technique as a form of treatment for physical or psychological problems either directly or indirectly. The information and recommendations outlined in this book are not intended as a substitute for medical advice; the reader of this book should see a qualified health care practitioner. The intent of the author is to offer information of a general nature to support caregivers and care recipients. In the event you use any of the information in this book for yourself or for another person, which is your constitutional right, the author and the publisher assume no responsibility for your actions or results. Names, characters, places, events, stories and situations have been changed to protect individual privacy. Any resemblance to actual persons, living or dead, or actual events is purely coincidental.

Library of Congress Control Number: 2014959669
ISBN 978-1-63047-535-2 paperback
ISBN 978-1-63047-536-9 eBook

Publisher's Cataloging-in-Publication
(Provided by Quality Books, Inc.)

Wilson, Pamela D.
The caregiving trap : solutions for life's unexpected changes / by Pamela D. Wilson. -- First edition.
pages cm
Includes bibliographical references and index.
1. Aging parents--Care. 2. Adult children of aging parents. 3. Caregivers--Family relationships. 4. Parent and adult child. I. Title.

RA645.3.W557 2015   649.8084'6
                                          QBI15-600066

A free eBook edition is available
with the purchase of this print book.

CLEARLY PRINT YOUR NAME ABOVE IN UPPER CASE

Instructions to claim your free eBook edition:
1. Download the BitLit app for Android or iOS
2. Write your name in **UPPER CASE** on the line
3. Use the BitLit app to submit a photo
4. Download your eBook to any device

Cover Design by:
Kathi Dunn, www.dunn-design.com

Interior Design by:
Bonnie Bushman, bonnie@caboodlegraphics.com

In an effort to support local communities and raise awareness and funds, Morgan James Publishing donates a percentage of all book sales for the life of each book to Habitat for Humanity Peninsula and Greater Williamsburg.

Get involved today, visit
www.MorganJamesBuilds.com

Habitat
for Humanity®
Peninsula and
Greater Williamsburg
Building Partner

Dedication

This book is dedicated to my husband, Sam, for his patience, understanding, and support for my career as a professional caregiver including the countless vacations, weekends, dinners and events I have missed over the years due to last minute and unexpected client situations. Your love and support have allowed me to achieve many of my lofty goals.

Table of Contents

Preface
Meeting Barbara

The red kimono stitched with black, silver, and tan flowers came into my possession as a memento by which to remember Barbara. Until recently I was unsure of its purpose or even what it represented; all I knew was that I could not give or throw away the kimono. As I write, it sits in my lap representing the intangible value of a human life—a life forgotten during the busyness of work and daily life but remembered in quiet moments of introspection. Barbara was important to me because knowing her changed the direction of my life and created a future that continues to unfold.

At the time I met Barbara, I was struggling in a lucrative corporate position that others likely envied. I was drifting off course, not because of work, as the result of the loss of my parents and several family members within a brief span of time. I wanted my destiny to show up, like an envelope in the mail, so I would not have to keep searching for my elusive next step.

My decision to volunteer changed my life. Meeting Barbara was the catalyst that gave hope, inspiration, and courage to a young and somewhat naïve woman that the idea of helping older adults might become a career path. Creating my new career has not been an easy road—it has been a road filled with potholes, unexpected challenges and experiences—making very clear my learning gaps and opportunities. I wake every day knowing that my efforts will be of value—that I will help someone—and I remember the wisdom of the words from one of my favorite clients, "God doesn't give you everything; you have to work for it."

I was determined to find purpose and meaning in my life but struggled to identify the exact path to make this change. Because of losses in my personal life, I had lost the emotional connection to a corporate position that had at one time been interesting and challenging. The idea of changing career paths to start all over again represented a huge personal and financial risk; I was told that I was crazy and that I would fail.

In July of 1998, I completed volunteer training for a program called the Caring Connection in Marina Del Rey, California. The program's goal was to connect volunteers with homebound and isolated older adults. I was introduced to a woman named Barbara, who lived in a towering apartment building on Washington Boulevard, a few blocks from the Venice Beach pier. Because of health and physical limitations, Barbara was homebound. Her brother, Harry, lived in the San Fernando Valley and visited weekly to deliver groceries. For a period of time, I visited Barbara weekly; as the result of a move, I visited less frequently and Barbara and I corresponded by mail.

1/25/1999—My dear Pam: I just want to tell you how much I enjoyed our time together. I love to talk and you are a wonderful listener and a godsend to an old sick woman. If I can write better, I'll do so later. It's two days later, and you must be told while I can still get a brain cell working. First, you are really special. Sunshine enters the room when you enter my cell. You are all kindness. All dreams are there in your beauty, my young friend. And giving your time and exquisite hand in friendship to me has been and will ever be a miracle. I'm grateful to whatever gods there be for just knowing you. Well my dear friend, I'm getting along, nothing really worth discussing. I wish I could see the Van Gogh display at the museum but I saw most of them in and around Paris. Lucky me. Just got off the phone—guess who? Sounds like music to my old ears; my best to the lucky man in your life. It will be good to talk. Dear friend, take good care of each other. My brother says hello. xx Barbara

2/17/1999—Dearest Friend: Forgive the late note. I have battled with a cold lately. Miss you and hope your trip is successful and that the weather is good. Be careful of your driving or just walking. It's been a heck of a few months. I can't keep warm. I hope you are comfortable and well. I look forward to seeing your lovely face soon. My pen just stopped trying to write. My fingers don't do as they should. Just saw a news item about a town in Poland that triggered a brain cell. It is Kovno, and my mother spoke of it as her birthplace. It was the town to go to for any help, work, etc. A beautiful city she recalled with pleasure. Enough of this. My love to you and fond regards to Sam. Come when you can. Mi casa is su casa. Barbara.

The next time I visited Barbara, her health had taken a turn for the worse. She was receiving care at a nursing home. Barbara was in good spirits: she was positive and mentioned tiring of life. She felt that her life lacked dignity because of the level of care required to support her health. She was embarrassed to have me see a catheter bag hanging from her wheelchair. I attempted to make light of the situation by saying that these things happen to all of us sooner or later. I did my best to be positive.

A few days after my last visit, Barbara passed away. Looking back, I know she waited for my visit so she might personally say good-bye. I received the following letter from Barbara's brother several days later:

4/22/1999—Dear Pamela: My sister Barbara passed away this a.m. Thank God she is no longer suffering. As her kid brother by twenty years, I did the best I could since 1993 to look after her continually almost on a daily basis. Your friendship and concern in the time you have known her has been a source of uplifting, the likes of which I have never seen—my sister was a "oner". I'll never forget her. She really loved you as a human being and was so happy when you visited or wrote. You brightened her life at its darkest period. God bless you and your husband, Harry

Harry's letter confirms what research affirms about the importance of social relations and interactions with other people as being an important component of the everyday life and well-being of older adults.

Relationships and connecting with others support feelings of self-esteem and purpose through a contribution to common goals and involvement in common interests.

According to research, participation in social activity by older adults results in a lower likelihood of a need for institutionalization, and a lower risk of declining health, institutionalization and death.[1] This research translates to the idea that older adults who remain socially active feel that they are able to make more choices in their daily lives to support independence. If and when health does change and a move to an assisted living or skilled nursing community is necessary, opportunities for socialization within these communities is critical to support ongoing well-being and purpose for residents.

My time with Barbara was joyful, and time passed quickly. My clients like Barbara—who are care recipients—tell me they feel trapped: trapped in aging bodies, trapped by having to take multiple medications to maintain their health, trapped because of the difficulty involved in leaving home. The individuals who provide care—the caregivers—tell me the same thing. Caregivers feel trapped by responsibility, a duty to provide care, guilt, financial contributions, expectations of parents or loved ones, and an inability to discuss their true feelings about the caregiving situation.

With Barbara, I was a visitor without the responsibility and duty of care experienced by family caregivers. By relating the role of volunteering to caregiving, I am able to translate life experiences—that make the role of caregiving and care receiving a challenge—and simplify these experiences to a very personal level that is often overlooked when swept up in the emotional turmoil that the experience of caregiving delivers.

How many of you volunteer? We volunteer because we want to give back, to do something that makes us feel good. One of the many rewards of volunteering is feeling appreciated by the people we help and by the volunteer organizations we support. This feeling of being appreciated makes us want to give more time and more money to a cause in which we believe. When volunteering begins, discussions occur about projects and support, a time commitment for the project, special skills required if any, and financial contributions if relevant. We agree and we sign up.

By contrast, caregiving begins through "implied consent." A parent asks an adult child to complete a certain task: for example, grocery shopping or picking up a prescription. The task is completed, which then leads the parent to believe that the adult child has and will continue to provide care. The requests grow and grow in scope and in time commitment until the time involved represents twenty or more hours a week—much more than the average volunteer project.

Further contrasting the role of volunteering with caregiving, in caregiving there is usually the absence of being thanked or feeling appreciated. Care and support are expected. The role of caregiving sneaks up innocently on family members by way of a simple request like grocery shopping. Suddenly this simple request turns into permanent responsibility and what may seem like a burden. Why does the role of volunteering make us feel so good and the role of caregiving make us feel so bad?

William Shakespeare said, "There is nothing either good or bad but thinking makes it so." How many of you would agree with the idea that the way we think about something—in this case, caregiving—makes the experience good or bad? Is caregiving a positive or a negative experience? It depends on whom you ask. Caregivers come in all shapes and sizes and backgrounds. Caregiving responsibilities may last for years resulting in loss of free time, financial expenditures, no time to pursue hobbies or spend time with friends, and late night emergency phone calls. And that project you've been working on for years that you never seem to finish? It's on your list. You'll get around to it—someday.

Personal experiences and interactions that impact caregiving relationships occur throughout our lives; these may not be viewed as significant when they occur but are significant at the time we become a caregiver. The first is "family ties" and the reality that every child has a different relationship with a parent. My oldest brother, Tom, was seventeen years and five children apart from me. By the time I was born he was leaving home to join the Marines. If you asked us both about our parents, it is likely we would relate very different stories because his experience of our parents and my experience seventeen years later were vastly different. Think of how you have changed in the span of seventeen years in habits, personality, likes, and dislikes. Parents aren't perfect and neither are children which can make for very complicated caregiving situations.

Then there's that "one thing." How many of you remember a time when your parents didn't allow you to do something or didn't give you something that you wanted: a bicycle, approval to attend a field trip at school, a pink dress for prom, a hamster to replace the one that unexpectedly took a trip down the heating vent? These little things are not forgotten and come up again at the time a parent requests help. "Mom [or Dad] wants X, and she [or he] wouldn't let me do this when I was younger—why should I be helpful today?" These early relationship fumbles come into play in parent-child relationships years later when care is needed. Then there are the relationship fumbles that may have occurred between brothers and sisters feeling that one was favored over another or given more privileges. These "little things" reopen wounds years later that result in difficult caregiving relationships.

Then there are experiences that bring the frustrations of being a care recipient up front and center. This is the time when you, the adult child, receive a diagnosis of something. High blood pressure, thyroid problems, or some other diagnosis and you are prescribed a medication that isn't optional. Talk about events that burst your bubble or take the rose out of your rose-colored glasses. Compassion grows when caregivers experience glimpses into the daily life and challenges experienced by a care recipient.

Broken promises are the promises that parents pressure adult children to make or that adult children make to parents that later have to be broken: "I promise to take care of you at home." "I promise never to put you into a nursing home." Promises that may be practical today become impractical tomorrow when life situations—like raising children or starting a new business—occur that consume the entire schedule of an adult child.

The same applies to the health of a parent: a parent may be healthy today but need twenty four hour care after a serious health diagnosis. It's impossible to predict the future, and promises made in caregiving situations are promises that will likely be broken. Caregiving represents an imperfect world—a world where situations change and where relationships are constantly tested—and while caregivers and care recipients feel guilty admitting that they feel trapped, many are trapped by situations that have spun out of control.

Since 1999, hundreds of older adults have come into my life, sharing their incomparable journeys and wisdom including their insights and fears about aging, so that I might help others in similar situations to feel less fearful and more accepting of the care recipient experience. Hundreds of caregivers have also come into my life, expressing fear and indecision about the caregiving role. Many caregivers are relieved to admit feeling trapped and frustrated by the situation—previously believing theirs to be an isolated situation—because of feeling guilty or "being a bad person" as the result of conflicting feelings of love and hate toward a parent.

My career is dedicated to helping care recipients and family caregivers make difficult choices about care when multiple variables complicate situations. Because of my experience as a legally responsible party—a guardian or power of attorney—I am faced with making emotionally difficult choices for my clients.

I have developed an innate ability to problem solve, allowing me to ask questions and to arrive at solutions that are not always obvious. I have developed a degree of persistence in identifying solutions that require greater effort and attention to detail to benefit my clients rather than taking the easy way out to agree to lower standards of care that would be detrimental to the well-being of my clients.

I have learned that situations are more challenging because caregivers feel overwhelmed and uncertain about available choices and options. There are times when caregivers must make prudent choices because of current circumstances that that may negatively affect the parent-child relationship. When caregiving becomes a role, life becomes complicated and circumstances may feel overwhelming for the individual accepting this responsibility. There are times when being the responsible caregiver means you may not be liked or popular by others—parents and family members—who disagree with your choices.

Without positive and resilient minds, caregivers may feel like each day is a struggle. We have all experienced days when a single interaction with another person changed a good day into a day of frustration and vice versa. These are the days when the car breaks down or when a co-worker is unintentionally rude. How amazing that a single compliment or an unexpected act of kindness can add light to a day that was marginal at best. Think about this when you are having one of those days, and offer a smile or a kind word to another person.

> *Do not forget to be kind to strangers, for some who have*
> *done this have entertained angels without realizing it.*
> Hebrews 13:2[2]

Short of my fortieth birthday, after the loss of a sister, my parents, a brother, my grandparents, and most of my aunts and uncles, I found my purpose in life. This event occurred the morning after I returned home to attend my mother's funeral. I slept in my old childhood bedroom and woke to sort through my bookcase, finding my life's purpose written on a yellowed list I had made more than twenty years earlier during my last year of high school: become a forest ranger, join the Peace Corps, fly F-14s in the Air Force and help old people.

I recall eliminating the first three as impractical. I pursued the last option on the list by applying and receiving a social work scholarship that I declined in favor of being practical—working full-time and attending evening college. The time wasn't right for me to help old people as a full-time career. I believe that purpose, through life experience, finds us when the time is right, when our experience is appropriate and when we are ready to pay attention to the lessons life provides. I became a willing student when life took away many of the people I loved.

Looking back, it would not have been reasonable for anyone to rely on an eighteen-year-old with no direct or actual experience in loss to educate or speak about experiences gleaned from information read in books about other people's life experiences. Life provided me with purpose and the ability to combine multiple experiences of loss and death with the components of education and work. Since 1999, my life has been a life of service supporting older adults and families.

Ten years into my new career, another door opened by way of an unexpected opportunity that allowed me to create The Caring Generation, an educational venture to provide support and education for caregivers. In April of 2009, a local radio-station representative contacted me about developing a weekly radio program for caregivers. My only media experience was working as a sales assistant at a local television station in Omaha many years earlier. On May 9, 2009, Mother's Day, I was live and on the air. The Caring Generation was developed through trial, error, and hours of research, featuring expert interviews, practical advice, and real stories about caregiving.

Feedback from radio listeners led me to the idea of *The Caregiving Trap*. Listeners desired answers but did not want to ask questions live on air for fear of being identified by loved ones or family. While caregiving is a rewarding and noble role, caregiving can also lead to feelings of being trapped in a situation over which one has little control. The events of later life are rarely discussed until they become our day-to-day reality.

Many individuals are swept into a whirlwind of caregiving when they fail to put in place a system of boundaries and alternatives to address care needs. *The Caregiving Trap* provides a foundation about aspects of caregiving that are apparent with 20/20 hindsight but rarely before. *The Caregiving Trap* provides unique insight into aspects of relationships and care needs to allow you to make the best decisions for you, your family and loved ones.

Many care recipients and caregivers fail to seek information because of exhaustion and feelings of overwhelm. The fact that you are reading this book places you in a select group of individuals who are serious about avoiding the pitfalls of caregiving and the care industry so that your caregiving experience will be positive and successful. End-of-chapter exercises will direct you to additional information on the website, including videos and podcasts offering insight and specific solutions for your individual caregiving situation. *The Caregiving Trap* is for caregivers desiring to be well informed and confident that the choices they make are the best for their individual situation.

Losses in life offer unexpected experiences and blessings that we may not realize for years to come. While the loss of loved ones during the journey of caregiving may be heartbreaking, the experience challenges us to find ways to support our own future journey of care. Thank you for taking this journey with me. You are in the right place to find information and to gain insight to benefit you and your loved ones.

—**Pamela D. Wilson**, The Care Navigator, MS, BS/BA, CSA, NCG

P.S. To avoid confusion, I've taken liberty with wording to describe those involved in situations of care. As you read, you'll notice that the words *caregiver* and *adult child* are interchangeable except where *adult child* requires specific use. The words *parent* and *care recipient* are also interchangeable, with the word *parent* also substituting for any individual who may benefit from care. The term *care navigator* is also used in place of *care manager* or *care advocate*.

PART ONE

FOUNDATIONS

Transitions and personal struggles are part of aging that surprise us. Caregivers wear many hats and fill different roles. The idea of caregiving falls into the "romantic" idea that one takes care of family.

Chapter 1

Discovery of Life
in a Cardboard Box

- Footprints
- Train Wreck
- Derailment
- Exercise: Connecting and Reconnecting
- Tales of The Caring Generation: The Baby

Footprints

The brown cardboard box sat atop the bed in the vacant room. Sunshine streamed from the window directly above the bed onto a few thirsty plants perched on the narrow windowsill. Inside the box was an oval plastic coin purse I imagined was purchased years earlier at what my parents affectionately called a dime store. Dark green in color and made of soft plastic, the coin purse had a slit down the middle that opened like a mouth when thumb and index finger squeezed both ends. Inside the

3

coin purse I discovered a silver dollar—imprinted with AA—a date and embellished with colored jewels glued in a circle representing the number of years sober. I later learned that being given this coin is a tradition of twelve-step groups.

In the box were the front pages of greeting cards with pictures of flowers, wheat fields, and open prairies; the other half that would have contained a greeting or signature was cut off in a jagged path by sharp scissors. Hidden inside the bottom of the box, were a wrinkled handkerchief embroidered with the initials *SH* and a pink crystal rosary. Absent from the box was a ring of purely sentimental value that was on her hand the last time I saw her, but not with her at the time the funeral home staff arrived to pick up her body. The missing ring was never found. An employee of the nursing home likely slipped the ring off her finger just prior to or after her death. These few belongings were all that remained of Sarah's life, and I was the only interested party available to collect them.

Sarah's death struck me as significant and melancholy. Sarah lived to the age of eighty-seven. There was no one except me to mourn her passing or to shed a tear, no one except me to know or care where Sarah was buried or to visit her burial place to acknowledge the life she had lived. Cemeteries are filled with stones bearing the names of people who no one visits. My clients tell me that their greatest fear is not dying but the fear of dying alone. It disturbed me that Sarah's presence on earth was memorialized by material belongings in a solitary cardboard box that now belonged to me. I wanted to believe that life—that all of our lives—offer some legacy to a world that we may no longer inhabit.

Holding the cardboard box of belongings gave me a better understanding of the isolation that many individuals experience in the latter years of life. While many of us take for granted frequent emails or phone calls from friends or the ease of going shopping or joining groups of friends, for many older adults advancing age and poor health prohibit participation in these activities. "People with stronger social relationships have a fifty percent increased likelihood of survival than those with weaker social relationships."[3] Having friends and participating in social activities has a positive impact on quality of life.

Older adults become isolated due to loss of friends or family, limited physical mobility, and reduced income that restricts participation in activities like going out for dinner with a friend or joining an interest group. Social isolation and loneliness negatively impact quality of life in many ways that include poorer health, increased medical expenses, and moving to a community of care much earlier than expected.

Today, families are spread across great distances. When older family members age and become isolated, family is many times unaware or uninvolved of daily struggles or health challenges. I know this to be personally true. This past holiday season I learned of the passing of an uncle who lived at a distance. Because contact with my uncle and aunt consisted of written cards and visits every several years I had no idea my uncle's health had declined and would have not known of his passing if his niece had failed to respond to my holiday card. As a result of receiving a note in the mail, I had a wonderful telephone conversation sharing memories of my uncle with his niece, who knew of me but whom I had never met in person.

Sometimes it takes great loss before we are fully able to understand the value of human connection. Life passes with time and we age. Remaining connected to family is important even if contact is by email or phone. If you doubt the human desire for connection, look at the popularity of Facebook and social media and the way these allow connection to those in our present and in our past. We seek to connect even if the connection is through the convenience of a computer and the Internet.

Even though many older adults are embracing the use of technology, older adults lag in use of technology behind younger Americans. Fifty nine percent of older adults, age sixty five or older, go online, 47 percent have a high speed broadband connection and 77 percent of older adults have a cellphone. In contrast, many older adults are largely unattached from online and mobile life—41 percent do not use the Internet at all, 53 percent do not have broadband access at home and 23 percent do not use cellphones. Those not using the Internet cite health or physical issues, a perceived lack of benefit from use of the Internet, and perceived difficulty in learning to use technology.[4]

These statistics lend support to one way in which Sarah's life became disconnected. She was connected while she was physically active and dedicated to a career. After retirement she slowly became isolated and then lost the ability to communicate and to connect with others in a socially acceptable manner because of a diagnosis of Alzheimer's disease. The result was a life of isolation and health declines during the final years of her life.

For many, like Sarah, life will become unexpectedly derailed by loss, a diagnosis of poor health, or other unexpected events. For many, the life hoped for in retirement will be very different from life changed by unexpected circumstances. Older adults, regardless of physical diagnosis, who are able to embrace technology and learn to use the technology, specifically the Internet, have the ability to remain socially connected to family and friends.

Train Wreck

Leaving with the box that represented Sarah's life, I recalled the first time we met. I walked down the long hallway of a familiar building that I had visited many times for other purposes. This particular building was the type of place older adults picture in their minds with visions of fear and disgust, the type of place that older adults hope to avoid calling their home. My footsteps echoed as I walked across the linoleum floors of the nursing home.

In this particular building, familiar scents of urine and bodily waste filled the air. Residents propelled themselves down hallways in wheelchairs, holding out their hand to greet me as if I was someone who knew them. I greeted each one with a cheerful smile and a comforting hello, hoping a kind soul would return the favor if I ever found myself in a similar situation. Soft voices cried, "Help me," similar to the pleas of a fairy tale princess imprisoned in a castle, pleading for rescue.

The hallways were dimly lit. Employees moved about slowly and deliberately. As is common in many nursing homes, rows of residents in wheelchairs were parked in front of the nursing station so they could easily be monitored. Most of these residents sat, bodies leaning forward uncomfortably with nodding heads, asleep in their wheelchairs, likely dreaming of the comfort and familiarity of a prior existence.

I made my way to the "locked" unit, a place where residents, many with memory loss and those considered wanderers or safety risks, made their permanent home. I sought out the nurses' station and explained the reason for my visit: I was the proposed guardian for Sarah.

The nurse and I spoke briefly about Sarah's background and about how she had come to live at Plum River Care Center four months earlier. Sarah previously lived in a week-to-week motel in an unsafe area of town. Her own home became uninhabitable due to hoarding and unpaid utilities; her yard was filled with junk automobiles and scrap metal. Sarah missed several rent payments at the motel, resulting in the property owner calling the police to evict Sarah or to encourage her to bring her rent payments current.

A resident of the motel, Betty, befriended Sarah. Betty told the police that Sarah did have money to pay—Betty reported Sarah to possess nearly half a million dollars. How is it that someone with resources of nearly half a million dollars became isolated, at risk, and lived in a dilapidated motel?

Further investigation by the police and county social service workers confirmed that Sarah had become a loner. Sarah was seen each day walking the neighborhood streets, wearing soiled clothing, muttering to herself. She appeared harmless and said hello if approached but rarely uttered more than a single word in response to questions.

Neighbors attributed her odd behavior to senility and left her alone. Her home, hidden behind a tall thicket, had grown unattended for years with rubbish collecting in her yard. Neighborhood children called her "crazy Sarah" and told tall tales that her home was haunted. Sarah's life was a train in slow motion moving toward eventual derailment.

Sarah told Betty she became fearful of strangers and began isolating herself after being threatened by a homeless man as she walked home from the bus stop. Shortly after this incident, Sarah reported that she returned to drinking alcohol.

Betty reported to police and county social workers that Sarah had a large envelope of cash that eventually ran low resulting in the situation of unpaid rent. Sarah could not recall the location of Sarah's bank. No mail was discovered at her home and no mail was forwarded to the motel. Sarah was a person living under the radar of general society failing to call attention to her needs and barely existing with the help of a single honest individual.

Sarah was removed from the motel by county Adult Protective Service workers and placed at Plum River Care Center. After months of investigation, her family was located but declined to become personally involved or responsible for Sarah. In fact, her family wanted nothing to do with Sarah. She had two sons and extended family who harbored years of hatred for acts Sarah had allegedly committed many years prior.

Sarah's medical chart included a diagnosis of Alzheimer's disease, unspecified mental illness, and other chronic disease. I realized that Sarah's decline had begun many years earlier. With no consistent or regular personal contact, there was no one to notice or to suggest beneficial medical care. As do most individuals with a diagnosis of memory loss, Sarah lacked the mental insight to realize her memory and her health were failing. Neighbors watched her decline but had no idea how to help or if there was family to contact.

The nurse directed me to Sarah, who sat in a lounge chair near other residents. So as not to startle, I walked over and knelt down to be at Sarah's eye level. Before I could say a word, her blue eyes flashed, she waved both arms high in the air, and her sharp, high-pitched voice screamed, "Leave me alone! I don't want to be bothered!" Not wanting to make a scene, I quickly stood up, turned around, and walked back to the nurses' station like a child being sent to stand in the corner as the result of bad behavior.

The nurse looked at me, smiled, and whispered as if to console me, "Don't feel bad; she doesn't get along with anyone." Notes in Sarah's chart reported frequent verbal and physical altercations with other residents. If another resident was served a meal prior to Sarah, she attempted to grab their plate. If a resident using a walker attempted to pass Sarah, she struck out to reach for the walker or attempted to hit the resident. There were other documented incidents of Sarah tripping other residents by pulling on their dangling oxygen cords as they passed by in the hallway.

I suspected Sarah had a life of ongoing and unexpected circumstances that took her off course. I was curious and wanted to know more. I looked at Sarah and took a seat nearby to watch for clues about her behavior that might shed light on her personality earlier in life.

I watched as the fingers on her right hand shifted from one crystal pink bead to the next on the rosary she clutched tightly. I watched the resident to her left wrapped snugly in a hand-crocheted afghan as she slept peacefully in her recliner. The resident to Sarah's right listened to music through headphones a CD player perched in his lap. His head bobbed to the left and the right with the beat of the music. Suddenly a loud thud broke the silence. Another resident had accidentally knocked a pile of books off a table to the floor. A resident working on a jigsaw puzzle shouted profanities in disappointment as pieces of the puzzle tumbled and bounced across the floor.

The commotion startled the sleeping woman to Sarah's left who began to cry inconsolably. Sarah turned to the woman, smiled with her blue eyes twinkling, and took the woman's hand in hers to caress in an attempt to comfort and stop tears streaming down the woman's cheeks. In that moment of madness, books crashing to the floor, jigsaw puzzle pieces tumbling across the floor, and sweet dreams broken by noise, I witnessed a softening in Sarah's face along with an expression of compassion and kindness. I stood slowly from my chair so as not to cause further disruption. I called my colleague to accept Sarah's case as I walked out of the building.

After being appointed Sarah's guardian, I held a meeting with the staff at Plum River to learn more about her background and care needs. I discovered that the steroids Sarah was prescribed to treat frequent pneumonia had an adverse effect on her behavior, making her aggressive, agitated, and threatening toward others. Once the steroids were discontinued, Sarah became less agitated and more relaxed. There were no more altercations with other residents. She willingly accepted my visits and began telling me stories about her life.

My second goal was to find a care center more compatible with Sarah's prior life history. I found Green Meadows, a care center in a quiet suburb with an available room. Sarah was assigned the bed next to a window overlooking a small park where bird and squirrel feeders had been placed to entertain the residents.

At the time in life when a nursing home becomes a permanent home, the little pleasures like a bed next to a window with a view are a highly requested luxury. At a time of life when comfort, compassion, and preservation of dignity are deserved, many residents of nursing homes are assigned a shared room eliminating any sense of privacy.

For individuals who are still able in mind and body, life passes slowly in a nursing home setting. Residents become completely dependent on their own self-will and determination to remain connected through participation in activities and to maintain contact with friends from the outside world. While family and friends visit when loved ones first move, visits become fewer and far in between because many dislike visiting nursing homes. Some residents living in nursing homes never receive visits from anyone except staff members. For those who are forgetful or confused, the absence of human connection and contact leaves them in a world where bodies and minds fade away, little by little, toward eventual death.

As I grew to know more about Sarah's life, I discovered she was an executive assistant for an attorney who litigated high-profile cases. She told the story of marrying young and described physical and emotional abuse from an alcoholic husband. Her father was also an alcoholic. When her two sons were eight and twelve, she packed a suitcase and disappeared into the night, never to return. As was common years ago, her husband denied any part in her leaving by telling their two young sons that their mother took off into the night with another man. This false tale led to hatred that her sons and family were unable to emotionally resolve.

As much as Sarah reported that she attempted to mend relationships, her sons refused all contact. When I called to tell her sons of her impending death, their response was unchanged: they wanted nothing to do with their mother. Their only memories were of a selfish woman who left with another man, and never returned, presenting an inaccurate story that eliminated the possibility of any type of relationship with their mother.

As her Alzheimer's progressed, Sarah believed she lived in the small town where she was born. The park outside her window represented fields in walking distance of the back porch of her home. Her sons attended school and came home at the end of each day to study and to help around the farm. There was no mention of her husband, only her parents and pleasant stories of her mother. There were stories of Sarah's daily responsibility of milking cows and gathering eggs which she recalled as hard work—not with fond memories. Her father worked long hours in the fields and occasionally at the local rail yard. Sarah recalled he was never without a bottle of whiskey or a cruel word.

This was the mental world Sarah lived in until her death, a world in which she was content with memories of living with her mother and raising her two young sons. Maybe this was Sarah's way of mentally working through relationships that were imperfect during her life so that she could pass through this world into the next world at peace.

After her death, Sarah's sons gladly accepted ownership of property and funds remaining in bank and investment accounts as payback for a lost childhood. Sarah had done well for herself during her working years likely knowing that she would be alone and that family would not provide care for her when the time came.

Sarah's financial wealth could have paid for any type of preventative and ongoing care that Sarah might have needed. Due to the diagnosis of

Alzheimer's and no one available to support or to coordinate care before the disease advanced, the availability of money offered little benefit during the last several years of her life.

Absent were relationships with family or friends who might have helped to plan and provide for her needs. After I became involved, I did my best to ensure that Sarah did not lack for care at the end of her life. Her family remained uninvolved. I am the one to remember her fondly, to visit the marker bearing her name, and to honor her life.

Derailment

Connections with family, friends, and acquaintances become more important as we age. Many of us unintentionally allow connections to slip away by not maintaining regular contact. This happens little by little as our lives become immersed in work, raising families, committing to careers, and engaging in other activities. Distance also becomes a factor in remaining connected when moving away from a hometown or relocating for employment opportunities.

Connections and interpersonal relationships are important. Other than family members, how many close connections or friends do you have? Responses to this question today versus several years ago may be drastically different, meaning that most of us have fewer connections and less time to connect. The frenetic pace of life allows less time to devote to meeting new people, building relationships, and establishing friendships. Friendship is an activity that requires interest, time, and devotion much like courting a new partner. While friendships seem less important during the years when married or when raising children, friendships are an extremely beneficial and important component of life as we age.

It surprises me when I ask older adults about interests or hobbies and they respond with a blank stare or have no response. Older adults, more men than women, report having few hobbies or interests; they do not read, play board or card games, create woodworking projects, or participate in physical activity or exercise. The television has become a constant companion, a source of entertainment and many times the only source of interpersonal contact.

To support and maintain friendships, one must have something to offer and to share. Hobbies and shared interests support friendships and social contacts. If one has few interests, I suggest cultivating interests today that may be valuable in establishing and maintaining relationships. It is also important to learn the benefits of sharing interests and common goals, whether discussing hobbies or interests, chatting about news or societal trends, or sharing the physical interaction of a sport or exercising together. People are drawn to other people who are interesting. To make and maintain friendships one must become interesting, embrace learning, and have something to offer to others.

The benefit of connecting with others by establishing and maintaining relationships builds the ability to relate to others and to establish support networks. When life changes or throws an unexpected curve, relationships with others provide support. Relational skills include patience, trustworthiness, empathy, reliability, and influence. Building these skills requires the ability to remain open-minded, to seek new information, to be a good listener, and to assume responsibility for managing the change that occurs in life. Some of these skills are not easily learned for people who are impatient, who lack empathy or sensitivity, or who are unreliable. These are skills not to be taken for granted, especially in anticipation of the idea of eventually needing care and relying on others for support and assistance.

Let me give an example of a situation where one has the ability to use these skills but may miss an opportunity. You meet a stranger at a networking event or social occasion. This person says something in the initial conversation. Their statement may be as simple as an interest or an opinion of which you disagree. Rather than ask a curious question to understand a different point of view, your brain turns off. You are finished speaking with this person. End of story, bye-bye, you walk away. This situation represents a lost opportunity to make a potential friend.

How many times, when in this situation, did you exercise patience, continue the conversation, and find points of commonality and interest? How many times did you find value and interest in considering a different opinion and fostering a business relationship or friendship? How might it be a challenge to your brain to attempt to consider a different viewpoint? Differences and new perspectives can be fascinating if you choose to be open-minded.

Many individuals, especially those who are uncomfortable in social situations, will blurt out words, any words, as an opening line that fails because of social inexperience. Think of building friendships as an exercise in becoming attractive to others. This requires an opening line, a topic of discussion, establishing an activity or interest that two people have in common, and a little bit of patience. Rather than immediately judging a person and turning away, allow a few minutes to become acquainted and to establish commonalities. Then offer to reconnect at a later time or date and continue networking.

Maintaining connections has multiple benefits:

1. The ability to communicate with those in our past and the opportunity to reminisce
2. The ability to build and maintain extended family connections that provide opportunities to gather and learn about history and heritage
3. Building communication and follow-up skills by way of personal visits, phone calls, emails and other actions required to maintain relationships
4. The ability to value family and friends as important components of a successful and happy life

Health benefits accrue from being socially active. These include living longer and boosting the body's immune system. According to Krames Staywell, these include:[5]

- Potentially reduced risk for cardiovascular problems, some cancers, osteoporosis, and rheumatoid arthritis
- Potentially reduced risk for Alzheimer's disease
- Lower blood pressure
- Reduced risk for mental health issues such as depression

The benefits of being socially connected extend to other parts of life. Communication skills are important in the workplace, as well as the ability to follow through to manage aspects of home and personal life. Maintaining relationships offers support when help is needed; people need people. Life becomes richer and fuller as a result of connecting with others.

Opportunities to connect and to meet others exist if one is willing to make time and exert the effort associated with participating in activities, including having an open mind and a sincere interest in learning technology and in meeting new people. If one is retired, time to socially and personally connect should not be a deterrent. If transportation is a concern, many communities offer ride programs and local transportation for older adults. Volunteer groups from community organizations like the Red Cross have individuals willing to provide free or low-cost transportation.

Computers and the Internet offer significant benefits to reduce loneliness among older adults—especially those who are isolated because of chronic illness or physical disability—who have a positive attitude toward learning to use a computer and accessing the Internet. A study completed in the Netherlands served to reduce emotional isolation by supporting contact with family and friends through email, by providing participants with a meaningful way to pass time and by strengthening self-confidence as the result of learning to use a computer and the Internet; this self-confidence extended to other life activities.[6]

For individuals with a busy career and home life, time may be limited but should not be an eliminating factor in building social relationships. A practical goal to maintain and make new connections is to attend two social events each month. My suggestion is to find a career group and a group of personal interest and commit to monthly attendance. Once you have made new connections, missing monthly meetings will be viewed as a lost opportunity to spend time with good friends. Activities and events that take one out of a normal routine are beneficial to emotional well-being, self-esteem, and health.

Begin today to investigate potential groups of shared interest whether through in person groups or groups through the Internet. This action is especially important if you are one of the millions of unpaid family caregivers who give their time, who sacrifice their career opportunities or who provide financial support to a loved one. Dedicated caregivers often feel that the provision of care is a responsibility requiring 100 percent dedication and proceed to neglect their own emotional, physical, and social needs. Many caregivers become isolated as a result of caregiving responsibilities. Connecting with others in the role of a caregiver provides emotional support and allows the caregiver to know that the caregiving journey does not have to be a path of isolation but may be a path of community and sharing with others who have similar experiences.

A survey of caregivers for persons with Alzheimer's disease indicates that seventy-nine percent had limited social activities, for example visiting friends or family as the result of caregiving responsibilities. Poor health was cited by 31.4% of caregivers when the person with Alzheimer's lived with them compared with 67% who reported good health when the care was alternated with a nursing home.[7]

Caregivers of persons with Alzheimer's disease often sacrifice their own well-being as a result of the care provided for loved ones. Many experience high levels of stress and poor health in addition to becoming isolated from friends and family as the result of caregiving responsibilities that expand to twenty-four hour care situations. This experience highlights the importance of caregivers identifying social outlets and using sources of care other than the provision of care— solely by the caregiver—in the home.

Research by the Alzheimer's Association indicates a long list of risks for caregivers that include risks to physical and emotional health.[8]

- Women are more likely than men to be caring for a loved one who lives in their household and to be on duty 24 hours a day.
- 37% of caregivers agreed with the statement, "I had no choice in becoming a caregiver."
- Caregivers who believed they had no choice in accepting the caregiving role or who felt captured by that role perceived the emotional stress and burden of caregiving to be significantly higher than caregivers who felt they had a choice.

You might be surprised to know all that you have in common with 126 million family caregivers in the United States. Who are these caregivers, and what are their backgrounds? You will learn what you might have in common with these caregivers in the next chapter.

Individuals, care recipients, and caregivers grow mentally and physically old because of losing interest in life and human connection. Remaining socially engaged allows the mind and body to remain resilient. There are equally as many older adults who are unhappy and suffering from debilitating illness as older adults fully enjoying life. The mental aspect of aging, as well as living a healthy lifestyle, is critical to a positive later-life experience.

Many older adults I know look at life from a positive perspective and use humor to make light of situations rather dwelling on the negative. A positive attitude is important: being active and social is important, as well as maintaining friends, especially those who are young at heart. Many older adults report that the qualities of persistence and appreciation for the little things in life make the challenging days a little easier. Caregivers would be wise to follow the wisdom of maintaining a positive attitude, persistence, and appreciation of the little things in life.

Exercise: Connecting and Reconnecting

For older adults, there is a difference between knowing, wanting, and being able to build social networks. These actions present less of a challenge for those of us who are active and still employed. What might you do each week, if only for sixty minutes to build your social network? Give thought to the following questions and what steps you might take to re-connect or to develop new relationships:

1. Consider the quality of your existing family relationships. If the relationships are not ideal, what steps might you take to improve the relationships? Is this a good place to put your effort or would you prefer to concentrate on friendships?

2. Consider the quality of relationships with your friends. How many are close enough that you might ask a favor and reciprocate? How many "good friends" do you have? If the number is less than five, set a goal of meeting and having five good friends within the next twelve months.

3. Do you have "generational" friends or acquaintances—friends with an age difference of ten or more years? How might this type of relationship be mutually beneficial? Might having younger or older friends support open-mindedness and access to different life perspectives?

4. How much time do you contribute to maintaining connections on a weekly basis? How might your life change if you committed one hour a week to developing family and friend connections in person, by telephone or through the Internet?

5. Here are four tips for expanding connections:
   a. Host a quarterly Sunday dinner and invite immediate and extended family. Ask your family members to host dinners.
   b. Establish a weekly "friend" outing whether for a meal or to an event.
   c. Join a career or social group.

    d. Identify a volunteer opportunity and commit for at least one year.

Be open and interested in all the people you meet; one of them may become a lifelong friend. Friendships are truly one of the most wonderful aspects of life, especially when they sustain through the decades.

Whatever your background or interest, increasing social connections is beneficial and supportive in many areas of life. Social connections add to quality of life and support good health. If you are a caregiver, joining with other caregivers offers many benefits.

If you are interested in accessing more tips and information about ideas presented in this chapter and about related subjects, visit http:// www.thecaregivingtrapbook.com/store and select Life in a Cardboard Box.

Tales of the Caring Generation

The Baby

How many of you are the baby in your family? I am the baby in my family, born to my mother Rose when she was thirty-five, nine years after my older brother and sister known as "the twins". Babies believe we are special—and of course we are! The baby was the last child born—maybe a surprise after a number of years since the last child maybe the only long-awaited boy or girl. The baby in the family usually enjoys a great deal of attention. Some turn out to be spoiled children, but the cuteness factor often outweighs most of the annoying behavior. Since the baby is used to being around lots of people, like older brothers and sisters and family members, the baby of the family is usually very social. There are benefits to being the baby, and no matter how old the baby becomes, he or she is still known as the baby.

How many of you have fond memories of moving away from home and being closely connected to your mother? There are so many things I remember quite fondly. Every year on my birthday—no matter where I was, usually sitting at my desk at work—my mother would call me at 1:00, the time of day I was born, to wish me happy birthday. Every year she made homemade German-chocolate cake from scratch—not out of a box, with the coconut-caramel frosting that had to be cooked over the stove. There was no better birthday cake. Three layers of chocolate cake with two thick layers of frosting—still my favorite cake to this day.

When I lived in Omaha, there were times I returned home from work to find things—food in my refrigerator that was not present in the morning when I left. I walked through my living room to discover a new photo of my parents in a frame sitting on a bookshelf. New towels in my linen closet sometimes my lawn was freshly mowed. There was always some nice type of surprise left by Mom and Dad.

After I moved to California, I returned home during the holidays when the weather was freezing cold. Note to self: Omaha is not the place to travel for Christmas when one lives in Southern California where the weather is warm all year round especially during the winter holidays. What did I find upstairs in my childhood bedroom lying on my bed but a pair of flannel pajamas, thick stockings, and slippers! The upper level of my parent's home had only two heating vents, which meant there was usually ice in frosty patterns appearing on the window panes. The wooden floors were freezing to stocking feet.

Then came the 7a.m. calls on Saturday mornings, usually because Mom knew that if she couldn't catch me then, she would not catch up with me because we would be out participating in activities all weekend, dawn to dusk. That's what twenty-and thirty-something babies do—we play.

The downside of being the baby is that even though you may be the youngest, it is likely that you will outlive most of your family members and experience several "last moments." If you have not experienced a last moment, these occur like any other moment during any given day. My sister Becky was twenty-nine years young when she made plans to drive to Chicago to live with friends and to find a new job. On I-80 eastbound, she fell asleep at the wheel of her car that flew into the air and off a bridge onto railroad tracks beneath, leading to her immediate death. I had no idea that the night before when I said goodnight, that would be the last time I would see Becky.

Amazing how life repeated itself, at least in my life. Mom had surgery after her sixty-ninth birthday and was recuperating in the hospital. The last time I saw her she was sitting up in her hospital bed. I told her I would see her for Mother's Day. She passed away weeks later. No matter how many times I called the house to speak with her she was always sleeping—or maybe pretending to sleep—I believe she knew we would never see each other again and didn't have the energy to have an emotional telephone conversation.

My father also left suddenly. He went into the hospital for a routine procedure and called me Halloween night to report his joy that Notre Dame had won a football game. We had a great conversation. Dad suffered a heart attack during the night, never regained consciousness, and passed away the next morning.

If you have mothers, fathers, brothers, sisters and other family still living, make the best of the time you have because you never know when your last see you later or talk to you later will be one of those last moments that will have to last you a lifetime. When I came home for my mother's funeral, the church was filled with neighbors and friends. I looked just like Mom but at a younger age, I recall Mom's friends and neighbors approaching: they said, "You must be the baby."

Chapter 2

Removing the Rose-Colored Glasses

- Who Are the Caregivers?
- End of the Innocence
- Risks of Average and Borderline
- Unexpected Surprises of Chronic Disease
- Exercise: Managing Caregiver Stress
- Tales of the Caring Generation: Karen and the Peanut Butter Sandwich

Who Are the Caregivers?

Who are the family members, the superheroes, the caregivers who give selflessly to others, and why do they act in this way? "Four in ten Americans are caring for a loved one with significant health issues."[9] "Almost half (46 percent) of family caregivers performed medical/nursing tasks for care recipients with multiple chronic physical and cognitive conditions."[10]

23

Giving consideration to family caregivers and the number of paid or professional caregivers, it is clear that a significant number of Americans provide services for individuals requiring support and who are unable to take care of themselves.

According to studies by AARP and the National Alliance for Caregiving, "The average U.S. caregiver is a forty-nine year-old woman who works outside the home and spends nearly twenty hours per week providing unpaid care to her mother for nearly five years."[11] When caregivers are asked why they believe their care recipient needs care, the two most popular responses are old age and Alzheimer's disease.

For most, caregiving is an unexpected journey. By the time a caregiver calls to set an appointment with me, many confess that they have carried my business card in their wallet for more than a year. Other caregivers tell me that not one but several professionals or acquaintances have recommended a meeting with me. Caregivers tell me they have listened to my radio program, visited my website, and read my articles. Why then the delay to pick up the phone? "It wasn't that bad until recently," or "I thought I could do it all" are common caregiver responses.

Many family members early in the caregiving journey are happy, energetic, and helpful, ready to jump in to rescue a loved one in need. The word *no* is absent from their vocabulary; they give and give and give. The big red *S* for superhero is secretly and proudly displayed on the caregiver's chest. Able to sweep a flight of stairs, clean filthy toilets, grocery shop at the speed of light, and make the bed after flipping the mattress, caregivers feel invincible until an event changes their daily routine. Suddenly the caregiver feels trapped in an unsustainable situation, unappreciated and resentful of the role of caregiving.

Time for caregiving is stolen from other parts of a caregiver's life. Time previously spent in healthy pursuits has evaporated: exercise or attending the gym, time with friends, participating in social activities, time with a spouse, or reading bedtime stories to a young child. The joy of caregiving disappears. The caregiver feels angry or resentful; subsequently, a sense of guilt makes the caregiver feel like he or she should be ashamed of the way they feel, and the caregiver continues in the selfless pursuit of providing care while a volcanic eruption builds inside.

Who of us hasn't experienced a similar situation, whether at work or in another role in life? We arrive to save the day, to keep the ship afloat. For a period of time, feelings of jubilation, excitement and glee light our hearts, making all the hard work and sacrifice given to this wonderful cause worth every moment of devotion. Overnight, a game-changing event sneaks up on us and deflates all remaining devotion and compassion toward our cause. The effort to save the day has become like kryptonite to Superman, destroying our inner light and energy.

Similar game-changing events happen in caregiving situations that begin with a small time commitment that then increases and extends year after year after year with no finite end in sight. Many caregivers ask themselves how they arrived at this point and what now can be done to decrease participation and the associated level of stress.

Similar to couples having their first child—and not knowing what to expect relative to the care of a newborn—is the naiveté of a caregiver not knowing the skills or actions to be taken as the health of a loved one continues to fail. While couples raising a child might recognize the added financial expense of each child, many looking back view the journey of child rearing as worthwhile. The difference is that most children are planned or at least welcomed as an unexpected blessing.

Caregiving is rarely planned. Depending on the physical, emotional, and financial consequences, caregivers may be unable to look back and see the journey as worthwhile. Some caregivers admit, honestly and with an expression of guilt, that they anticipate the day when the role of caregiving ends much like a parent anticipates the day when children move out of the home.

The feeling of "how did I get here?" occurs and is barely noticeable over time until the care recipient becomes the sole focus of the caregiver. The care recipient becomes totally dependent on the caregiver, making the caregiver feel that the responsibilities of care are the sole burden of the caregiver. At this point warning signals should be sounding. An iceberg is lurking ahead, and the caregiving ship is about to crash and sink. This sinking feeling of realizing that the caregiver has few options represents the self-fulfilling prophecy of caregiver superheroes and the caregiving trap.

Also existing are self-absorbed caregivers who desire to have total control over the care recipient and the care situation. While this situation happens unintentionally, other helpful family and friends are driven away by the negative behaviors of the caregiver. The caregiver expresses territorial tendencies and refuses outside assistance. This is another situation of danger because the care recipient becomes isolated with no one but the caregiver to whom concerns may be expressed. Situations of isolation support the potential for abuse—physical, emotional, or financial.

The feeling of "how do I work this?" is the discussion about care needs, the act of caregiving and planning that is a critical part of life not to be neglected or swept under a rug until the caregiver suddenly feels trapped after providing care for a substantial period of time. Care recipients express shock when caregivers, who have willingly sacrificed time and effort without expressing concern, all of a sudden say "no more." This sudden change represents an unfortunate situation for both individuals whose emotions run high due to feelings of being unappreciated or abandoned.

One of the most important considerations in caregiving is for caregivers and the care recipient to have ongoing discussions about concerns in order to avoid relationship breakdowns. These discussions are beneficial and practical. For family caregivers, understanding the expectations of the care recipient is critical in order to avoid situations where expectations are impractical or unreasonable. For care recipients, understanding the degree to which family caregivers are able to participate may bring disappointment. However, these honest conversations have the benefit of preserving, rather than destroying, family relationships as the care situation advances.

Hiring support by retaining professional services allows family caregivers to preserve relationships with a parent rather than becoming the resentful caregiver performing tasks. The family benefits from having a care navigator responsible for making recommendations, providing oversight, and managing the care situation. The care recipient benefits from the expertise of access to beneficial care and socialization provided by a paid caregiver or companion who offers a fresh face and a change in routine and conversation.

In caregiving situations, money is a controversial topic, especially for parents who clearly need care but who refuse to pay for professional services. The ideal care situation exists when financial resources are available for care oversight and management. A tug-of-war often occurs between the caregiver and the care recipient who balks at spending money on outside care services because finances are limited or because there is a desire to preserve money for the estate.

Depending on the prior support of family caregivers, hiring professional services may be more difficult because of an inability of family caregivers to say no to the care recipient when additional caregiving responsibilities are requested. As family caregivers do more and more, a false sense of stability and security occurs as the care recipient believes that family caregivers will continue to provide increased levels of care and support.

End of the Innocence

When we meet, caregivers tell me, "I've never been sick in my life, "or "I'm never sick," as if the current experience of not feeling well because of caregiving responsibilities is a shock or surprise. These statements of denial are the first in a long sequence of excuses by caregivers for not taking responsibility for the consequences of their actions. "I'm never sick" is a reality check that the rapid recovery and ability to bounce back quickly from health issues occurring in our youth is a reality of the past. As we age, recovering from a cold or flu takes longer than the recovery time experienced in our youth.

"I've never been sick in my life" is a reminder that caregivers can no longer abuse their bodies by not sleeping, not eating properly, not exercising, and not paying attention to stress that affects the body and mind. A single episode of not feeling well should serve as a reminder that remaining healthy and resilient as we age takes effort and work. A similar experience of abusing or not giving health-appropriate attention or consideration may be the reason our care recipient needs care. Flip the mirror and a caregiver may be looking at their own future if refusals to reduce stress and support good health are ignored.

Caregivers telling me, "I've never been sick in my life" are adamant that there is no time to attend to their health or to see the doctor. This is when I pose the question, "Then you do have time to be sick?" A caregiver recently told me that caring for her mother took such a toll on her health and well-being that she retired from her job to take care of her mother. To make sure I understood her statement, I restated, "You retired from your job so you could spend even more time being ill and burdened by caring for your mother?" The caregiver smiled back at me and nodded her head, realizing now that this may not have been the best choice. Hindsight is 20/20.

Logic is absent from many caregiving situations as emotions take over the driver's seat. Excuses and poor decisions are made rather than taking a step back to evaluate the consequences of decisions and actions. Heaven forbid that a caregiver might respond no to a request to add one more project to an already overscheduled schedule. Caregivers say yes because of a lack of skills to cope with what may be perceived as a negative response from a care recipient, and their schedules continue to spiral out of control.

As mentioned above, caregivers find attending to their own health issues to be too much work. "I'm not that sick"—yet. A caregiver will rarely admit that caregiving is too much work until there is no other option. A situation will arise when the caregiver is forced to take a step back and look at the current situation because of a serious health issue that must receive attention or because of repeated statements of concern from family members that have become final demands. Many relationships and marriages are ruined because of illogical caregivers who continually insist they have to run errands, grocery shop, clean house, pick up prescriptions, pay bills, or complete other tasks.

Unhealthy caregivers are ineffective. Ailing bodies move and react slowly. Sluggish or exhausted brains are not as quick to respond. Faulty decisions are made because of distractions and feelings of overwhelm. Rather than being helpful, caregivers place care recipients at risk as the result of the side effects of their illness. How logical is it that a caregiver suffering from a cold and fever care for a frail older adult with greater health vulnerability who may then be diagnosed with pneumonia as the result of exposure to the caregiver's cold? In these situations, the caregiver clearly places the well-being of the care recipient at risk.

Healthy individuals who become caregivers experience a higher prevalence of chronic disease as a direct result of the act of caregiving. Many caregivers over time acquire a greater number and severity of health conditions than their care recipients. This is the result of caregivers who selflessly provide care to the detriment and neglect of their own health and well-being because of a strong sense of responsibility and duty. Other caregivers provide care because of guilt: for example, based on a belief that adult children should care for parents.

A well-known term, *caregiver burden*, describes the stress experienced by caregivers resulting in negative impacts on physical and mental health, including more frequent episodes of anxiety and depression. Caregiver burden increases as the care recipient begins to experience health declines, increasing loss of physical abilities, and activities and decreases in mental function. This means that as care recipients require more care in the way of time, physical assistance, and verbal reminders, caregiver stress increases.

The time frame of caregiving is uncertain, ranging from one year to the lifetime of the care recipient. The uncertainty of time needed for caregiving, when prior discussions were not held, places significant stress on the caregiver. Caregiver health fails as a result of not attending to medical care on a regular basis. The stress of caregiving has a negative effect on self-care, nutrition, and exercise as these aspects of well-being are often neglected due to a perceived lack of time. Many caregivers are unaware of the potential effect of caregiving on their mental and physical well-being until well after problems occur.

The effect of caregiving stress is supported by the life experience of Dana Reeve, wife and caregiver for her husband, actor Christopher

Reeve who experienced a horseback-riding accident that left him paralyzed in 1995. Dana cared for her husband until his death in October 2004. Eight months later in July 2005, Dana aged forty-four and a nonsmoker, was diagnosed with stage 4 lung cancer. She died March 2006, seventeen months after the death of her husband. Dana's death supports the idea that the act of caregiving significantly increases mortality risk.

Caregivers able to separate the role of caregiving from their personal identity are less likely to suffer negative effects to mental health and well-being. Caregivers who are able to recognize the importance of maintaining family relationships versus being task focused—meaning, feeling that the caregiver must complete a long list of tasks versus spending quality time with the care recipient—fare better in balancing the role of caregiver. This division is not always practical or easy if you are a sole family caregiver who bears total responsibility and duty, but it is possible.

Being a caregiver may be comparable to stepping into a pool of mental quicksand. Having one foot buried by sand may feel confining: an initial struggle may occur over "do I or don't I?" As caregivers continue to add more responsibilities because of a sense of duty, they find themselves knee or waist deep in mental quicksand. This is often when questions arise of "how did this happen?" or "how did I get myself into this situation?" Only when caregivers begin to feel stuck are they able to recognize that aspects of the current situation may be unsustainable. It is also at this point of feeling stuck in mental quicksand that many caregivers do not know how to move forward or to become unstuck from situations that they accepted or initiated.

For both caregivers and care recipients, accepting help is challenging. Accepting change is even more complex. Is it possible that caregivers are as stubborn and unyielding as the care recipient who initially refused all offers of assistance? Similar to innocent statements of "I hope I never become like my mother," many caregivers become a replica of the care recipient who previously angered and frustrated them by refusing or failing to consider beneficial support and assistance. Caregivers become their own worst nightmare, especially when the caregiver's health and well-being suffer.

How do caregivers recognize and change unsupportive or negative behaviors? Denial occurs as the result of stubborn behaviors and refusing to believe that the role of caregiving does not have negative effects on mental health and well-being. Changing mind-sets that may be stuck occurs when caregivers are able to acknowledge that they are not superheroes and that the experience and advice of others with similar experiences offer value.

Change occurs by acknowledging that "doing it all" is not practical if caregivers hope to preserve personal health and relationships. Behaviors change when we are able to ask for and to accept help and support by learning coping strategies and by realizing that life does come full circle and that we as caregivers will someday need care. Some individuals will be able to easily balance the role of caregiving with other aspects of life. Other individuals will choose to be a caregiver with no boundaries, resulting in a life of emotional ups and downs and unexpected complications.

Research and real-life situations prove that the risks and complications of accepting the role of caregiver are significant. Caregivers and care recipients resist advice and hesitate to act because the advice represents change that requires more effort and energy than the individual feels he or she is able to commit.

The role of caregiver offers many positive aspects that include the personal satisfaction derived from caring for others. If this were not true, the number of family caregivers would be significantly less, and fewer individuals would seek caregiving as a profession. With this in mind, it is important for caregivers to realize the consequences of their actions today and how these relate to their own ability to provide care for care recipients and themselves.

Risks of Average and Borderline

The media promotes youth and vitality. How many television, radio, and Internet commercials tout products and procedures to delay the appearance of aging: mommy makeovers, Botox for wrinkles, the repair of hair loss, and other treatments? If you dislike any aspect of your appearance, the media assures that you are better informed about your options and that change is the solution. What happened to the idea of aging with character and a few wrinkles? For those in middle age, accepting gray hair and wrinkles is an idea that may have passed with our grandparents' generation.

We live in a fast-paced environment, susceptible to the media and perception that older adults, who may be slower moving and slower thinking, are hindrances to society. How many times have you been at the grocery store and witnessed an older adult struggling to walk or fumbling for change at the cash register? The first thought that pops into your head—rather than being one of compassion and understanding—may be a feeling of impatience and maybe even dread. Your mind fills with unkind thoughts about the mental faculties, appearance, or dress of slow-moving older adults. You believe you will never be that person, yet just as certain as taxes and death, you will eventually join the ranks of the millions of aging older adults.

In our youth and during most of our early adult life, many of us feel physically invincible. Brief illnesses, like colds and flu, pass quickly. Bones break and heal without incident or significant physical effect. You hear your friends say, I'm never sick. You may even say I'm never sick. This may be true—until the first time you are diagnosed with a chronic disease that challenges your mental health and well-being. These unexpected diagnoses alter that false sense of security you had in believing that you would remain eternally young and healthy.

How many of you are diagnosed with "borderline" something: borderline high blood sugar, high blood pressure, borderline depression, or borderline obesity? Physicians comment about the condition but never seriously discuss the consequences, so most patients let the information pass through one ear and out the other. This is similar to noticing early events that lead to care situations: comments may be made, but serious discussions about future consequences are never held. We are creatures of habit in avoiding discussions that may be unpleasant. The idea of having to work to age successfully may be less appealing than the idea of taking a pill or applying a magic lotion.

In the case of a health diagnosis, failure to discuss consequences may be the result of a physician who has also failed to be responsible for his or her own care and appearance and feels that he or she is unable to judge or provide recommendations. How many of you have physicians who appear to have their own chronic health conditions? Some physicians are overweight or have a physical appearance that is demotivating to patients. I imagine it must be difficult, if not impossible, for a medical professional to preach to patients when he or she fails to take their own advice.

Lack of serious discussion between physician and patient may also be the result of perceived futility by the physician. Physicians make daily recommendations and suggestions to patients that fall on deaf ears. At some point or another, I imagine that physicians cease to make recommendations because patients have expressed ongoing disinterest in change or fail to take any actions that show that they are interested in making positive changes in their own health.

This disinterest results in patients missing the consequences of borderline. Only during borderline periods does the opportunity exist to eliminate the condition through deliberate attention and action. The condition eventually becomes permanent, or chronic, and will be with you the rest of your life. Older adults frequently hear comments of a little memory loss and fall into the common belief that advancing memory loss will not have serious consequences.

This little factor of borderline—of not realizing the effects of future consequences—repeats in many areas of our lives. We hear information that might be relevant to a certain part of life and fail to listen. Weeks, months, or years later we look back and think I wish someone had told me, and we realize that it may be too late to turn around a situation that has already progressed too far in magnitude.

In healthcare, as in many aspects of life, there is a standard or system of averages. How many of you dream to be average? The healthcare system is a system of averages—average weights, average ranges for blood test results, average results for procedures for generally unhealthy people. What if you want to feel better than average? Will your doctors provide a list of the requirements to reach better-than-average or will he or she recall responses of disinterest from other patients and offer no information? It is not enough for your physician to tell you that your results are average; an explanation of what average means holds more value. Average results might place you in the company of people who are chronically ill.

Missing from discussions is consideration or correlation of how multiple diagnoses are interconnected. The ability to correlate information and to offer preventative advice to patients who are interested is lacking from the practices of many physicians today because of time pressures and insurance restrictions. I attended a physician appointment with a client and asked why the side effects of a particular medication were not explained. The physician's response, "That happens in only 30 percent of patients, so I didn't want to worry anyone." Unfortunately, my client happened to be in the 30 percent of patients experiencing side effects, and we had reason to be worried.

A simpler aspect of health maintenance is the regular tests physicians recommend for patients. It is helpful to know your blood pressure, cholesterol, triglycerides, blood cell counts, and what the numbers mean. You have a right to obtain copies of your lab work; it is important to understand and track the results of all testing. Knowing your numbers, especially if they are out of a normal range, provides the opportunity to make lifestyle changes so that you may avoid the advance of chronic disease.

I suggest starting a file in which you keep copies of lab results, medical tests, and a health history. Then research your health condition and ask questions at medical appointments. This ensures that you are aware of your health diagnosis and that you know more about yourself than your doctor so that you can obtain the best care possible.

Why do doctors fail to speak about prevention, consequences, or the management of chronic disease? Part of the answer is that these conversations are difficult—even for doctors. Some physicians may fail to present unfavorable information about a treatment they recommend if they feel the recommendation will be easily accepted rather than questioned by the patient. This lack of not presenting thorough information—including the pros and cons of treatment and the eventual outcome—occurs frequently between physicians and patients. Patients have a responsibility to ask the difficult questions. Many fail to ask because of fear that the news will be bad.

A specific example of the provision of too little information is patients who choose to participate in dialysis and later report that if they knew when making the decision—what they know today—they would have declined treatment. Dialysis involves insertion of catheter into a vein to filter waste from the body. Treatment frequency varies for each individual and ranges from 3-4 hours per day up to several days each week. Some dialysis patients feel that they are "tied" to the machine and have little control over their life. After dialysis is initiated, the decision by a patient to end dialysis will result in death as waste builds-up in the body. Many dialysis patients feel trapped by the requirement of ongoing treatment.

In my conversation with Dr. Alvin Moss on the subject of palliative and end of life care, we discussed patients receiving dialysis treatment and the ethical duty of physicians to fully discuss details of the treatment, related chronic disease diagnoses, and expected outcomes for each individual considering dialysis. While some patients are excellent candidates for dialysis, there are others for whom dialysis prolongs life without improving quality of life.

Discussions about diagnoses, consequences, treatments, and difficult decisions are best scheduled with your physician and care team. Assuming that you want the best care, you must advocate for yourself and loved ones. You must ask difficult questions that will sometimes result in answers you may not wish to receive.

Even though many individuals have been previously cautioned about health habits, many prefer to remain in a state of pleasant ignorance or denial. How many times do we hear, "My doctor didn't tell me"? Where does the ultimate responsibility lie for our own health and well-being? It is possible to prevent medical conditions from advancing if action is taken early and immediately after diagnosis.

It seems that many individuals remain in denial or are unwilling to change habits and make good choices. If the consequences were fully explained, would patients respond differently or would they remain in a sense of purposeful ignorance? I believe this answer lies in the individual personality traits of each individual and how one responds and reacts to situations and change. Some individuals will take action; others will allow situations to force action.

In the medical world, it seems that every week, new findings refute previous research. Eggs are bad for you—eggs are good for you. Consuming alcohol is bad— red wine is good for the heart. Chocolate is bad—dark chocolate is better. How do we know what news to trust? You know your body and the way it reacts better than anyone else. This leaves the responsibility up to you to investigate and advocate for your own healthcare.

As with many events in life, do-overs are not always possible. You have today and the results of the choices you make or avoid—including the opportunity to become informed and to advocate. Our choices and responsibilities are important because the last several decades of life represent continual transitions. Responsibility and the consequences of a lifetime of choices have a significant impact on the management and future consequences of chronic disease.

Unexpected Surprises of Chronic Disease

The world is growing older, not younger. A knock on a neighborhood door might result in an answer from a young person or one of advanced age. In 2010, 40 million people or 13 percent of the population were aged sixty-five and older.[12] According to the U.S. Census, by 2030, persons over the age of sixty-five will number 72 million, representing 20 percent of the population. Women past the age of sixty-five are more likely than men of the same age to be widowed—40 versus 13 percent—

and are twice as likely to live alone—37 versus 19 percent.[13] Similar trends exist worldwide.

By 2050, 22 percent of the world's population will be over the age of sixty. The reality of an aging population with care needs poses a worldwide economic and fiscal challenge.[14] This shift to an older population will shape the economic future of the world. Why are these statistics important? What economic impact does an aging population present? Persons aged sixty and older generate fewer tax dollars and represent higher expenditures for healthcare. Advances in medicine have extended life, but at what cost? Caregiving costs are the result of a chronically ill and aging population.

Chronic disease is defined as a disease that is incurable but not immediately life-threatening; a condition that a person generally lives with for years that negatively affects quality of daily life. If you have a diagnosis of heart disease, high blood pressure, diabetes, a breathing condition like asthma or COPD, cancer, or mental illness, you have a chronic disease.

According to the Partnership to Fight Chronic Disease:[15]

133 million Americans—45 percent of the population—have at least one chronic disease. People with chronic conditions are the most frequent users of health care in the U.S. They account for 81% of hospital admissions; 91% of all prescriptions filled; and 76 percent of all physician visits.

The prevalence of chronic disease spreads across all age groups; illness and chronic disease is not limited to the very old. The advancement of a chronic disease over time, unless action is taken to reverse the disease, is an indicator of an absolute need for care.

To make a point about the serious long-term effects of chronic disease and how this relates to caregiving, let me illustrate how a diagnosis of diabetes affects multiple body parts and leads to significant disability and illness if ignored. This progression of disease and the effect on the body are common to many other health diagnoses, for example heart disease that may lead to a stroke and the eventual diagnosis of dementia.

The Centers for Disease Control and Prevention list multiple complications of diabetes including heart disease, kidney disease, stroke, eye conditions including glaucoma and cataracts, painful nerve damage, skin conditions including difficult to heal foot ulcers, gastroparesis, and peripheral artery disease.[16] In 2014, nearly twenty-nine million or 9.3 percent of the U.S. population had a diagnosis of diabetes. Diabetes is a serious illness that can be treated and managed by healthful eating, regular physical activity and medications to lower blood glucose levels. Diabetes was the seventh leading cause of death in the U.S. in 2010.[17] A diagnosis of chronic disease, like diabetes, that is not appropriately treated or managed by the person with the diagnosis, results in a need for caregiving.

In order to ensure that the role of caregiving is viewed positively from family generation to generation, family caregivers who are aware of the effects of good health and how health affects long term care needs should serve as educators and leaders for younger family members. Discussions about health and well-being are important. Discussions about caregiving and care needs, including the related costs, should also be included in family discussions. While many older adults say that they do not "wish to be a burden to their children", actions speak louder than words and those who have not supported good health or prepared financially will ultimately represent a burden of care for their children.

The ability to maintain a positive mindset about the role of caregiving is equally as important as the ability to set personal boundaries. My life as a caregiving professional began in 1999 after years of my role as a family caregiver. In the past fifteen years I have learned to set boundaries to protect my emotional and physical health. I have learned that some care recipients prefer to complain and will never take action to change situations. I have experienced the kindness and graciousness of other care recipients who willingly accept and appreciate support. I have supported care recipients who have lived past the age of one-hundred in good physical and mental health. There is no substitute for taking action to protect your health today. Your future care needs depend on the choices you make today.

Exercise: Managing Caregiver Stress

Uncertainty and lack of control are two frustrating aspects of care situations. Moving the situation forward is a process that involves scheduling a family meeting with those involved in the care situation to identify and discuss concerns so that a plan of care may be established. After confirming a date and time for a family meeting and sending invitations the following are steps to simplify the process:

1. Prior to the meeting, the care recipient and family caregivers each write a list of concerns and questions. Each person has an equal time limit (five to ten minutes) to express their concerns.

2. If possible an independent and uninvolved person, called a "group leader" is asked to serve as a moderator for the meeting. Family meetings without a leader easily spiral out of control.

3. Ground rules for the participants are to remain open-minded and accepting of opposite opinions and to *listen*. One person speaks at a time and has a time limit of five to ten minutes (the group can decide on the time frame). Attendees may *not* interrupt or comment until everyone has had an opportunity to express their concerns. During this time, the group leader listens and compiles a list of concerns for the group to discuss.

4. After everyone has had an *uninterrupted* opportunity to express concerns, the group leader "ranks" concerns by a group vote.

5. The team leader selects one concern at a time and again sets a time limit of five to ten minutes for the group to brainstorm solutions and options. If time is extended, the entire group must agree on the time extension.

6. Where agreement is possible, the group identifies next steps and a backup plan in the event the decision does not work according to plan.

7. When consensus or agreement is not possible, the consequences of taking action (or not taking action) must be identified so that all involved have a clear understanding of potential areas of concern.

8. The meeting concludes with attendees identifying their level of participation and commitment to take next steps. The next meeting date and time are established as ongoing monitoring and check-ins are beneficial to the situation.

As in all aspects of life, it must be recognized that individuals, both caregivers and care recipients, have the right to make poor choices. The goal of this exercise is to open communication, to reduce guilt, and to provide peace of mind that discussion is possible in situations where not everyone agrees on how, who, or where care should be provided for a loved one.

Many caregivers find themselves in care situations where parents hesitate to participate in change. In other situations where parents are willing to participate, there may be guilt on the part of the caregiver relative to making changes and the uncertainty of the results of the change. While no one is able to predict outcomes, proper planning and discussion gives confidence that plans put in place will have a greater chance of success.

If you are interested in accessing more tips and information about ideas presented in this chapter and about related subjects, visit http:// www.thecaregivingtrapbook.com/store and select Removing the Rose-Colored Glasses.

Tales of the Caring Generation

Karen and the Peanut Butter Sandwich

Karen found her home inhabited by strange people called caregivers. She and her husband had lived in their home for more than fifty years. Her husband, Ted, had passed away six months ago. Karen's life seemed to change in an instant. She remembered that Ted did everything—managed the money, took care of the house, and organized Karen. Since he passed away, Karen felt that life quickly spiraled out of control.

One afternoon while driving home from the grocery store, Karen had a car accident; the other driver came out of nowhere. Karen's car crashed into the passenger side door and was totaled. It was clear that he—not she— had run the stop sign, but the police believed she was at fault. She was examined at the hospital, and a doctor told her it was time to stop driving because her memory was faulty. There seemed to be one challenge after another, and now people were telling Karen she was becoming forgetful and needed help caring for herself.

Karen didn't really mind the company of the caregivers since she was used to having her husband around, but she did mind being told that she was becoming forgetful. Karen remembered everything that had happened forty or fifty years ago. How could anyone call her forgetful? Even the thought that her memory was failing was an insult.

As a follow-up to the car accident she was to see her physician who diagnosed a kidney infection. He wrote a prescription and sent her and the caregiver on their way. They stopped at the grocery store on the way home to pick up her favorites: apple mint jelly, vanilla ice cream, and peanut butter. After dinner, the caregiver handed Karen a prescription medication. Karen refused because she was certain that she never took medications.

The caregiver explained about the doctor appointment, the kidney infection, and the prescription. Again, a situation of other people making up stories to make Karen think she was losing her mind. Karen did not recall seeing her doctor or receiving any type of prescription. This was some foolish attempt by a caregiver to drug her for some unknown reason, and there was no way she was taking any kind of pill.

Karen woke up in a fog. She was in the hospital with doctors and nurses talking about a kidney infection that had worsened during the past two weeks. She had no idea how she had arrived at the emergency room but didn't feel well enough to argue. She allowed the staff to do whatever they wanted as she drifted off to sleep. The next morning Karen awoke in another bed that was not hers. A young girl wearing scrubs told her she was in a nursing home to get stronger while recovering from a serious kidney infection.

Karen thought, "More people making up stories about a kidney infection." There was certainly nothing wrong except for feeling a little tired. Karen noticed an IV in her arm that she promptly pulled out— it was time to get dressed and return home. Karen heard discussion of "sitters"—persons to stay with her so she wasn't pulling out IVs or becoming agitated. Of course she was agitated; people kept making up stories about her memory and some silly kidney infection and refused to allow her to return home. What was wrong with these people—for heaven's sake—Karen thought the entire world had gone mad.

The next day when Karen awoke, a stranger sat next to her reading a book. Karen felt drugged. Her arms were wrapped in bandages. People came and went. Her mind was too foggy to answer questions about the day of the week, where was she, or the season. Why didn't they stop asking her silly questions? All she knew was that she was feeling absolutely nauseous and had a major stomachache but no one seemed to be paying attention to what was wrong.

Karen heard talk about failing to thrive and deciding to give up. Karen thought, "They must be talking about someone else. I am certainly here and I'm not giving up. I can't get the words out of my mouth to explain how I feel or what is wrong. Why don't they ask me instead of talking around me and not to me? Don't they know that only three weeks ago I was up and about, walking and doing everything on my own?"

Karen felt like a victim in a movie who wanted to scream but no sound came out of her mouth. She thought, "This doctor is going to kill me—he will let me die—and there is no one to tell him how I feel, no one to speak up for me!"

The next day a woman who looked familiar stopped by to visit. She related that she had spoken with the doctor and that she was going to make sure Karen received the care she needed. Thank heavens—someone finally able to speak up for her! She overheard the woman and the doctor speaking, "Yes it is a puzzling situation, not sure what caused such a decline." She closed her eyes and went back to sleep.

It was a warm summer day; the caregivers were with Karen. They were enjoying a picnic in the park—peanut butter and mint apple jelly triple decker sandwiches and iced tea. Her memory was still foggy. Life was back to normal. Karen took a bite of the peanut butter sandwich—the taste of mint apple jelly reminded of her childhood—she lifted her face to feel the warmth of the sun and to enjoy the warm breeze. Today was a good day.

Chapter 3

Sticker Shock—
Who Really Pays?

- The Effects of Caregiving on Health, in the Workplace, and in Retirement
- Caring for the Caregiver
- Costs of Care
  - o Care Navigation
  - o In-Home Care
  - o Retirement and Communities of Care
  - o Naiveté
  - o Rehabilitation and Skilled Nursing
- Exercise: Time Off
- Tales of the Caring Generation: The Best of My Father

The Effects of Caregiving on Health, in the Workplace, and in Retirement

For a family caregiver working a full-time job, adding twenty hours a week for the role of caregiving is similar to accepting a part-time job in addition to an already full work schedule without the associated financial reward a real part-time job might offer. For many, the reward of caregiving is personal satisfaction. However many fail to realize that the act of caregiving poses negative effects on the caregiver's health, ability to work, and to save for retirement. The role of caregiver also may increase the likelihood that the caregiver will need care, sooner rather than later, because of diagnosis of a chronic disease.

The effects of chronic disease in the American workplace are significant:[18]

- One-third of working Americans ages nineteen to sixty-four suffer from at least one chronic disease increasing the likelihood of random or even prolonged absenteeism
- Twenty one percent take from one to five sick days per year when they don't feel they can give one-hundred percent on the job
- Twenty seven percent have missed six or more days of work

Poor health costs the U.S. economy $576 billion a year. Of that amount, 39 percent, or $227 billion is from lost productivity from employee absenteeism due to illness or what researchers call presenteeism, defined by employees who report to work but illness prevents them from performing at their best. Of the remaining $576 billion tallied in the report, the cost of wage replacement is $117 billion from absence due to illness as well as workers compensation, and both short and long-term disability. Meanwhile, another $232 billion of poor health costs come from medical treatment and pharmacy related costs.[19]

The idea of caregiving falls into the "romantic" idea that one takes care of family. Yet the personal costs of caregiving to health, well-being, and finances are unimaginable until you find yourself in this role. About 70%

of people who die in the United States each year succumb to a chronic disease.[20] More than half of all Americans are diagnosed with a chronic disease. A caregiver with a chronic disease is likely to experience more health challenges because of the emotional stress of caregiving. Even though many caregivers would never consider saying no to the role of caregiving, the prevalence of stress, anxiety, and depression contributing to chronic health conditions is significant. Caregivers unable to set boundaries must identify alternatives and lay out a road map for the future rather than naively participating in actions that harm personal health and well-being.

Chronic health conditions result from relationship stress between the caregiver and the care recipient and from family relationships where conflict and differences of opinion exist. In many caregiving situations, the chronic health conditions of the caregiver escalate more quickly than the chronic health conditions of the care recipient. These health conditions negatively affect the caregiver's ability to continue to work to retirement age and the caregiver's ability to provide care for the care recipient.

Caregivers already diagnosed with chronic disease who experience increased stress due to the act of caregiving may become permanently disabled, having no other option but to end a career prior to retirement age. Other caregivers with chronic disease continue to work until retirement age and require care earlier than expected from family members, making the role of caregiving a recurring family event. There is no question that the act of caregiving has negative effects on the caregiver and on the workplace. What is the answer for family members who choose to become caregivers?

How do we prevent caregivers from needing care? How might the workplace support the issue of caregiving as this aspect of life becomes more prevalent as a result of an aging population? Do companies bear the responsibility to provide support to caregivers? Should caregivers be more sensitive to the effects of their personal situations on workplace productivity? What are the significant issues experienced by caregivers? Will bringing caregiving issues into the workplace unleash discussion about a variety of other issues, including the responsibility to be proactive about health? What responsibilities do individuals have to care for their own health to minimize future caregiving needs? There are more questions than concrete answers.

As mentioned at the beginning of this chapter, many caregivers are employed full-time. Many employed caregivers are fearful of advising supervisors of caregiving demands upon their lives as the result of a parent or loved one needing care. Concern exists about being viewed as a less than able employee, while in many situations work performance does suffer and employers unaware of the reasons may institute corrective action.

Most employees desire to fulfill work responsibilities without allowing personal lives to interfere. Caregiving becomes a tug-of-war between work, personal life, and the responsibilities of caregiving. A requested change in work schedule due to caregiving may result in conflict between employee and the employer. Caregivers requesting time off during the week to care for loved ones or to attend medical or other appointments may throw a kink into high-demand businesses where employee absences negatively affect company sales. These absences directly affect co-workers. Supervisors are also negatively impacted by the need to cover work projects for absent employee caregivers.

Individuals in the role of caregiver are often oblivious to the negative effects of their workplace absences because they are so focused on the needs of the care recipient and the daily responsibilities of care. Any woman who has cared for a newborn is able to relate to how all-encompassing caregiving can be when there are no free moments in the day. A similar situation exists when a spouse or a parent requires 24/7 care. While many employers are patient and understanding caregiving has negative effects on the workplace.

What might the workplace do to support caregivers? In my opinion, increasing workplace sensitivity is important, however boundaries—as in all areas of life—must exist. Educating managers and supervisors to the issues surrounding caregiving and loss is important. Achieving a level of sensitivity may be challenging, if a manager has not had a similar life experience. Posing questions relative to employee job commitment and balancing caregiving are reasonable so that sensitivity to company operations may be considered with sensitivity to the personal caregiving situation of an employee. Communication between manager and employee is critical.

Another area of company-to-caregiver support is the availability of resources and education. Many large companies offer employee-assistance programs. However programs for caregivers may not be offered within these programs, or, if offered, may not be common knowledge to employees. Many employees are concerned about using assistance programs for fear that a supervisor will discover their participation.

Making the subject of caregiving a common topic in the workplace may alleviate employee concern about stepping forward to accept assistance. Most employees glow about the experience of raising children that is not without challenges. Employees should also be able to discuss realistically the challenges of caring for aging parents without embarrassment or fear.

Because of the aging population and the increasing number of employee caregivers, employers who are proactive in becoming more educated about the personal and workplace effects of caregiving will be better equipped to respond to the effects of caregiving upon the workplace. Determining avenues of support may alleviate stress experienced by employee caregivers and company personnel responsible for supervising these employees. The numbers show that the effect of employee caregivers upon the workplace is significant and only likely to increase in the future.

For employers, the total cost of absences averages 36 percent of base payroll each year. More than 20 percent of Americans are absent from work to take care of their family. According to a survey on the subject of unscheduled absences:[21]

Only one-third of the workforce happens to be sick when they take an unplanned absence. The other two-thirds of the time, they are dealing with personal needs (18 percent), family issues (22 percent), entitlement mentality (13 percent) and stress (13 percent).

Personal issues experienced by working caregivers are significant. Some reduce work hours or leave employment to care for a parent. Risks for women caregivers who choose to reduce work schedules or to completely opt out of the workforce are significant including a short- or long-term loss of income and a subsequent inability to fund costs of living and care in retirement years.

It is important that all caregivers, especially women, avoid being naïve about the short- and long-term effects of caregiving. When women consider opting out of the workforce to caregive, it is important to examine the present and future financial costs by consulting a CPA, a financial advisor, or a retirement planner. The effect of choices—illustrated by hard numbers—may change the decision for a woman to opt out of the workplace to accept the role of a full-time caregiver.

While women have been traditional caregivers because of a desire to have children or because of a sense of duty or responsibility to care for parents, hindsight is frighteningly clear when women struggle to pay daily living expenses during retirement years. In many marriages the husband's health fails prior to the health of the wife. Marital financial resources used to pay for care of the husband may deplete resources so that when care is needed by the wife, she may be unable to receive care in a home setting. Women, who generally live longer than men, have no other option but to live in a nursing home on public assistance when care is needed because social security income and retirement savings combined are insufficient to pay the cost of living in a traditional assisted living community.

Long-term care insurance is a protection that women should strongly consider. Long-term care policies provide for costs of care for a specified period of time and a dollar amount. While policies have annual premiums ranging in the thousands of dollars, depending on age and health at the time of purchase, a policy should be considered protection for women who accept family caregiving responsibilities of raising children or caring for aging parents. While men tend to avoid discussions about long-term care and end of life, women are wise to initiate these discussions early and if married, insist on obtaining a policy. Long-term care insurance policies provide for care in a variety of settings. Policies often make the difference between receiving care that is needed versus delaying care until there are no other options.

The act of caregiving has significant effects on financial well-being. Forty-three percent of caregivers surveyed stated that caregiving had increased their financial worries. Individual caregivers reported that caregiving not only had an adverse effect on their financial well-being but on the overall quality of life.[22]

Caregiving is exhausting and emotionally overwhelming; health fails, life and work situations change, and well-being in retirement is compromised. In addition to financial worries are the emotional worries resulting from the act of caregiving. While caregiving is noble, needed, and beneficial to society because of uncompensated family caregivers, when the time comes, who will provide care for the caregiver? How can the caregiver ensure that he or she does not risk their financial, health, and emotional well-being? Support and educational resources are available for caregivers so that the caregiver does not feel he or she has to bear the total burden of care.

Caring for the Caregiver

While many caregivers insist that they have to "do it all" as statistics indicate, the idea of having to do it all is a faulty belief that results in a poor outcome for the caregiver financially, physically, and emotionally. Resources for education and personal support for caregivers exist. Support is available through many national and local organizations like the Alzheimer's Association, the Parkinson's Association, cancer care centers, and other specific disease organizations.

Books and Internet websites like my website, The Caring Generation, offer a wide range of information on many topics. A caregiver's desire for information is only limited by available time to research, read, and participate. Admittedly many caregivers, because of feelings of overwhelm and exhaustion, do not set aside time for research. This time constraint will be addressed below in the section called "Care Navigation."

Support groups and individual counseling are beneficial. Many caregivers tell me there is little time for individual counseling or group meetings, yet I know others who would not forgo attending these meetings. Some caregivers report that they lack energy and are unable to take the initiative to join a group or to meet with a counselor because the role of caregiving is time-consuming and draining. If caregivers refuse to consider options that may offer benefits, the caregiving situation will continue to remain time-consuming and draining. Changing attitudes about care situations is as difficult for the caregiver as it is for the care recipient. Until one or the other decides upon change—or an outside catalyst changes a care situation—the situation will likely remain static.

If a caregiver has attended a support group to gain a sense of the group dynamic and information offered, attending the group on a regular basis may be an intimidating thought for multiple reasons. Hearing others talk about aspects of a loved one's advancing disease or the difficult experience of an individual caregiver may bring up feelings or emotions of which the caregiver is unprepared or unable to manage. In this situation, seeing an individual counselor may be more beneficial to address fears, frustrations, or other feelings that may be arising as a result of the caregiving experience.

Below are considerations in determining if a support group might be a good fit for you:

- You may see and hear aspects of caregiving that may be frightening. The benefit is that rather than being shocked or surprised by potential or future aspects of caregiving, you will be aware that these events may occur, and you will be more prepared to respond.
- You will meet others who have been where you are today. You will have someone to call when your patience has run thin and you seek empathy or suggestions.
- You will learn that you are not alone, that your experiences are not unusual.

- You will be able to honestly share your feelings in a group who experience similar feelings of anger, guilt, and frustration as well as positive feelings about caregiving.
- Your role as a caregiver will eventually end. Group participation offers access to others with whom you might establish friendships and who may remain your friends when it is time to rebuild your life absent of caregiving.

The idea of respite for caregivers is another beneficial concept. Respite means a break from caregiving activities, whether for a short period of time, a day, a weekend or longer. Removing yourself from a situation perceived to be stressful is beneficial for mental and physical well-being. There arrives a point in caregiving where caregivers tell me they want to scream and run away. Enough is enough. This is the experience of a caregiving phenomenon called compassion fatigue.

When you reach a point where you feel unable to listen to your care recipient who constantly complains about his or her woes, you may be experiencing compassion fatigue. Who knew there was a term for lacking sympathy or empathy to the situations or experiences of others in care situations? Symptoms and feelings of compassion fatigue include hopelessness, stress and anxiety, sleeplessness, and a persistent negative attitude. As caregivers become drained emotionally and physically, being compassionate becomes more challenging. For many, it is difficult to maintain a positive attitude in a situation that seems never to improve or to end.

In situations of compassion fatigue, respite is one course of action to break the pattern of feeling hopeless. Think of enjoyable activities, make a list, and commit to taking action. A short list may include soaking in a hot tub, eating dark chocolate while enjoying a glass of wine, reading the newspaper in the quiet of the morning, or taking a walk with the dog, or getting away for an entire weekend. When caregivers are overwhelmed, it may seem impossible to take a break however, if a daily routine of small breaks is implemented the benefits to attitude and outlook will be quickly realized.

Self-care is extremely important for caregivers who experience challenging family situations where multiple parties are involved but do not always see eye to eye. Family relationships change over time. The care situations and the needs of loved ones are unpredictable. Accessing professional support for care situations is important and beneficial.

Many families are unaware of the services and support available that include three of the most commonly utilized support services: care navigation, in-home care support, and retirement communities. While many parents prefer to have family provide care because there is no associated expense, this is not always practical or realistic in the long term. However, upon investigation of available services and options, some families experience sticker shock.

Costs of Care

Costs of care are often a surprise. Employer healthcare plans during working years shield individuals from the true cost of health-related care. After retirement, healthcare costs may increase drastically especially if a diagnosis of chronic disease exists. I consult with caregivers and care recipients who believe that Medicare and social security will fund all costs related to care. This is a faulty belief.

Discussions surrounding money to pay for care rarely occur until the time of need or an emergency: for example a hospitalization or rehabilitation stay. Many family members and individuals believe these healthcare institutions will provide care for an indefinite time period. Surprise occurs when notice is given about a family member being immediately discharged from the hospital or being discharged in several days from a rehabilitation center and it is clear, at least to the family, that the individual is unable to live alone without substantial assistance. Few families realize the importance of care planning when a loved one is admitted to a hospital or a care community providing rehabilitation. These stays are temporary and not long-term.

This lack of urgency on the part of family members to make plans for a loved one to return home results from naïveté about the care situation. The reality of healthcare is that insurance companies have strict requirements for admission and for remaining in the care of a hospital or rehabilitation center. Hospitals, nursing homes, and rehabilitation centers are intended for short-term medical care reimbursed by Medicare or private health insurance, not for a long-term stay.

Admissions, social work, or discharge planning staffs in these healthcare organizations provide explanations about length of stay however, families, because of stress levels or distraction fail to recognize the immediate relevance of the information provided and the impending near-term consequences. I commonly receive phone calls from panicked family members unsure of next steps, reporting that their loved one is being released from the hospital on Friday afternoon or is being released from a rehabilitation center in three days.

Family members in these situations are angry that no one in the hospital or in the rehabilitation center told them discharge was a possibility. In most if not all cases family caregivers were informed but did not realize the importance of asking the right questions or of making an immediate plan.

In these situations, making a plan may include a difficult discussion about money and available funds to pay for care. This is when sticker shock occurs because neither Medicare nor social security pays for the type of care most individuals require to remain safe and independent at home. This type of care, paid for privately, is commonly called custodial care and may be provided at home or in retirement communities offering a variety of care levels. Care navigators exist to guide families through the process of identifying, evaluating, planning, and implementing options.

Care Navigation
Professionals called care navigators have a duty and responsibility to make sure that recommendations are offered to provide family caregivers and care recipients' options relative to care situations. Care navigators offer a level of objectivity that allows care recipients and family caregivers to look

at care situations with clarity, to set boundaries, to review alternatives, and to lay out a plan for the short- and long-term future.

Before a significant crisis or health emergency has occurred, monitoring daily activities of a parent and care of the household often provides one of the best indicators of whether a parent is able to provide self-care and the extent to which the ability to organize, recall information, schedule activities, and plan exists. More often than not, care of the person or the household will begin to show signs of wear and tear in conjunction with the advancement of medical or physical conditions. Physical abilities and an increase in health concerns affect mobility and the ability to manage day-to-day activities.

By evaluating the ability of a parent to manage day to day, including examining the ability to manage health, a more accurate picture of the ability to live independently may be gained. At this time discussions and plans for the future are best made so that hasty decisions are not made about care when an emergency occurs. The ideal goal is a plan to support a parent living as independently as possible for as long as possible. This is one example of a situation where a care navigator is able to provide insight and guidance.

Utilizing a care navigator is a prudent first step to identify needs and to make a short and a long-term plan with backup options. I assess individuals relative to healthcare needs, available services for remaining at home, transitioning to care communities, and determining whether recommendations by providers are appropriate and prudent. I help family caregivers work through the stress and guilt of having to make difficult decisions on behalf of a loved one that include evaluating in-home assistance, the viability and services offered by retirement communities, and a variety of other available services.

Family caregivers, because of familiarity and lack of knowledge, may miss the small signs of decline that indicate a loved one would benefit from support today before a situation advances and more care might be needed. More often is the case that children see parents and miss the little signs indicating that a physical or mental change or decline has occurred.

Parents (mine were no exception) are excellent at stepping up their game to appear to be in total control for short periods of time while family is visiting so that no potential faults or risks are detected.

As might be expected, many families wait to contact a care navigator until an emergency has occurred, like a hospitalization or a rehabilitation stay. In other situations, a parent's memory loss may be increasing, and safety concerns may exist relative to the parent remaining at home, but no steps are taken until a running faucet floods the house, an oven fire occurs, or perhaps a serious car accident. Regardless of the care situation, an experienced care navigator is able to save families time, worry, and expense by making beneficial recommendations and by offering continued involvement. The support of care navigators is beneficial for families who are at a distance and for those who are local but who lack the time to provide ongoing oversight of care or for families who prefer to focus on the relationship with a parent minus the task work

In my business, The Care Navigator, I serve as court-appointed guardian, medical and financial power of attorney, and personal representative of the estate. I provide assessments for care situations, and I make recommendations for family that my staff implements. We provide oversight of ongoing care situations, including support in transitions from home to retirement communities. I routinely report that there is not any service that we are unable to provide because of the breadth of our services and the number of ancillary service providers with whom we have relationships. Our goal is to support independence as long as possible by providing and coordinating services to address daily living needs and health. At the time a higher level of care is needed, we remain in place to provide ongoing support and oversight.

Care navigation services are valuable in situations of care. Since care navigation is a relatively new profession, many individuals entering the industry possess book sense but few years of practical experience. This is no different from other life situations where personal trainers, not in the best physical shape, advise and train clients hoping to lose weight or to improve diets. Similarly, therapists counsel clients to navigate life and interpersonal issues but lack the skills to implement the same recommendations in their own lives. Practical experience in all professions is beneficial.

Book sense offers benefits in theory, but not in navigating challenging situations. One can read a book about how to ride a bicycle and still not be able to ride a bicycle. Before you retain a care navigator or any professional in the care industry, take steps to ensure the individual has the education and career experience to support the needs of your situation. Critically evaluate years of experience, educational background, membership in community organizations, and community service.

Care navigators are fluent in a wide variety of care situations; some specialize in small niche areas—for example, worker's compensation or cancer care. Ask about common situations and outcomes that might be expected. While no care navigator is able to guarantee outcomes, due to unpredictable events, the navigator should be able to explain in detail other outcomes he or she has delivered in their practice.

Rates for care navigation vary from fifty to two hundred dollars an hour depending on the expertise of the individual providing the service and the type of service provided. Some states, like Colorado, have a senate bill that provides compensation guidelines for care navigators who act in a fiduciary capacity like a guardian or power of attorney.

In-Home Care

I often receive questions from family members about "the right time" to begin in-home care services or the best time to move to an assisted living or other care community. These are individual choices that depend on aspects of the care situation and personal preferences. In a perfect world, in-home care services and assisted living are put in place long before an emergency occurs; in reality this is a rare occurrence.

For individuals who wish to delay a move to a retirement community or who have the financial means to remain in their homes, the rate for in-home care services averages between twenty to thirty dollars an hour depending on the type of assistance offered. These services are not reimbursed by insurance but paid for privately or are reimbursed by some long-term care insurance policies.

Companion care offers the services of light housekeeping, laundry and meal preparation, while nursing assistants are able to offer the services of incontinence care, physical mobility support and transfers, and personal care related to bathing and dressing.

There are situations where having a paid professional caregiver visit several times a week to provide meals and other support adds sufficient assistance to allow an individual to continue to live independently at home. In other situations, providing daily activity and exercise benefits the physical body and the mind of the care recipient. As we age, we become less physically active and more isolated, both of which contribute to declines in physical strength and memory.

If financial means are available, remaining at home is the best course of action for an individual who would benefit from care and desires to avoid moving into a care community. Hiring the right in-home caregiving agency can provide peace of mind and great benefit. The caveat is that the family or the care recipient must manage and direct the agency and their caregivers.

Caregivers are generally unsupervised and require oversight by family or a care navigator to make sure that the care recipient receives the appropriate care and that no adverse situations occur. Caregivers commonly become too familiar with a client resulting in the caregiver having poor professional boundaries. Familiarity results in actions like arriving late or leaving early for shifts (while billing the client for the entire shift), using a personal cell phone while working, bringing children or other family members into the home of a client, and performing other actions not approved by the care agency. Many care recipients are taken advantage of by caregivers because they do not wish to complain to the care agency, thereby getting their caregiver "into trouble."

If you are a family caregiver whose loved one desires to remain at home, consider hiring a care navigator to oversee the care of an in-home caregiving agency. This will allow your family member to continue living at home without your having to manage many of the details of care, including supervising agency caregivers.

Retirement and Communities of Care

When the idea of moving becomes a topic of conversation, it is best to introduce the idea as early as a possible in anticipation of a change in care or lifestyle needs. While many older adults wish to remain in their homes, this is not always possible or practical as aspects of daily life change. "Involuntary movers are forced to leave their current living situation against their wishes due to changes in their functional abilities, financial resources, or care support options." [23] There are times when an involuntary move occurs because of an unexpected event like hospitalization for a broken hip and the realization that returning home is impractical. Events such as the death of a loved one also result in involuntary moves.

Voluntary moves may involve some of the same factors but also focus on positive aspects such as the availability of social networks and the ability to participate in retirement activities. In general, the attitude and personal beliefs of the individual who is moving is an excellent predictor of the success of the move. For example, if an older adult resists moving because he or she desires to remain in their home, resistance to participating in activities that support integration into a community after the move may occur. On the other hand if an individual realizes that a move is practical and the individual has a positive attitude toward integrating into a new community—including participation in activities—the move will have a significantly greater chance of success.

The promise of care communities is that new residents will not isolate in their rooms but will enjoy participation in meal times, activities, and social events. This promise—while well intended—must take into consideration the past social style of the individual. A person who has always been an introvert will not transform into a social butterfly as the result of a change in physical location.

For some individuals a move to a retirement community is a practical choice when the costs of in-home care approaches the monthly cost of a care community or when an individual wishes to be in a community where social activities, meals, and other services are easily accessible. Some individuals prefer to move into a campus-like environment where independent, assisted living, memory care, and skilled care, called nursing-home care exist in a single location. This allows an individual to remain in the same community for the remainder of their life unless significant changes in health occur. Other individuals choose freestanding communities offering a low level of assistance, knowing that they will have future moves.

More times than not, the idea of a move to a retirement or care community is initiated by a family caregiver who bears the responsibility of care. When considering a move, consider both the short- and long-term possibilities related to health and well-being that may result in multiple moves.

For older adults, the idea of an initial move is intimidating. A parent may have lived in the family home for decades. The idea of leaving a familiar neighborhood, church community, and friends may be so daunting that the move is delayed and delayed. Another factor that delays moving is the daunting thought of sorting through an entire household to decide what to keep and what to leave behind or donate.

Assisted living communities have a wide range of rates from as low as three thousand dollars a month to twelve thousand dollars a month. Continuing-care retirement communities typically have buy-ins of several hundred thousand dollars that reduce monthly costs. Rates in most care communities increase on average 6-8% percent a year.

Choosing the right community should be based on a number of factors, including lifestyle, personal preferences, hobbies, interest in socialization and communal activities, current and future health factors, finances and other considerations. Because of statistics indicating an increase in the aging population, the number of communities built each year is increasing at a rapid pace.

It is often difficult for family members or individuals to know what questions to ask when interviewing different communities. There are many communities, but not all are the right fit for each care situation. Know that community sales and marketing staff are under significant pressure to maintain a high census, meaning having no or low vacancy. This factor results in some sales staff appearing to be high pressure or offering multiple incentives to entice individuals to select their community.

There are also housing services that bill themselves as "free" to the family. These services receive fees from communities they recommend that are equal to one to two months of the rental rate. If you choose to use a free service, be sure to ask the dollar amount the service provider receives from each community, as this will allow you to be discerning and not be led to choose the community paying the greatest fee. Ask if the service offers access to all available communities. Know that communities refusing to pay referral fees may not be included in their offerings, and one of these may be the perfect community for you or a loved one. Make sure that you are satisfied with the full disclosure of the company before moving forward and that the company has all the normal standards of an ongoing business: for example, business, workers comp, bonding, and liability insurance.

Families are often confused by the type of care provided in assisted living, memory care, and skilled nursing communities. Retirement communities—assisted living, to be more specific—offer assistance such as meals, medication reminding, housekeeping, laundry, some personal care, and social activities. Assisted living communities do not provide "total care," often assumed by families to be medical care. Persons living in assisted living are generally expected to be able to care for themselves relative to medical needs and to request assistance as needed.

Many consumers are surprised to learn that assisted living communities are not regulated by federal guidelines. To provide an example of the variances in state guidelines, at present in the state of Colorado, the licensing requirement to open, to own, and to operate an assisted living community is a thirty-hour course with no requirement for continuing education. If you are curious about the guidelines in your state, contact the department of health who will be able to direct you to the location of this information. Many states are in the process of reviewing guidelines and creating higher standards for community operations.

By definition, assisted living community staff may not provide medical care. Some communities advertise being "nurse owned" or having a nurse on staff. While this information may be accurate, state regulations prohibit nurses from using their professional skills while working in or managing an assisted living community. Medication management and oversight is one exception. When in question, research your state guidelines relative to regulations for assisted living.

All assisted living communities should have a detailed agreement describing the services they provide and do not provide. While the agreement may be thirty to fifty pages thick, I recommend taking the time to read the agreement thoroughly, as this will avoid many common misunderstandings or misperceptions about the level or type of care provided. Many community agreements have arbitration statements that may be declined. Pay particular attention if this is part of your assisted living community agreement and ask if a signature is legally required. This portion of the agreement is more beneficial to the community rather than to the consumer. There are also reasons an assisted living community will ask a resident to leave. Make sure you read the fine details of the contract before you sign.

Within the assisted living category there are various levels of service and types. One type of assisted living community is called a personal care home or a family home. These homes are typically found in neighborhoods and provide assisted living services to a small number of residents, usually four to ten. Some will allow individuals to remain through the end of life with hospice care visiting the home. Individuals who prefer a quieter setting without all the extras offered by larger communities are a good fit for this type of community. Make sure that the community you choose is licensed by the state, as not all personal care or family homes are licensed.

Memory care communities are a specialized type of assisted living community providing care for individuals with dementia, Alzheimer's, Parkinson's, and other types of memory impairments. These communities are usually designed into smaller neighborhoods of ten to thirty residents. Special activities and care tailored to individuals with memory loss are provided in these communities. Many are gated to ensure that individuals diagnosed with memory impairment do not wander out of the building.

Naiveté

Careful planning is required to ensure choosing the right community of care. Caregivers, not realizing the importance of planning for the long term, will move parents from the family home into one type of community—believing that they will be able to remain there for years. A health event occurs that precipitates the need for a move and the individual quickly makes another move.

Adult children investigating care communities often approach this transition with an overly-optimistic point of view due to lack of experience into planning for future care needs. Three types of moves generally occur after retirement. The first relocation focuses on amenities and lifestyle, for example, moving to a warmer climate or to be closer to friends. The second move is the result of physical decline bringing parents closer to family or under formal care, for example, an assisted living community. The final transition, if necessary, results in a move to a nursing home when care needs exceed service levels of assisted living type communities.[24]

This naïveté often results in multiple moves when questions are not asked to ensure that a community is able to provide the level of care needed by a parent for the foreseeable future. "Moves can generate enormous stress, particularly when they're prompted by medical emergencies, which typically require quick action. The faster the decision needs to be made, the more you will need help," reports Dr. Philip Sloane.[25]

A loved one with significant medical needs is a red flag that additional investigation should be completed prior to selecting an assisted living community. If your loved one is considered high need for health oversight, a skilled nursing community may be the best choice to ensure that health concerns do not advance. If you wish to choose a lower level of care, like an assisted living community, then you or a care navigator should visit frequently to provide care oversight so that if a change in condition occurs, immediate plans may be put in place to address the issue. Caregivers retained from outside the community may also be beneficial in providing more frequent insight into daily needs of a loved one.

Some family members see retirement communities as the perfect answer to relieve a caregiver's responsibility and burden. Other family caregivers know that a move is necessary and experience a great degree of guilt when the time comes to move a loved one. While retirement communities offer a range of services, family oversight or oversight by a care navigator remains beneficial for a number of reasons.

Moving a loved one to a care community and never or rarely visiting is a true recipe for disaster that may potentially result in neglect of care needs. It is true that the squeaky wheel receives attention. Communities who know that family rarely visits are likely to be less attentive to a resident with whom no one on the outside ever visits.

Retirement communities provide different levels of care and support. Oversight is beneficial from the standpoint of the family or a care navigator having in-depth knowledge about an individual, including their health history and habits. Often this knowledge proves invaluable in ensuring that an individual receives appropriate care. As mentioned previously, loved ones with complicated or multiple medical diagnoses do require family or care navigator oversight as assisted living communities by state regulation do not provide medical care or oversight.

This is especially relevant as early identification of escalating health concerns is important to ensuring that a loved one receives appropriate care. Here are several examples where intervention or communication might have avoided potential care issues. A parent who eats slowly or has special eating requirements may be ignored or rushed to eat quickly in a larger community with set time frames for mealtimes. The parent begins to lose weight and is diagnosed with "failure to thrive" by a visiting physician who has not investigated why the parent may be losing weight. The physician recommends that the family place the parent on hospice care, and the family, not feeling comfortable questioning the physician, agrees.

The parent dies within a matter of weeks because family was not willing or knowledgeable enough to ask questions about the weight loss and to ask what type of support might have been beneficial at mealtimes. Some family caregivers have little way of knowing the options in these types of situations and often leave decisions to medical professionals, believing that they know best. In this case, the eating difficulty may have resulted from denture pain, a tooth infection, or difficulty chewing that went uninvestigated.

In another situation, an individual with memory loss complained about dental pain for several days. The community care staff, believing the complaint to be unfounded because the individual frequently mentioned imagined events did nothing to investigate the reason for the pain. Nor did they mention the concern to the family. The individual succumbed to a severe dental infection three days later and died.

Another resident had a rapid change in health condition. He became delirious and talked about seeing dead family members. The care staff, certain that the individual was actively dying, failed to send the resident immediately to the emergency room. Staff contacted me as the guardian for this individual. I ordered the community staff to follow the directive on file, to send the resident to the emergency room for evaluation.

At the hospital, my client was diagnosed with a urinary tract infection and pneumonia that was treatable. Because the care staff placed their own personal bias and judgment upon the situation—their belief that my client was actively dying—their choice not to follow my directive would have been irreversible and my client would have died. Poor care results when community staff is too busy, fails to notice issues, allows their personal bias or judgment to enter into care decisions, or fails to take action by contacting family or the responsible person for direction.

Language differences also represent significant risk. I have a Korean speaking client who was unable to respond to questions posed by a physician. The physician made the assumption that my client wanted to die and spoke to me about placing my client on hospice. Knowing my client and the difficulties posed by the language barrier, I disagreed with the physician and retained the services of a translator. My client was able to explain his wishes to receive beneficial medications and to participate in therapy; his wishes were not to die. Had I not retained a translator, the physician would have placed my client on hospice, stopped treatment, and sped him to an early death.

Age represents another risk factor for caregivers unwilling to disagree with physicians. Some physicians believe that because an older care recipient is a certain age that they should not receive care or treatment. I have had many physicians say to me, "he or she is 94." My response is yes—he or she is 94 and deserves care, treatment and your respect.

These are all real-life situations in which I have personally been involved. Care staffs, possessing insufficient patient background, make uninformed or poor decisions when they do not consult the decision maker relative to concerns or questions. Medical professionals assume that caregivers and care recipients understand medical terms and prognosis—this assumption has the potential to result in decision makers making uninformed and faulty decisions. While care communities including assisted living, nursing homes and hospitals are beneficial, care advocacy and discernment are critical and beneficial for those who hope to receive better than average care.

Rehabilitation and Skilled Nursing Communities

The daily cost to remain in a nursing home or rehabilitation center averages $300-500 a day or $106,800-178,000 a year. Nursing homes and rehabilitation communities provide the highest level of care at the greatest cost. While Medicare and private insurance do not reimburse for long-term care, many families will exhaust all available financial resources and apply for Medicaid, a government program that reimburses for care in this type of community.

Confusion exists over the term used to describe this type of community. In reality the terms *nursing home* and *rehabilitation community* represent the same type of care. Research shows that individuals respond more favorably to the term *rehabilitation community* versus *nursing home*. As a result, most communities of this type market their services as "rehab."

Know that the care provided in this type of community, regardless of name, is similar. These communities are federally regulated. Marketing and consumer perception of nursing and rehab communities may lead families to choose a community based on visual appearance rather than the quality of care provided—caveat emptor. Not all communities are created equal. Communities with an older façade provide equally as appropriate care as those recently built.

In situations where parents are hospitalized and sent for rehabilitation, the ongoing involvement of family is critical. Because of insurance requirements, patients are evaluated week to week for "functional progress." If your loved one does not meet week-to-week improvement in functional progress, care communities will discharge or release your parent home with as little as three days' notice whether or not your loved one can physically care for himself or herself.

This dilemma represents a catch-22 for many individuals and families who are unprepared for this news and who have no plan for what to do next. My recommendation is to make a plan to return home or to investigate other options the first day your loved one is admitted for rehabilitation. Planning early ensures a no-surprise experience.

If the plan is for your loved one to remain in a rehabilitation center or nursing home for the remainder of life, care oversight is critical. Higher needs for medical care and attention require a greater degree of involvement to avoid situations of poor care or potential neglect. If this is the situation and funds will be exhausted within a few months, make sure you are aware of the qualifications and application process to apply for Medicaid. Also confirm that there are Medicaid beds available in the community where your loved one resides so that if relocation is required, you may make immediate plans.

There are many care options to support caregivers in providing and managing care for a loved one. While these options may initially seem like more work to investigate and put in place, care navigators are able to relieve family caregivers from day-to-day hands on care, including some of the emotional and physical effects of the role of caregiving.

Exercise: Time Off

Many family caregivers view the opportunity to provide care and to take time off from work as a semi-vacation. Caregiving is hard work, and you will quickly learn that there is no vacation involved. Opting out of the workforce requires careful consideration and a firm plan that addresses financial loss, daily responsibilities, timing, and a backup plan in the event that you need or wish to return to work prior to the end of the need for caregiving.

If you are a family caregiver or a friend and are contemplating a change in employment to become a family caregiver, ask yourself the following ten questions:

1. How will opting out and later returning to the workplace affect my career prospects relative to income potential and advancement?
2. What is the current value of my retirement account?
3. Do I have long-term care insurance, and will I be able to continue to pay the premium?
4. What is the value of savings, potential employer contributions, and social security that I will give up if I opt out of the workforce? What impact will this loss of income have upon my ability to save for retirement?
5. How will I financially support myself when I am not formally employed?
6. Is there a written caregiver agreement between me and the care recipient outlining all the details of the care situation?
7. For what period of time do I agree to be a caregiver?
8. What happens if this time must be extended or if I wish to end this time prior to the agreement date?
9. What actions must I take regarding updating my skills in order to return to the workforce?
10. How will I explain my caregiving time off to future employers?

If you find yourself considering opting out of the workforce to become a full-time caregiver, it is important to consider and understand all aspects of the care situation. In many situations, emotions overtake logic. Caregivers find themselves looking back and realizing that they did not fully take the time to investigate becoming a full-time caregiver before jumping into the role. Returning to the workforce is sometimes more difficult than anticipated.

If you are interested in accessing more tips and information about ideas presented in this chapter and about related subjects, visit http://www.thecaregivingtrapbook.com/store and select Sticker Shock—Who Really Pays?

THE CARING GENERATION®

Tales of the Caring Generation

The Best of My Father

I was born nine years after my next older brother and sister, the twins, that made my life feel as if I were an only child. At the time of my birth my oldest brother joined the Marines and the twins were nine years old. My father worked to support the family and my mother stayed home to raise six children and did not return to work until I was in first grade. Being born late gave me the best of my parents—especially my father.

Dad played with me, pretending he was Indian Joe from The Adventures of Huckleberry Finn. He enjoyed fishing and taught me, not only how to bait a hook, but also how to catch night crawlers for bait. We had a large front yard with a tall sloping bank. On Friday evenings Dad watered the bank just before sunset. We sat on the front steps until the fireflies came out. That was the signal that it was time to hunt for night crawlers. My dad had a large flashlight that he covered with red cellophane

71

paper stretched tight with a rubber band so that the bright light would not scare the night crawlers back into their earthly homes. He shined the light, making it easy for me to see the night crawlers half-resting outside their underground homes in the moonlight.

If you've hunted night crawlers, you know the trick is to figure out which end of the night crawler is closest to its underground home and then quickly and gently grab for that end and then slowly pull the night crawler right out of its home. We kept the night crawlers in a milk carton filled with dirt in the garage overnight, where the temperature was cool. In the morning, before sunrise we set out for a nearby lake with four fishing poles, the night crawlers, and a cooler of food that Mom put together for us. This was our weekend pattern from early June through late August.

August began football season. Dad was one of several custodians and groundskeepers for Central High School in Omaha. Central was Omaha's first all-grades public school, opening in 1859. From Central graduated people who later became famous—movie stars Henry Fonda and Dorothy McGuire, pro football players Gayle Sayers and Keith Jones. The building was surrounded by what seemed like acres of land with flowering peonies in the spring and rows of rosebushes in the heat of summer. Today Central High School is included in the national register of historic buildings.

My father loved sports. He had free passes to all of the high school football games, and on Friday and Saturday nights into the fall, he and I attended every game. He knew all of the players by name, and they knew him because he helped in the locker rooms and watched them during daily practice.

For college football, Dad followed Notre Dame. One of his early heroes, Knute Rockne, was the coach of Notre Dame from the year my father was born in 1918 until 1930. Dad rarely missed a televised game. After Dad retired, a friend of my brother who graduated from Notre Dame was able to secure tickets. We traveled to South Bend for a football game; this was an experience Dad talked about for years.

Spring was time for gardening. Dad started tomato plants from seed inside the house on the kitchen windowsill when it was still too cold outside to plant a garden. When the days warmed, we planted the seedlings in the backyard garden twenty feet deep by forty feet wide. Dad drove to the nearby stockyards for free manure that he mixed with dirt as fertilizer. Every year he and my mother had a garden filled with tomatoes, lettuce, cucumbers, radishes, strawberries, carrots, cauliflower, broccoli, and onions that they shared with neighbors.

Dad taught me to ride a two-wheel bicycle when I was five and to mow the yard when I was ten. He was particular, always wanting straight mowed rows. He sat and watched as I mowed, calling his activity directing. He loved the garden and sat outside in the early mornings talking to the plants and encouraging them to grow.

Dad remained fairly active most of his life, walking through the neighborhood for exercise and visiting with anyone he came across. He woke up early each morning around 5 a.m. to make coffee and to read the newspaper. He enjoyed doing dishes and cleaning the kitchen, calling it KP duty as a carryover from his years in World War II, which he rarely spoke about. His shoes were always shined, and he was a neat dresser. His hair, longer when he was young, was styled in a crew cut as he grew older. Dad enjoyed music and had a voice that rivaled Bing Crosby and Frank Sinatra. On Sunday mornings after attending church, he would turn on the radio and croon to the oldies.

On Halloween, the night before he passed away, we talked on the phone after he watched Notre Dame win against their opponent. He was in the hospital having a routine procedure and did not wake the next day. At his funeral, a twenty-one gun salute and taps were played. For those of you with fathers and grandfathers who are still living, appreciate them, visit often, talk with them on the phone, and enjoy a hobby or activity together. Let them tell you stories of their youth, the war, and raising your family. Record the stories—time passes in the blink of an eye.

Chapter 4

The Oreo Cookie—
Stuck in the Middle

- Health Literacy
- Hindsight is 20/20
- It's No Wonder—Things Go Wrong
- Unexpected Traps
- Skill Gaps
- Advocating for Better Than Average
- Exercise: Learning to Advocate
- Tales of The Caring Generation: Pauline and the Elephants

Health Literacy

The fact that you are reading this book places you into a select category of individuals who continue to read and have an interest in learning. Literacy rates have a significant effect on the ability to successfully navigate daily life and to advocate for and to receive appropriate care.

Shocking statistics on the topic of literacy include:[26]

- 33 percent of high school graduates will never read a book after high school
- 42 percent of college students will never read another book after they graduate
- 50 percent of U.S. adults are unable to read a book written at the eighth-grade level
- 46 percent of American adults can't understand the labels on their prescription drugs

Studies in adult literacy indicate challenges in managing life on a day to day basis related to having knowledge in a variety of areas: "nearly 21.3% of adults in the United States were functionally incompetent relative to health and an additional 22.6% functionally incompetent relative to knowledge of community resources."[27] The ability to apply everyday life skills to situations requiring problem solving ability represents another area of challenge for many adults.[28] Individuals who become independent of government programs become self-sufficient and fare better in life by contributing to society and supporting the national economy.[29]

Your interest in learning also places you in a group of individuals serious about learning how to navigate the role of caregiving. Life skills and the ability to read, to ask questions, to advocate, and to evaluate and understand information has a direct effect on your ability to advocate for beneficial care for yourself and for a loved one.

Adult literacy studies have great significance for those of us living today. If nearly 43.9 percent of adults have difficulty with health and community resources this indicates a significant gap in the ability of adults to advocate for themselves relative to aspects of health and well-being. Many of these knowledge challenged individuals are our aging parents, neighbors, and the older adults we see driving down the street shopping at grocery stores and attending church. These individuals are the caregivers and the care recipients of today who are challenged to learn and to possess the skills to advocate.

Every day we make decisions about health and well-being as we shop in grocery stores, exercise at the gym, or visit our doctor's office. Research indicates that most adults possess poor health literacy. Poor health literacy results in the inability to properly advocate in many areas of life—including caregiving and healthcare—often resulting in unintended and unexpected consequences.

In a report, "The State of Aging and Health in America 2013," health literacy was defined by Healthy People 2010 as "the degree to which individuals have the capacity to obtain, process, and understand basic health information and services needed to make appropriate health decisions."[30]

Limited health literacy occurs when individuals are unable to find and use needed health information and services. For example:[31]

- Nearly 9 of 10 adults have trouble using the everyday health information that is routinely available in our health care facilities, retail outlets, media and communities.
- Among adult age groups, those aged 65 or older have the smallest percentage of people with proficient health literacy skills and the largest percentage with "below basic" health literacy skills.
- Without clear information and an understanding of the information's importance, people are more likely to skip necessary medical tests, end up in the emergency room more often, and have a harder time managing chronic diseases such as diabetes or high blood pressure.

One effect of poor health literacy is the significant number of older adults who have difficulty managing their health through the activity of taking prescription drugs correctly. This results from an inability to read and understand directions on the prescription label. Many older adults have multiple health diagnoses requiring use of multiple prescription drugs. As the number of prescription bottles increases, so does the mental acuity required to manage multiple prescription medications relative to ordering, reordering, and taking medications properly.

An aging body more slowly processes prescription drugs. This means that prescription drugs remain in the body for longer periods of time. "Taking medications improperly—whether by accident or intent—can worsen an older adult's health. Older adults who take prescription medications improperly have a higher risk of accidents, falls, and injuries." [32] Adverse drug reactions (ADRs) "cause three to six percent of all hospital admissions and are responsible for about five to ten percent of inpatient costs. ADRs represent an important medical problem in older people." [33]

Another result of poor health literacy is that many individuals sign hospital treatment forms and readily participate in tests and procedures that they likely do not understand because of a fear of asking questions or appearing ignorant. Many have documents placed in front of them that they sign without reading. Other older adults with hearing or vision loss sign forms for procedures that have not been read or explained to them. Others fail to ask the right questions because of feeling rushed, intimidated, or because of a lack of education or a language barrier.

The value of family caregivers or care navigators must not be underestimated when care is needed. How often is it difficult for us to identify issues in our own lives, yet others on the outside easily identify the issues and provide suggestions? How many times does the problem or solution evade us because of a lack of knowledge and ability to problem solve? How many times are we so overwhelmed that we fail to believe a solution exists? Many times when we are in the thick of caregiving situations, it is nearly impossible to "see the forest through the trees." This is exactly when an advocate is beneficial.

"The rate of growth in healthcare spending in the U.S. has outpaced the growth rate in the gross domestic product (GDP), inflation, and population for many years. Total spending on health is projected to reach $4 trillion, 20% of GDP by 2015." [34] Another study reports that patients with chronic illness in their last two years of life account for about 32 percent of total Medicare spending; much of the spending is attributed to physician and hospital fees associated with repeated hospitalizations.[35]

These statistics are staggering and indicate that healthcare costs will continue to increase at a rapid pace. What questions should we be asking? Are we spending money on healthcare treatments that may extend life but not improve quality of life? Do we believe that we deserve the best and most expensive treatment even if the outcome will not change? What do individuals want at end of life? Most patients with serious illnesses report that they would prefer to die at home. Yet studies report that most patients die in the hospital, and the care provided at the time of death does not match patient desires or preferences. Where is the disconnect? Both of my parents lived at home until prior to their deaths, yet both died in the hospital—rather than at home.

The value of education and advocacy in the areas of aging and healthcare should not be understated or underestimated. The value of expressing your end-of-life wishes and appointing the right person to implement these wishes is critically important. Waiting to make these plans may have disastrous results if you are involved in a tragic or unexpected accident.

If you believe an unexpected accident will never happen to you, visit The Caring Generation website and watch the video on the main page titled "Eat Cookies." David Drummond's life experience may change your mind about not needing or delaying completion of legal documents expressing your wishes or appointing a power of attorney.

Hindsight is 20/20

If only we knew at an early age what most of us know today; would our lives be different? How might our later years fare better as the result of an earlier awareness of the long-term consequences of our choices? Our lives are formed of building blocks. These include our health, daily activities like work or career, family and social ties, hobbies, interests, and other aspects that form a full and rewarding life of meaning and purpose, or for some, a life of regret.

While traditional education is important, so is the importance of acquiring life skills and having a realistic outlook related to aging. Many people who are aging tell me that they avoid thinking about the future because they realize "the end is coming day by day." While aging certainly poses challenges, older individuals have much to offer in the way of wisdom, experience, and stories. They also have the ability to remain active and engaged participants in life rather than focusing on the end of life.

Many previously active older adults defy the vision that it is common to be sick and old. They continue to exercise and focus daily on health and exercise. They remain socially engaged in communities and active as volunteers. End of life does not have to be filled with sickness and depression unless the choices one makes leads to this physical or mental state.

It is best not to sweep aside or delay discussions about care needs, tasks, and other practical concerns that become more relevant as we age. Depending on whom you ask, the idea of care presents a contrast of opinions. In my opinion, caregiving presents two opposing roles: one role represents task work, while the other role represents focus on relationships. It is best to be optimistic and realistic about both.

Task work focuses on the practicalities of caregiving such as meal preparation and cooking, cleaning, laundry, shopping, and other tasks that do not require one-on-one interaction with the care recipient. The relationship aspect focuses on developing and supporting the relationship between the caregiver and the care recipient and the relationships with other involved family members. In my opinion, focusing on the relationship is the more important aspect of caregiving. Tasks can be done by supporting characters. Material belongings offer little consolation in the absence of positive memories with loved ones.

The life of your aging loved one has a time limit, a finite end. In my opinion, a caregiver's time is best devoted to making the best of the time remaining and in making memories to be cherished. The aftereffects of the caregiving journey are the wisdom, experiences, relationships, and personal stories that families and caregivers will remember long after loved ones are gone.

By utilizing a system to set boundaries, identify alternatives, and lay out a plan for the future, including the practical aspects of care, caregivers are able to focus on the relational aspects of a loved one's care. In the midst of fears, frustrations, and uncertainty in the role of caregiving, it is critical to remember that the care recipient is a person with wisdom and insight that might surprise you—if you ask.

It is easy to take our eyes off long-term goals when immediate caregiving needs compete for our attention. Few individuals possess insight into how to plan for long-term care; for the most part, only those who were exposed to caregiving at an early age can understand the aspects that might be involved in caring for a family member.

Except for physical education, classes about health and good nutrition are absent from school curriculums. Yet, independent of the benefit of formal education, good health, and nutrition habits have one of the most significant positive effects on the human body. If there is hope of changing individual reliance on the medical profession to solve health problems, recognition of the importance of education and self-advocacy must occur. Diverting for a moment to the bigger picture, let's look at a few statistics that might surprise you.

It's No Wonder—Things Go Wrong

Education is a privilege. Its value is misunderstood and underestimated throughout the world. Take a look at Afghanistan, one of the least developed countries in the world. Afghanistan has an educational system comparable to that of the United States in the year 1900. The average life expectancy of a person born in Afghanistan is fifty-years. Seventy one percent of the population is illiterate, unable to read or write. About thirty-five percent of its population is unemployed and thirty six percent live below the national poverty line suffering from shortages of housing, clean drinking water, and electricity.[36]

The benefit of education is more significant than we realize. A high school education reduces government spending on healthcare, crime, and welfare, and results in higher tax revenues. Let me paint a picture of a country where "about one-third of all students who enter high school do not graduate on time if ever. More than two-thirds of the inmates in state prisons are school dropouts."[37] A country where 1.2 million students drop out of high school each year; this equals one student dropping out every twenty-six seconds or 7,000 a day.[38]

A country where nearly eighty percent of dropouts depend on the government for healthcare assistance, where each youth who drops out and enters a life of drugs and crime costs the nation between $1.7-2.3 million dollars in crime control and health expenditures. It's no surprise that the children of dropouts are more likely to drop out and to live in poverty.[39]

What country would support such dismal educational outcomes? *These are education statistics for the United States of America.*

Each day in the U.S., people spend on average four hours watching TV, five hours with digital media like the Internet and cellphones, about one and a half hour listening to the radio, and thirty minutes reading the newspaper or magazines.[40] Fifty percent of adults are unable to read an eighth grade level book. Forty-two percent of college graduates never read another book after college. Eighty percent of families didn't buy or read a book last year; fifty-seven percent of books started aren't read to completion.[41]

Millions of books sit idle in public libraries each year. Yet the cost to check out a library book in person or online is nothing, zero, nada. My mother took me to the library at the age of five to attend Saturday book club; she supported my love for books, newspapers, magazines, and education. I continue to be fascinated by the knowledge and education books, magazines, and the Internet provide. Not enough time exists in any given day for me to read.

As you walk by a newspaper stand, drive by a bookstore or a library, or search the Internet, consider the benefits of reading and the benefits of education. Think about how fortunate you are *not* to have been born in Afghanistan; think about how fortunate you are to have been born and to live in the United States—to have access to education. Talk to your children, to the young people you know, and encourage them to stay in school. If you have the time and interest, return to school. It's never too late to learn. Education is never wasted. The ability to advocate in care situations because of knowledge possessed is more valuable than you might imagine.

Unexpected Traps

The role of caregiving poses many unexpected challenges. While the process of bodily aging means that many of us will eventually need and receive care, it is also likely that we will receive care from professional caregivers. Professional caregivers come in a number of backgrounds, shapes, and sizes that include physicians, nurses, nursing assistants, hospital or care community staff, care managers, in-home caregivers, occupational and physical therapists, hospice staff, attorneys, CPAs, bankers, and any individual involved in supporting health or well-being. Professional caregivers are, in reality, anyone who provides support and who is not a family member, friend, or acquaintance.

Involvement and support from professional caregivers is valuable to the point that the support benefits and improves quality of life. However, many of us find that the care we desire for a loved one is not always the care that results. Involvement with professional caregivers who fail to meet our expectations can be equally, if not more, frustrating than dealing with difficult family members.

Professional caregivers who are experienced and ethical provide value that is of significant benefit to care situations. Others who choose the care industry to work through their own personal caregiving issues or those who lack professional boundaries can be extremely damaging to care situations and family interactions. Many times it is difficult for family to distinguish between ethical and professional caregivers of questionable character until situations have gone past the point of no return.

Caregiving families in unfamiliar territory often rely on the expertise of those in the healthcare and aging professions. While advice and experience are the reasons professionals are utilized, families must also be discerning in developing these relationships. In many situations, understanding industry limitations and asking the right questions help avoid frustrating experiences on the part of families seeking care and support for a loved one. The challenge is that these limitations are not always evident. Family caregivers assume that healthcare providers are able to provide a higher level or a greater number of services than industry standards permit.

Americans are living longer and therefore are accumulating more diseases and disabilities. One in five Americans will be eligible for Medicare by 2030. Statistics also indicate a shortage of healthcare providers certified or specializing in geriatrics.[42] If you have attempted to find a physician accepting Medicare or a psychiatrist or psychologist providing mental health services, you may have already discovered a lack of available providers. If you or a loved one has received services from home health or in-home caregivers you may also be experiencing challenges finding qualified and caring assistance in your home.

Nursing home direct care jobs have few skill requirements, minimal selectivity in hiring, cursory initial orientation and on-the-job training, low wages and benefits, and supervision focused on completion of defined tasks. Workers are treated as unreliable and easily replaceable.[43] This description is accurate of most direct care workers in skilled and non-skilled home care and those working in assisted living communities, in nursing homes, and in hospitals and is fueled by the idea of a "low road" enterprise.

The term *low road* enterprise was initially coined by the manufacturing industry, where focus was on jobs geared to specific tasks requiring narrow skills with no discretion over the task and the provision of relatively low wages. In a sense, a worker was hired to place a widget into a piece of machinery and repeated this task hundreds if not thousands of times throughout the day.

How many of you remember the television series, *I Love Lucy*, and the episode with Lucy and Ethel wrapping chocolates on the assembly line in a candy factory? Google "I Love Lucy's Famous Chocolate Scene" and you will see a funny but simple example of a low road enterprise.[44] Today fast food restaurants like McDonald's and Burger King and some care communities may be considered low road enterprises. It is important to understand that many of the individuals caring for your loved ones have low levels of training and skills. This does not mean that these individuals are not caring and committed however it may mean that you may wish to seek advice from individuals with greater education and qualifications.

We know that family caregiving is difficult from an emotional perspective due to the stresses involved in caring for parents. Imagine how the dynamic changes for professional community care staff who are not only required to manage the care of ten individuals in their daily schedules, but who also come into direct contact with concerned and demanding family members every single workday.

Having this insight may allow you to manage expectations regarding care. This also presents an opportunity for you to openly discuss care needs with professional providers and to set expectations that may reasonably be met, avoiding frustration on your part and the professional provider organization. Many families fail to have these discussions because of the perception that the care provided is at a higher level than may be realistic.

Because the senior care industry is considered a booming industry, the number of entrants in all business categories from in-home care to care communities to case managers to physicians specializing in elder care, is and will continue to be significant. This presents many inherent risks of which consumers should be aware. Rather than taking experience at face value, investigate the background and the qualifications of the individuals from whom you seek support. Are the individuals or organizations part of national certifying organizations? Do they possess advanced degrees? How many years of experience do they have and in what capacity?

So many areas in healthcare remain unregulated. Lack of regulation poses danger for the average consumer who may lack literacy skills to thoroughly investigate service providers.

In 2011, Michael Berens, a *Seattle Times* reporter, completed an investigative report called "Seniors for Sale: Exploiting the Aging and Frail in Washington's Adult Family Homes."[45] Since this time, other investigative reports have surfaced including the 2013 report by PBS's *Frontline* called "Life and Death in Assisted Living."[46] As mentioned in the previous chapter, standards for qualifications and levels of care vary throughout the healthcare industry. As a consumer of services, the benefits of being informed are significant, or you or your loved one may be at risk.

Skill Gaps

Whether care communities or in-home care agencies, all types of traditional healthcare and service providers face challenges as the number of older adults needing services exceeds the ability of companies to hire, train, and retain qualified employees. Lacking is a sufficient number of individuals interested in working in an industry with high emotional and physical demands and low pay, like care agencies and care communities. This represents a significant industry challenge relative to quality of care and customer satisfaction, of which many families are unaware.

The in-home care or non-medical caregiving agency niche is challenged to hire reliable and qualified workers. With a pay rate averaging nine to twelve dollars an hour and a general lack of healthcare benefits, employee turnover averages 50 percent or more each year. Because of an employee pool that receives low wages, caregiving employees frequently fail to show up for work, call in sick, or leave to find a better-paying job. This revolving door of staff change results in frustration by family members who feel that caregiving agencies are unable to provide consistent and qualified caregivers for loved ones. The reality is that this expectation by family members may be impossible to meet until wages and service rate increases are accepted by the consumer.

Frequent turnover fails to support the industry model of culture change and person-centered care—that despite significant national efforts since the 1980s with the goal to improve quality of care—has not been successful in achieving this goal across all care models. Care remains substandard in many areas of the industry.

Companies, employing professional caregivers in the areas of nursing and long term care, find it challenging to provide consistent and well-trained employees in part, because of high levels of job turnover. Also challenging is the transfer of consistent and accurate communication across members of the care team to ensure that care recipients receive appropriate and beneficial care.[47][48] Other challenges include poor organizational response to changes in internal processes. Equally challenging are uncontrollable external environmental changes.[49][50]

Non-medical caregiving is an industry where caregivers are largely unsupervised because their work environment is in the home of the care recipient. Without a great deal of training in ethics, character, honesty, and setting boundaries, employees often act in a manner that does not support company policies. Individuals seek this type of work because they care. In more cases than not, employees lack common sense and make errors in judgment that cause harm rather than benefit to care situations.

Great temptation exists on the part of non-medical caregiving employees to accept gifts or items that the care recipient wishes to give the employee. Care recipients and their family members often cross professional boundaries because they become personally involved with the caregiver and want to express appreciation by giving items the family may no longer need but that the caregiver may not possess. These actions result in unintended consequences—caregivers are terminated for disregarding company rules about receiving gifts—and families are angry with care agency staff because their favorite caregiver was terminated.

For family caregivers who hire in-home caregiving agencies, it is important to understand that care agency guidelines exist to set boundaries for care. Remember that these caregivers are employees, not your friend and not your family. Keeping this in mind will stop you from crossing an employer-employee boundary that may result in the termination of your favorite caregiver.

Similar hiring, retention, and literacy issues exist with professional caregivers: nurses, lab technicians, and others who lack skills to read manuals or to follow verbal or written instructions. Professional caregivers represent diverse populations. Cultural backgrounds and language barriers exist when care recipients, community residents, management staff, and caregivers have differences in native languages and especially when English is a second language.

Many nursing assistants and caregivers possess a servant's heart and a sincere desire to help but lack an appropriate level of literacy to communicate with residents. I have been in care communities where care staff fear losing their jobs if management recognizes that they have poor skills in reading or writing in English. Yet on the other hand, the care staffs fail to understand the negative effects of poor literacy on patient care that might potentially result in care mistakes or unintentional deaths.

Care recipients with racial biases also present challenges. Diverse caregivers are often on the receiving end of discrimination and negative comments by care recipients. While few want to acknowledge the prejudices of older adults toward caregivers of different races, race and prejudice have been and will continue to be issues in the provision of care that must be addressed proactively by professional care companies and family caregivers.

The fact cannot be ignored that issues with literacy and a poor command of the English language have the potential to result in serious issues—for example, improper reporting or transposition of the numbers of a blood pressure or a blood sugar reading that results in a medication change or dispensing error. Cultural backgrounds and language barriers must be acknowledged and addressed by the provision of ongoing education by caregiving companies.

For all caregivers, many of the frustrations related to receiving or providing care are the result of the challenges of balancing a multitude of aspects of daily life with a lack of problem-solving and critical-thinking skills. The ability to solve problems, to cope and to respond to change, is supported by education coupled with experience and common sense. This is an area where family caregivers must also be discerning, relative to evaluating information and services provided.

Inaccurate information and opinions from industry professionals complicate care situations. Some caregiving professionals may offer advice that is faulty, especially if the professional is not an expert in the field of which they are advising. This professional advice often makes decision making a challenge for family caregivers hoping to make the right choices and decisions for a parent. Just as you would expect a CPA to know tax rules, asking a tax question to your financial planner may not result in an accurate response. Many specialties exist, and it is important to rely only on individuals you know who specialize in the subject at hand.

Competing and self-interests of hospital conglomerates, insurance companies, individual healthcare providers, and the many other providers in the industry also make navigating the system a challenge. For example, one of the more controversial portions, Section 3025 of the Affordable Care Act, establishes the Hospital Readmissions Reduction Program that requires CMS to reduce payments to acute care hospitals with excess readmissions, effective for discharges beginning on October 1, 2012 for the applicable conditions of heart attack (AMI), heart failure (HF) and pneumonia (PN). In 2015 the conditions expand to include chronic obstructive pulmonary disease (COPD) and total hip (THA) and total knee (TKA) replacements. [51] [52]

Admittedly, the rates for hospital readmission are high and the cost of readmissions expensive to the healthcare system. However, my suspicion is those who wrote this section had no idea of the extent to which hospitals would change aspects of care to avoid financial penalties. I have personally experienced battles in having many of my clients become admitted to hospitals for needed care.

Hospitals and insurance companies are holding patients on observation rather than risk an admission that might turn into a readmission with a related penalty. This holding for observation results in greater cost to patients and lessens the risk of financial penalties to hospitals. For older adults who need care, having to battle the system to receive care, in my opinion, is deplorable. Many older adults lack the ability to advocate for themselves.

Navigating the complexities of healthcare and aging services become a puzzle for caregivers who may not know what questions to ask. The skills of advocating successfully in the healthcare and aging environment might be compared to asking a person to change the oil in their own car when they have no prior experience. If the role of caregiving is unfamiliar, there is a greater likelihood of making poor choices and of experiencing poor outcomes.

When decisions relate to the life and well-being of a loved one, we all hope or expect to receive better than average care or results. Possessing the confidence, skill, and ability to question care recommendations is a critical and beneficial skill. Certain recommendations may financially benefit the provider but have no or little benefit to the care recipient.

Several years ago I had an experience with a client diagnosed with Alzheimer's disease for whom I was guardian. We were directed to a breast-imaging center for a second opinion by my client's primary care physician because the original mammogram appeared suspect. I took my client for additional testing. After the test, the nurse mentioned that the individual reading the test wanted to perform a needle biopsy and additional testing.

I questioned the nurse, and she directed me to the technician reading the results. Standing in front of the scans, the individual pointed to multiple calcifications. I asked if the calcifications were cancerous, he said no. I asked, "In how many years might these calcifications transform into cancer?" He replied, "Two to ten years." I explained to him that my client had advanced Alzheimer's disease and that I had no intention of placing her through the stress of additional tests for calcifications that currently were not harmful and "might" be cancer in two to ten years, as we would not treat the cancer. He was visibly angry and disagreed with my decision.

On the way back to the dressing room, the nurse thanked me and said, "You have no idea how many people we put through unnecessary tests in a given day because the procedures generate revenue." I thanked her for her honesty. I knew I had made the right decision for my client. Many family caregivers, not knowing the right questions to ask, may have been intimidated by refusing the recommendation of the technician. In this case, continued testing would not have changed the outcome for my client. Testing would have resulted in costs for my client and contributed to profits for the testing center and a possible bonus for the technician.

My advice is to question medical diagnoses, to question procedures, and to question the need for surgery to make sure there is a clear understanding of the recommendations and of the expected benefits and risks. Also important is to ask about the prognosis or outcome. While physicians—especially those involved in cancer treatments—become personally involved with families, many hesitate to give bad news unless pressed for the information.

I have experienced the failure to give bad news or to discuss a prognosis in situations where there is motivation to continue experimental treatments that give hope but no positive results. The patient participates in extensive and sometimes painful treatment, and death is still the result.

Time and preparedness are also factors in receiving better than average care. Because of the constraints of the healthcare industry relative to insurance, the time scheduled for in-office visits is extremely limited. If patients or family caregivers are not prepared with a list of questions, there may be little time to discuss preventative strategies or actions that may be taken to decrease dependence on a certain medication or what actions might be taken to reverse a newly diagnosed condition that has not yet advanced to a point of no return.

Physicians and the healthcare community have recommended to patients to exercise, to lose weight, to avoid alcohol and drugs, and to stop smoking. Patients for years have ignored these recommendations. Consumers pay for this ignorance and denial by way of a system that prescribes pills or recommends treatment rather than investigating permanent solutions for change. When traditional methods fail, I recommend investigating alternative therapies, many of which are not reimbursed by health insurance.

Advocating for Better Than Average

We are living with a fragmented healthcare system that requires consumer activism and advocacy in order to receive above average care and treatment. We live in a system that manages from averages and minimum standards of care. This is why the care in many communities, medical offices, and hospitals appears to be substandard. Insurance reimbursements dictate available treatment and care. Hospitals, medical offices, and doctors are restricted in the services that can be offered due to insurance reimbursements and government regulations.

For example, new regulations from the Affordable Care Act, as previously mentioned, demand that hospitals reduce readmissions or experience financial penalties. This is the side of the healthcare system of which consumers lack awareness that results in significant risks. Providers are well aware of system limitations but fail to offer explanations due to concerns of lawsuits that might arise from the perception of poor care.

The unfortunate reality is that many caregivers and care recipients accept low or poor standards of care because most lack the ability to advocate. Most of us fare better by having someone else advocate or speak up for our needs. If you are in a situation where you feel uncomfortable advocating, retain a care navigator to advocate on your behalf. As care navigators, we persist in asking the tough questions. We also mediate situations with caregiving families. A care navigator is the expert needed when a caregiver knows he or she should take action but due to the situation feels immobilized to move forward or to act.

The details involved in care planning may be compared to assembling a stereo system. If you are familiar with the parts and have the mechanical aptitude, the outcome will be a sound system run by remote operation that provides beautiful-sounding music. In caregiving, if you lack understanding of all the planning components and how they work together, putting a plan together for a loved one may result in a faulty plan and a situation that fails to work as expected.

The school for caregiving may be compared to the school of hard knocks. The act of caregiving is learned through trial, error, and experience. Unfortunately, most family caregivers lack the time to learn these skills because of being thrown into an emergency situation that requires immediate response and action.

Should a loved one be the recipient of a family caregiver's lack of expertise? In many situations, a care navigator will shorten the caregiver's learning curve and provide invaluable advice regarding the care needs of a parent. Sometimes an hour-long consultation will provide the insight and direction needed. In more complicated situations, as we will examine in the following chapters, ongoing coordination of services and recommendations is beneficial. As in all things, and especially in caregiving, we don't know what we don't know. A lack of knowledge or sense of naiveté can be dangerous in care situations.

Exercise: Learning to Advocate

In care situations, becoming the squeaky wheel and knowing what questions to ask offer the best outcome. When you or a loved one needs care, do not be a shrinking violet or feel that your desire for information will be bothersome to a provider. It is the provider's responsibility to make sure that caregivers understand diagnoses, systems, and procedures. If you don't ask, the provider has no way of knowing that you have questions or lack understanding.

Below are three scenarios to help you identify questions to ask when working with individuals in care situations:

1. When working with staff at a physician's office, document vitals like weight, blood pressure, etc. and ask if these numbers are within range. During the visit, ask questions about any information, word, or description you do not understand. Ask the doctor to explain what he is examining and why. Before leaving ask, "Is there anything else I should be asking that I am not asking?" Prior to leaving ask for a detailed visit report. This will allow you to review the practitioner's notes from the visit and to follow up to ask questions you may have not considered during the appointment.

2. Get to know the nurse on staff, the director of nursing, the director of healthcare, or whoever has oversight of the care of a loved one in a care community. If in a hospital or a nursing home, I recommend daily phone calls or contact with the nurse on staff especially if conditions are being treated. It is easy for a significant change in condition to occur unexpectedly and for staff to be so busy that they fail to notify family members. If your loved one resides in an assisted living community or skilled nursing community and health is stable, weekly contact is recommended. Communities are to contact responsible parties regarding any change in health or condition.

3. For all other professionals with whom you work, ask about their background, years of experience, certifications, association

memberships, and experience specific to your situation. It is common for caregivers to assume that because an individual works in a particular setting, they have the associated level of education, skills, and experience. Never assume—always ask.

Situations quickly become complicated as care needs increase. If you are in a care situation and you feel that you don't know the right questions to ask or you are unsure how to advocate for your needs or the needs of a loved one, becoming more educated offers benefits.

If you are interested in accessing more tips and information about ideas presented in this chapter and about related subjects, visit http://www.thecaregivingtrapbook.com/store and select The Oreo Cookie—Stuck in the Middle.

THE CARING GENERATION®

Tales of the Caring Generation

Pauline and the Elephants

From a young age, Pauline had an interest in teaching. She enjoyed being the center of attention in a group. She played teacher with small groups of her friends after school. After Pauline graduated from high school she went to a teachers college. She was highly intelligent, always making good grades.

Her mother, Bridget, worried that her reliance on intellect would one day have a negative effect as she believed Pauline's social skills to be somewhat lacking. Because of her inability to make friends with others considered her peers in college, Pauline adopted people with problems and then poured her life into fixing or controlling their lives.

As one might imagine, Bridget's advice and concerns for Pauline's well-being fell on deaf ears. She and her husband remained as supporters in the background of Pauline's life. Pauline never married, telling her parents she never found anyone suitable; her mother believed that she never found anyone willing to live under her controlling personality.

Pauline was a tireless educator, teaching English and history at the high school level. Her students found her tough but were filled with respect for her knowledge and talent. The faculty found her an odd personality, keeping mostly alone. Her efforts resulted in successfully educated children. Even though she was perceived as odd, the administrators could find nothing lacking in her academic efforts and pursuits.

As she grew older, she took an interest in travel. Her idea of summer vacation was to substitute teach in other countries where she could sightsee on the weekends. She taught one summer in Africa and took a liking to elephants that she began to collect in various forms. In her home on shelf after shelf posed elephants made of wood, plastic, papier mache'—stuffed elephants, elephants of all types.

When Pauline was seventy-five, she was hospitalized. A neighbor reported not seeing Pauline for several days. Emergency personnel found her lying on the floor at home from an apparent late night fall in which she had broken her arm and could not get up to call for help. Upon entering her home, they discovered piles and piles of paper, items stacked so high that one could barely walk a path through the house. It seemed that all of those years of trips abroad resulted in things too treasured for Pauline to throw out or give away. Her treasures filled her home from floor to ceiling.

Her behavior was erratic, and the physicians at the hospital questioned her ability to care for herself. She was evaluated by several psychiatrists, who recommended that she have someone to manage her day-to-day affairs. There was no family available, as her parents had passed on years before and she had no brothers or sisters. No friends came forward for the task, so professionals were appointed.

Pauline lived in her own world, believing to be years younger; anyone approaching her was a student, someone for her to educate and direct. Many attempts were made to find suitable housing for Pauline but each time she always found something wrong—she complained about the food, the other residents, a room too small, or a bed too hard.

It was finally decided that Pauline would live at Kennedy Village, a memory care community with staff specializing in working with difficult people—those with undiagnosed personality disorders. On any given day, Pauline was kind one moment and accusing the next. She changed clothing multiple times in a single day, rearranging drawers in her dresser, removing everything from her closet only to return it after rearranging clothing by color or length. She spent most of her time alone, as being with other people only agitated her—they were always doing something wrong.

One day a week, a former student visited. James was Pauline's only connection to her past, a past in which she remembered him as a young boy of fifteen in her history class. James's mother, diagnosed with Alzheimer's disease, lived at the same community. James visited and reminisced with Pauline about school days and her travels. He remained a loyal friend and visited until her death.

Many individuals find themselves alone at end of life. If you have distant family, find ways to keep in touch, if only with occasional phone calls and cards. If you have time, volunteer or adopt an older adult living in a nursing home or care community. The act of volunteering might serve as a good example to young children of the value of caring for older adults. Your life will be enriched in many unexpected ways and you will bring light into the life of an isolated older adult, and the good deed may be returned in an unexpected manner at the time you need care.

PART TWO

THE FAST MOVING TRAIN

Setting boundaries and taking a break from caregiving responsibilities allows a fresh perspective and many times a new start. An afternoon at the movies, lying in a hammock in the backyard or a drive in the country may relieve feelings of stress and frustration.

Chapter 5

The Starry-Eyed Caregiver

- When the Bubble Bursts
- The Midnight Phone Call
- Oblivion and Assumptions
- Who Will Provide Care?
- Exercise: Avoiding Surprises
- Tales of the Caring Generation: The Story of Mr. D.

When the Bubble Bursts

As children and young adults, life is filled with hope and possibility. The end of life, precipitated by loss of physical ability and declining health, remains an unknown. When we are young, our concerns relate to being accepted by friends, pairing with a first boyfriend or girlfriend, deciding whether to attend college, and making choices about career. Depending on parental values and lifestyle, children may grow up in a family where relationships were emphasized, or children may have experienced a lifestyle of materialism, toys, and gadgets to replace time not spent with parents.

I grew up in a family where everything I needed—not necessarily wanted—was provided. It was not until I attended high school and noticed the material belongings of my classmates did I realize that everyone did not live the same lifestyle and have the same values as my family. I rode the bus to school during all four years of high school. Most if not all of my classmates were given cars as gifts for their sixteenth birthday. I was aware that my parents were barely able to pay my high school tuition, so I did not ask for extra money to join groups or to attend high school trips.

When children progress through grade and high school and make friends, many become more focused on wants and needs for things and activities rather than on family. Events may be missed that allow insight into the fact that life may be fading away from Grandma or Grandpa. Discussions surrounding grandparents needing care or eventually dying are delayed or discussion is not initiated by parents who choose to protect children from death until it actually occurs.

I recall my mother being involved in Grandma's life, yet there were never specific discussions about aspects of Grandma's aging or failing health. When these discussions do not occur, children become sheltered from the reality of failing health and death. While the loss of a grandparent may be a young child's first experience with death, children rarely understand the impact felt by a parent when losing their parent.

This lack of understanding is supported by a parent's desire to present a strong outward appearance to their children. Parents avoid talking about the grief they feel at the loss of their parent. This absence of discussion places a protective layer of naiveté around young children so that discussion about the eventual loss of their parents is delayed until many years later when the failing health and potential loss of a parent become a harsh reality.

In my opinion, the significance of the experience of losing a grandparent is overlooked as an opportunity to present death as part of life to young children. There is benefit from awareness that life does turn full circle, that children may care for elderly parents and that parents eventually die. If these discussions happen early in life and are presented as a normal part of life, how might this knowledge support care toward the end of life versus resulting in the shock that many adult children experience when the role of caregiving surfaces?

There is no class, no book, or a movie that prepares us for the events of life including college, marriage, raising children, or the process of aging or dying. Television commercials entice us toward consumerism—buy, buy, buy. Advertising about retirement fails to advise that our later years might be filled with unexpected pitfalls and challenges.

Until we arrive at retirement age, there is little insight that many of our peers, if not us, will have health problems that result in later life being more about taking pills and attending medical appointments instead of the dream of participation in exciting events or travel. Many of my clients tell me that the silver lining imagined in retirement quickly becomes tarnished.

Most of us live in a bubble of good or at least stable health. We are immune to the health challenges that other people face. Then one day— often suddenly—the bubble bursts, and change personally affects us, or the need to provide care for a loved one arises. Little do we realize until we are personally affected that these challenges occur every day to other people in other situations in other parts of the world.

A baby is born with a defect that will require a lifetime of attention and vigilance. Excited, expectant parents are forced to change gears from the role of a parent-caregiver for a bubbling, laughing bundle of joy to a caregiver experiencing sleepless nights and constant worry. Worry exists about how to provide care, how to pay for medical expenses, and concerns linger about the life experience of this child. This child will require constant care, if not from parents, then from someone else. This child will require support and oversight that will extend past the lifetime of his or her parents.

Another scenario, a young adult is involved in an automobile accident, a skiing accident or chooses to drink alcohol after taking a handful of prescription drugs. Life changes in the blink of an eye. Rather than a movie star found dead after a prescription drug overdose this brother, sister, husband or wife survives but only after heroic measures to revive are taken by the staff of the hospital emergency room, returning life to a body without oxygen for an indeterminate amount of time. This life will never be the same. This life will require significant care.

Guilt results; the family blames themselves. The husband should have been in that car. The brother should have made sure that helmets and protective gear were worn skiing. The often professed statement "I'll never take another drink" should have been met with disbelief at least one more time by the family member on the other end of the phone line hearing the repeated and often broken promise.

A healthy-looking middle-aged man is suddenly diagnosed with leukemia. A life of military service, of work, and of raising a family is cut short by an unexpected diagnosis. In spite of treatments and participation in clinical trials giving hope for recovery, after eight months he dies, leaving behind a wife and two children.

For those whose lives do not end but continue, for individuals plagued early in life by chronic disease, poor health, or physical disability, the experience of living may seem like an altered reality. Healthy individuals have little experience in common with the daily challenges experienced by the early disabled or by those whose work careers ended early due to health issues or an unexpected accident.

From a physical standpoint, the human body is like an automobile that benefits from ongoing maintenance like oil changes and replacing worn-out parts. The human body benefits from having fluids checked, batteries recharged and tires kicked. From a young age, the way one attends to health and physical well-being has a major effect on the same aspects in later years. While hereditary factors and genes contribute to our longevity, lifestyle choices may have an equal if not greater impact. If control over the quality of life as we age is desired, attention must be given to the individual aspects when younger that enable us to control future outcomes.

Individuals considered healthy today may have taken action to change health and lifestyle because of seeing a parent or other family member whose life was greatly affected by poor health, multiple medical appointments, frequent hospitalizations, and a self-expressed misery of living. Individuals attentive to their health through diet and exercise view this action as a moral imperative with the goal of making it less likely that someone, like adult children, will bear the responsibility of their care. Older adults I know hope that they will not be burden to anyone, especially their children.

With age, many individuals become unable to manage or to hide the effects of declining memory and other physical losses—until those problems accumulate and result in disaster when an elderly driver mistakes the gas pedal for the brake. Patients diagnosed with heart disease or other chronic diseases are often able to manage on their own until their physical condition declines to the point where self-care becomes challenging, if not impossible.

It is easy for adult children or friends to miss signs that indicate care and support are needed. This occurs when each situation or event is viewed as a single episode that does not appear to be significant. A friend may notice one concern. A child notices another, and a second child observes yet another. When events are combined and accumulated, the overall big picture of the inability of a parent to care for himself or herself becomes significant, shocking and eye opening. How is it that a need for assistance was not noticed earlier, sometimes even years earlier?

No one escapes this world without becoming physically old or frail unless life is ended unexpectedly by an accident or terminal health diagnosis at an earlier age. Whether the need for a caregiver results from a long-hidden health concern that takes years to surface and finally attracts the attention of loved ones, or the need results from a sudden, unexpected emergency, the result is the same. Life will never be the same for the person needing care. Relying on others for help and support with aspects of everyday life is no longer optional but necessary.

The Midnight Phone Call

The ringing of the telephone on the nightstand next to my bed jolted me from a sound sleep at 3 a.m. It was a phone call I expected and had dreamt about weeks before to soften the blow when the news arrived. My dream predicted both the phone call and the event. On the other end of the phone was my oldest brother—his words broken—telling me that Mom had died.

Unable to fall asleep after the call, I dressed and drove to the Los Angeles airport to make flight arrangements to return to Omaha. While on the airplane, I imagined my brother and sister in other parts of the country also sitting on airplanes returning to Omaha to be with my father and to say a final goodbye to Mom. I was thirty-five, the age of my mother when I was born, too young to lose a mother.

I remember walking through the familiar front door of our family home where Dad waited to greet me. He gave me a big hug. He was sobbing, tears streaming down his cheeks. I could not recall a time when I ever saw my father cry. He was a World War II veteran, one of the stoic and strong who never spoke about the events of the war. He was not a person to get overly emotional—except over a Notre Dame Football game or the subject of money, specifically related to the memory of his father losing the family's money during the Great Depression.

My mother's calls for help began years earlier. Mom wondered what I was doing when I constantly spent time with friends, beginning Friday night after work and extending through Sunday evening. These were the days of early adulthood when I had had very few responsibilities and spent hours at play. By midweek, my main concern was the activity for the coming weekend and with whom I would be playing. I had a wonderful group of friends, some of whom I am still in contact with today. We were together most weekends and always managed to find something fun and interesting to do to consume our free time.

Mom knew my schedule and waited, or it seemed she waited, to call on Sunday evenings, when she knew she could reach me. The request seemed to repeat, "Can you drive me to the emergency room?" These little phone calls became life- and habit-changing. Whenever the phone rang late at night or early in the morning, I was as well trained as Pavlov's dogs. The ring meant bad news from my mother—another health crisis or request for me to drive her to the hospital emergency room. I always wondered why I received the call when my father clearly could have served as chauffer; I later realized that Mom hoped to shield Dad from the seriousness and responsibility of her health issues.

This is the path of an unexpected caregiving journey that includes midnight phone calls, trips to medical offices, test results that indicate bad news and the ever-failing health of a parent. Just as family caregivers fail to notice the little signs indicating care is needed, family caregivers fail to consider the long-term significance of health events because there is the desire to believe everything will be just fine. Fine is good. Fine is comfortable.

Adult children, spouses, and other potential caregivers walk a path of denial, trying to ignore the reality of providing care. This denial allows the illusion that loved ones will live forever and that loss will never be experienced.

In hindsight, the timing of my mother's need for care was perfect. I was young and had ample time to do whatever was asked or needed. If the same situation occurred today, I would not be as available. While family members want to be helpful, timing and life situations dictate the ability to be available.

Years ago, family members were expected to take care of each other no matter what—even if caregiving meant delaying marriage or sacrificing the opportunity to attend college—to provide care for elderly parents. Today the obligation to take care of family is largely canceled out by the increasing complexity of ordinary, everyday life.

Family dynamics in particular have become complicated. Parents who grew up believing it was a child's duty to care for parents in their old age often fail to consider how caregiving may affect their adult children in today's society. It is difficult for parents to understand that the stress of caregiving might end a son's marriage or negatively impact a daughter's career. Parents, after hearing concerns expressed by adult children, may consider their children to be selfish and insensitive to the need for care.

To a parent's way of thinking, caregiving simply should not cause marital problems (even though it does), and children should be required to take care of parents no questions asked (even though *many* questions should be asked). Older parents often have little or no understanding of the demands of a career—or of simply remaining employed—in a shaky economy, nor do they fully understand why their caregiving child who is also self-employed has to devote sixty or more hours a week to their business just to keep it afloat.

When I was in my early twenties, I worked and attended college in the evening. My days, nights, and weekends were filled and scheduled down to the hour of each day so that I could juggle projects that had to be completed including my first experience with caregiving.

After my Aunt Bernice passed away, my Uncle Bennie invited me to visit weekly if not more frequently; he lived in the same neighborhood as my parents, so I was able to visit both at the same time. When I visited Uncle, I limited my visit time to an hour because of the long list of other things I had to fit into my weekend. Uncle had a very difficult time understanding why I did not have more time to spend with him or why I was unable to visit more frequently. I explained that my schedule was limited because of the demands of a full-time job and that my free time was devoted to my desire to complete a college education.

Retired for nearly twenty years, and without the companionship of Aunt Bernice, Uncle had hours to fill in each day. His frame of reference relative to family relationships and expectations was based on his life experience that significantly differed from my life experience. He had attended high school and worked in a meat-packing plant eight to ten hours a day. He married my dad's sister; they never had children. Much of their life revolved around how to use free time enjoying social pursuits and activities.

I was employed full-time in a demanding marketing position where I worked on average fifty hours a week including most Saturday mornings. I attended college four evenings a week after working a full day which resulted in hours of homework on the weekend. I was responsible for myself by way of grocery shopping, housekeeping, yard work, and other projects.

My uncle had great difficulty understanding that I had very little free time. His wife had not worked; she had stayed home to take care of the house and Uncle. I was self-sufficient with no one to take care of me. Uncle was unable to comprehend the opportunity cost of my spending time with him, the value of the time that I gave him relative to the trade-off of projects I could be completing if at home. If you are not familiar with the term *opportunity cost*, it is the value of an activity that is given up to pursue another activity. The role of caregiving represents a significant opportunity cost for family caregivers.

The time I was able to visit Uncle was never enough; my visits failed to meet his expectations. The demands of my schedule were an ongoing debate that eventually resulted in my decision to end visits with Uncle because of his inability or refusal to understand the schedule of my life. The opportunity cost of visiting with Uncle had become too great.

For some older adults, adjusting to a new way of thinking or considering ideas that are foreign become difficult as cognitive abilities decline. At the time I had no idea that Uncle was experiencing the beginning stages of Alzheimer's disease making my attempts to explain or to reason with him unsuccessful because his brain function had declined beyond the point of comprehending my repeated explanations of my busy and demanding schedule.

My experience with Uncle is common in caregiving situations for several reasons. Parents scold adult children about not visiting, about not being able to drop work responsibilities to show up at their homes when an emergency occurs. Parents scold adult children who are unable to fly across country at the drop of a hat to provide assistance. Another complicating factor is discussions that repeat or seem to go nowhere—not because of a lack of intellect on the part of the parent, but because of compromised cognitive ability that is unrecognized as early memory loss.

The responsibility of care and of care planning lies with the care recipient who rarely plans for needing care but depends on family members to pick up the pieces when life falls apart. Denial of care is often the first point of contention in caregiving situations, especially when parents are stubborn or in denial about health and related needs. Parents dig their feet in the sand, like young children, and refuse to accept paid assistance or refuse to move closer to children who might provide support when an emergency occurs.

This paradox exists because many older adults, like my uncle, had a very different life experience. An inability or refusal exists to acknowledge the time constraints and responsibilities of working children because career and work thirty to forty years ago was very different from today. For many caregivers, time spent caregiving averages ten to twenty hours a week or more and equates to an uncompensated part-time job with no time frame or end in sight.

Giving this amount of time to care for a parent guarantees that other parts of the caregiver's life must be compromised. For many who find it difficult to achieve a work-life balance, it is more challenging to achieve a work-life-caregiving balance. This lack of balance is the reason the role of caregiving becomes a point of stress, disagreement, and dysfunction within families and often feels like a never-ending trap.

Identifying and accepting responsibilities related to caregiving may be an unappealing project. Do any of us wish for a longer list of projects to accomplish? Caregivers experience emotional ups and downs that result from decisions that must be made in addition to a lack of definition of their role as a caregiver. Individuals new to caregiving have no experience to rely upon and have no comfort zone or belief that the situation might be manageable.

Feelings of being overwhelmed are common especially when there is no family support to soothe feelings of frustration or to provide direction. This "supporter" was the parent who served as an adviser, the one to call when problems arose. Without a parent in this role, adult children are challenged to identify a clear path of action when roles reverse and managing the life of a parent becomes a reality.

Further complications result from rusty relationships and the unknown realities of potential health diagnoses creating feelings of being trapped. If an adult child chooses not to provide care for a parent, who will? What then?

When caregiving is a new role, how are we to know what actions to take or what decisions are to be made? Depending on the situation and family members who might be involved, caregiving and the related emotions, relationships, tasks, duties, and responsibility may feel rewarding and memorable or draining and exhausting. The involvement of caring family members and friends paves the road for a positive caregiving experience. In situations where a single adult child holds responsibility or multiple children are involved but divided, the caregiving experience may be extremely challenging.

When the journey of caregiving begins, the idea of loss relates more to losses experienced by the caregiver including loss of sleep, time absent for enjoyable activities, loss of freedom, and other restrictions imposed by the caregiving role. These losses, if not placed in perspective and managed properly, have the potential to consume and destroy the health, relationships and daily routines of caregivers.

Nearly impossible to comprehend, when one is consumed by the act of caregiving, is that this role involves supporting parents and loved one nearing the end of their lives. Many caregivers are oblivious to the realities of final loss because of the constant irritating emergencies of the present day. Focus remains on work, care of family and parental caregiving tasks. Beyond treading water to survive the present day, the faraway horizon of end of life is rarely considered or recognized.

When talking with caregivers I focus on the difference between tasks and relationships. Anyone can clean a toilet, change the bed, or make a meal. Not just anyone can reminisce with a parent about childhood years, write down favorite recipes, or document family history. So often, relationships with ailing loved ones are placed at a lower priority than completing tasks of care. I encourage family caregivers to hire care navigators and other professional assistance and support so that supporting a relationship with a parent may be the focus of the caregiving journey.

Oblivion and Assumptions

When my parents were living, I was their organizer, the child who did their annual income taxes and helped with other financial or business matters. I had no idea until after my mother passed away that she never knew how to balance a checkbook. While she maintained a checkbook ledger and filed bank statements in a drawer, it was curious to me that there was never any written reconciliation on the backs of the statements.

The bank ledger showed that she made deposits or transfers to checking from a savings account to maintain a balance greater than zero. This revelation occurred to me as I helped my father work through financial transactions after Mom passed away. Financial management and balancing the checkbook were areas where I could have assisted if only I had known there was a need.

I made a monthly budget and balanced my checkbook to the penny every month. I believed that I inherited this ability from my mother, since she was careful about managing money. Little did I realize she was careful because she did not know how to balance the checkbook ledger. Like most caregivers, I assumed my parents were capable of managing every aspect of their lives even as they grew older.

Today I realize that parents may be concerned about negative perception from their children if they ask for help. It never occurred to me to ask my parents if I might help with practical things because I assumed they knew what I knew, if not more. After all, they were my parents. Mom and Dad taught me most of the practical skills I learned. I now realize there was no reasonable foundation for my assumption that my parents were as educated as me. One parent graduated from grade school; one did not. I worked during the day and began attending college at night immediately after graduating from high school. By my early twenties, I had more years of education than both parents combined. As my dad would often say, "what was I thinking?"

I was oblivious to the benefits of having an advanced education because I assumed everyone was equally knowledgeable and interested in learning. I remember my mother voicing concern about her ability to pay the bills if my father passed away. This was a frequent and repeated topic of conversation when Mom was with my brothers, my sisters, and me. None of us took her comments seriously; none of us ever told her not to worry. None of us offered solutions or suggestions or had serious conversations with her about money or with each other about what would happen if my father died first. Mom voiced concerns; her children allowed her words to fall on deaf ears. What were we thinking?

Today I wonder if constant worry about money contributed to the fact that my mother died before my father. We were five children making our own plans for our parents. To our way of thinking, Dad, who was older, would pass away first. Mom, with multiple health complications, would move about the country, living with her children for several months at a time. We never discussed any of this with our parents. We never made a formal plan for what we would do after one parent—either parent—died.

Our parents had their own assumptions about what would happen if the other one became ill or died first. They made comments that we ignored. We never initiated any serious discussions about what *would* happen. My parents attempted but did not demand that their children participate in this important discussion.

This situation is common in most families. Adult children may give thought to the care of a parent, but seldom do children open the conversation because it is an uncomfortable topic. Parents may be in denial, or they may actually have given thought to who will care for them, but they fail to initiate the conversation. Both sides thinking, neither side speaking, silence drowning out the thoughts, feelings, and potential plans for the eventual need for care.

In my family, signs that our parents needed care were in front of our eyes and we were oblivious. Mom hesitated to travel far away from home after her heart bypass surgery as each time she did she was admitted to a hospital out of town because of heart irregularities or high blood pressure. My parents stopped traveling because my mother was afraid of becoming seriously ill while away from home. My father, still relatively healthy and desiring to travel, stayed home to be with Mom. They were married for forty-eight years and were inseparable.

Their remaining children—a retired son, a nurse, a Franciscan priest, a skilled trades worker, and a career-oriented daughter—lacked the foresight to see that the scenario we planned for our parents was not only unlikely but was also totally impractical. Today I know what it means to "not see the forest for the trees."

We failed to notice the little signs. Hope that had no foundation in reality enabled us to believe everything would be okay. But rarely is it the case that everything will be okay when parents begin to age and experience health issues. We never had those all-important discussions and never did that all-important planning simply because we didn't want to talk about death and because we were oblivious and didn't know the importance or relevance of having the conversation.

To add to the challenge, caregivers—and prospective caregivers—must engage in quite a bit of detective work to determine when a parent begins to shift from independence to dependence, especially when parents refuse to be forthcoming about their declining health or failing abilities. Siblings end up engaging in a family project of discovery, clandestinely comparing notes from visits and conversations with parents.

Lack of caregiving experience results in children overlooking signs and verbal and physical clues indicating a need for care. Many children move away, return home for a visit and are shocked to see that Mom or Dad has gone downhill. Little things like small changes in health, if noticed early, have the greatest potential to be managed or at least maintained for a period of time.

The need for caregiving usually arises suddenly with no one prepared for the possibility that Mom or Dad will need care. The shock is lessened if the parent has experienced longstanding health issues, required regular medical care, or had frequent hospitalizations. In these situations, family involvement and discussions may have taken place at a high level, but it is rare even in these cases that detailed plans for caregiving have been identified. Sudden situations like heart attacks, hip fractures, or strokes—especially when they happen to an independent and healthy parent—are more shocking. The family's daily routine is interrupted, and someone must create new systems and routines for care.

When parents experience worsening health problems over time but keep them hidden from their children, parents like mine say, "We didn't want to worry you." Adult children are often shocked and understandably angry when they hear their parents make this statement and then an unexpected event—that might have been prevented—occurs. I imagine situations where the caregiving parent enters into a secret pact with the care-recipient parent not to divulge information about their day-to-day care needs or troubling diagnosis to anyone, especially their children in the hope that nothing will happen.

But then one day, a health crisis blows the lid off a situation that has been simmering for some time. Mom is transported to the emergency room because she failed to manage her blood sugar levels, she forgot to take her medication, or she is exhibiting delusional behavior due to an undiagnosed urinary tract infection. Or it may be Dad who went to the grocery store, drove into an unfamiliar neighborhood and was stopped by the highway patrol because he was driving the wrong direction on I-70 in Kansas while attempting to return to his Colorado home. Dad denies that there is any cause for alarm; he simply made a wrong turn and decided to take a Sunday drive.

Denial about care needs is one of the most significant challenges faced by caregivers. Care recipients deny the need for support firmly insisting that no help is necessary and then go to great extremes to prove independence. No one wants to "need help" or feel inferior about their abilities, as this may indicate acceptance or recognition of a loss of the abilities. Repeated professions of "I don't need help" complicate the daily struggles adult children experience with parents who forget or refuse to eat, who refuse to take medications, or who refuse to move to care communities when their behaviors and abilities indicate that living at home alone is unsafe and unwise.

Acknowledging a need for help is viewed as a personal failure by parents who need care. One of my clients told me that she did not want to accept help into her home because she was afraid others would realize how much help she did need and then her "secret" would be known by her friends. She was a career military nurse diagnosed with pancreatic cancer. She had previously been independent and capable of caring for herself. Accepting that it was the little things that made her feel humbled—for example, being unable to stand at the kitchen sink to prepare a meal without becoming totally exhausted, she willingly accepted help and support. She asked me to share her fears with others in similar situations so that family caregivers would better understand the actions of loved ones who would benefit from care but who resist.

There will be a point when a need for care can no longer be hidden or disguised. Minus midnight phone calls or significant emergencies, many adult children today are oblivious to the eventual care needs of parents who live independently without intervention or support for years. These same parents with careers raised children, made friends, participated in social activities, and entered into retirement with the goal of setting an example for their children to do the same. What most parents failed to do was to talk about and to set an example of caregiving for their children based on their own experiences of caring for their parents.

Who Will Provide Care?

The quality of the early relationship between children and parents is a predictor of the type of relationship that adult children will have with parents when caregiving becomes a reality. Some children remain close in proximity and maintain relationships. For these children, while caregiving is a shock, caregiving responsibilities are more readily assumed because there has been frequent and ongoing personal involvement over the years.

For children who move away, the expectations and responsibilities of caregiving may represent a physical and psychological burden. Caregiving from a distance adds stress because of attempts to manage a situation not directly seen or touched. There may be a sense of desire to swoop in and control aspects of life that parents may not believe need fixing, resulting in a sinking feeling of nervousness in the pit of the caregiver's stomach. If there are disagreements about care, conflict may occur in the parent child relationship.

I am told by parents that they avoid discussions of a need for care with children because of hearing shocking stories from peers about poor treatment by adult children. Reports of adult children selling their parents' homes for their own financial gain, and then depositing their parents in nursing homes or assisted living facilities against their will have parents thinking twice about appointing children to act on their behalf. (There's more than a little wisdom in the T-shirt slogan "Be nice to your children— they choose your nursing home.") Older adults also watch peers sacrifice their own financial well-being by giving money to adult children who are in a position to work (but do not) and who fail to manage their finances and continue to ask their parents for cash gifts or loans.

In some situations, overly demanding and controlling children become nightmare caregivers for parents. To be fair, some situations are brought on by the parents' own questionable decisions, either by their failure to plan for the possibility of declining health or by such actions as giving power of attorney to a child who has done a poor job of managing their own financial matters. Suddenly the child, who is power of attorney, moves the parent into a retirement community, with or without agreement of the parent. Peers looking in from the outside may blame the children, but it is very possible that the parents have a share in the blame.

Family dynamics and the relationships between parents and adult children are a significant component in caregiving. Early discussions regarding care are beneficial. Recognizing that care will eventually be needed allows practical planning. For adult children, learning early about aspects that contribute to care needs when older provides the best opportunity for future planning.

It is also best to realize that depending on the present circumstances in the life of an adult child, caregiving may be practical and possible at the present time. For other adult children, the present life experience may make it impractical and impossible to provide care; imagine a child who has just started their own business or a daughter who just had twins. In caregiving as in many areas of life, timing is relevant.

Exercise: Avoiding Surprises

Being aware of family history and identifying actions you might take today to avoid care related surprises in the future are beneficial. Unexpected surprises result in unnecessary stress. Planning ahead, including taking preventative steps relative to health is important to your well-being and future need for care.

Below are ten questions to help you identify steps to avoid surprises:

1. What is your family history relative to caring for parents for example, did your parents provide care for their parents and at what level of involvement?
2. What is your parents' expectation of you at the time they need care?
3. What is your family history relative to health diagnosis and length of life?
4. Do you attend regular or annual medical appointments?
5. Do you attend regular dental appointments for cleanings and preventative work?
6. Do you practice good nutrition?
7. Do you exercise to maintain the recommended weight for your height?
8. Do you participate in leisure activities and have social contacts you enjoy?
9. Are you saving for retirement and the costs of future care needs?
10. What level of involvement related to care do you expect from your children or family members?

The shock of becoming a caregiver for an aging parent usually arrives suddenly. Many aspects of prior relationships are tested when caregiving becomes a role. Having an understanding of care needs and discussing family involvement is important to avoid family disagreements.

If you are interested in accessing more tips and information about ideas presented in this chapter and about related subjects, visit <u>http:// www.thecaregivingtrapbook.com/store</u> and select The Starry-Eyed Caregiver.

Tales of the Caring Generation

The Story of Mr. D.

The world lost an exceptional man. Not exceptional because of lofty accomplishments like winning a Nobel Peace Prize, inventing electricity, or discovering the secret of relativity—but exceptional because of his kind nature and his dedication to his wife, Betsy, who he knew was the "right one" from the moment they met. Exceptional because of his love for our country by serving in the navy during World War II and even more so because of the way he smiled and said "yes, dear" when I visited with him. He had a smile that could melt an iceberg. He charmed the doctors, nurses, and care staff who watched over him during the last two weeks of his life until the angels collected and flew with him to heaven. Those who never had the opportunity to meet John D. lost an opportunity to meet an amazing man.

We met in June of 2009 even though it seems we knew each other a lifetime—amazing the adventures and joy that can fill a time span of sixteen months. When I met him, John was living in a nursing home with no clear or easy way out. He had fallen months previous and broken a shoulder. The nursing home wanted to keep him, told his family he needed twenty-four hour care, that he could not leave—some of you may have had a similar experience with a loved one. John had already been privately billed for two months—a total of thirteen thousand dollars. To the nursing home, Mr. D. represented steady cash income—for the rest of his life.

To his family, he was a man wanting nothing more than to return home, to return to a more normal life or at least NOT to spend the last years of his life in a nursing home—which is exactly what would have happened had his family not contacted me. I became his power of attorney and sprung him from the nursing home shortly after I met him, much to the disappointment of the nursing home staff who told me I was taking Mr. D. "from them." My response to them: I was giving Mr. D back his life or as much of a life as possible considering his health and care needs for whatever time he had left. I moved him into a small assisted living community.

Mr. D served in the U.S. Navy in the South Pacific from August 15, 1942, through March 26, 1953. He had a work ethic absent in the younger generations today. There were letters from military personnel who commended him for being organized, punctual, and dedicated. When he returned home from the war, he met and married his wife, Betsy. Their home in Denver was modest and by today's standards probably considered sparse. There were a few pieces of furniture, some photo albums and two bicycles, one red and one black, in the garage.

It was the bicycles that began a story about Mr. D. teaching his wife to ride. There were days a picnic lunch was packed for a ride to Red Rocks to enjoy a warm summer afternoon. He and his wife were unable to have children; they tried to adopt but that was not possible. Being childless was okay because they had each other. He would have made a devoted father any child would have been fortunate to call Dad.

Those of us who watched over and cared for Mr. D. made sure he was able to enjoy simple pleasures. He had a sweet tooth for hard candy—we made sure there was plenty of candy around. He enjoyed sitting outside on the front or back porch, a soft breeze on his face, listening to the sound of the leaves rustling. He enjoyed drinking a beer or two while watching the Broncos play football. His eyes twinkled on the occasions love stories were read to him. He enjoyed attending an adult day program three days a week that changed his routine and allowed him to spend time with his contemporaries. He enjoyed watching classic movies. He was fawned over by staff that cared for him; people were drawn to be around him.

His health had its ups and downs. In spite of a broken hip and a couple of hospitalizations, he never complained; complaining was not his nature. The rare times he expressed frustration—it was done with kind words and a smile. Mr. D. joined the angels on Monday October 4, just three months after celebrating his eighty-seventh birthday. Those of us who cared for him are privileged to have known such a kind, dignified man who brought as much joy into our lives as we can only hope we brought to him.

If you have a loved one in a nursing home, know that in many circumstances, in spite of what you may have been told, it is possible to return home or at least move to a more homelike environment. Yes, it is likely your loved one will need care—probably a great deal of care and added oversight if health is compromised—but it is possible. What type of care, what type of life would you want if you were in a similar situation? Would you want to spend the rest of your life in a nursing home? The choice is possible to "make a wish" and to give a family member the best possible care during the last years of life.

Chapter 6
Family Ties

- Child and Parent Relationships
- Caregiver Burden
- Love and Hate Relationships
- Aging and Change
- Into the Looking Glass
- Exercise: Identifying Caregiving Traps
- Tales of The Caring Generation: George

Child and Parent Relationships

If one asked my brother and sisters about my parents, five very different responses would be expressed. I arrived seventeen years later and four children after my oldest brother. It was impossible to compare his experience of my parents nearly two decades earlier with my experience. In the span of nearly twenty years I imagine that my parents transformed in their likes, dislikes, activities, and preferences. While I have many of the same qualities that I had twenty years ago, I am truly a different person today because of my life experience.

I believe that that the relationships children have with parents form in their youth and support the type of relationship they have with parents later in life when they are adult caregivers. Two children with the same parents may have a totally different relationship experience. Important to remember especially in caregiving situations is that parents aren't perfect and neither are children.

My next oldest siblings, the twins, were nine years older than me. This meant that by the time I was in first grade, the twins were in high school. Mom, who stayed home to raise a family, was suddenly able to return to work to supplement my father's income and to save for retirement. This meant that my elementary, high school, and later years were very different from those of my brothers and sisters because when raising them my mother was not formally employed. Her days of work were devoted to caring for five children of different ages, all competing for attention.

My older brother and sisters will say that I was the spoiled child. If I was spoiled, I lacked this realization. My birth order was pure and simple timing. I am similar in many respects to an only child. Rather than growing up with brothers and sisters my age and competing for the attention of my parents, I grew up with parents who spent a great deal of time with their brothers and sisters, my aunts and uncles, and family members of an older age because they had more time as they were moving into the position of an empty nest. I grew up knowing that I had brothers and sisters but I did not rely on them for attention or support because they had already left the household.

My playmates, besides my schoolmates, were Grandma, aunts, uncles, and cousins whom Mom invited to visit our house or whom we visited in their homes. I believe this early life experience of watching my mother's enjoyment of spending time with older family members served as a halo effect resulting in my love of older adults.

I remember visiting Aunt Zos's apartment in downtown Omaha; she lived in a fascinating building in the shape of a triangle called the Flatiron.

Aunt Zos played the piano, never married, and was very independent all of her life. There was the annual phone call that came the Saturday before Easter culminating in a drive to Aunt Jenny's to pick out one of many cakes in the shape of a lamb that she decorated with brightly colored coconut frosting to represent wool. She strategically placed jelly beans for the eyes and nose. Going to her home was like attending a family reunion, as there were always cousins and other family who we had not seen in some time, also visiting to pick up their Easter lamb cakes. I later realized how ingenious the Easter lamb event became as it was her way of making sure that almost all family members visited her at least once a year.

There were visits with Grandma Mary in her apartment above the White Eagle bar on the corner of Thirty-Third and L Streets that was owned by my grandfather. I recall the smell of the old wooden building and the creaking flight of brown painted steps. These family visits were delightful events that taught me the value of being in the presence of those much older and wiser who doted on me when I was a child. Unaware to us both at the time, through these visits Mom taught me to be a caregiver.

As we realize when we look back at our childhood, we rank our siblings and have very different perceptions about the relationships we each have with our parents. The time when we are young and living under our parents' roof may result in a more competitive environment than years later when we move away and live independently.

I remember comparisons: one child received this or that; one was smarter and did not have to study to make A grades while the other studied for hours to barely achieve C grades. The two oldest and most independent left home, one for college and the other to join the Marines. My middle sister did not leave home until she married and remained the child most dependent on my mother for support, perhaps because she had the only grandchildren. It is interesting how these rankings and inequalities come into play when adult children become involved in the care of parents and must, or should, work together to provide care.

As children grow up and move away from the family home, distance may benefit the child parent relationships because of feelings of increased independence by both parties. Other times distance results in less frequent contact because the adult child wants to establish a life away from the supervision or judgment of parents. Children who remain in physical proximity to parents have a higher degree of probability of remaining involved on an ongoing basis with parents because they are close enough to support frequent contact.

Many parents enjoy regaining independence when children move out of the home. Life returns to a focus on marital relationships and social activities. Until one day years later when an event occurs and support is needed from adult children. The event may be as simple as coordination of a tax return or assistance with a home repair. The realization that the ability of parents to care for themselves is changing may concern adult children. More concerning is the idea of providing care for parents by adult children who have moved on with aspects of their own lives like raising families or operating their own businesses. Adult children become thrust into the role of caregiver out of necessity, usually with little or no prior discussions about participation or expectations. Caregiving is a role more commonly assumed rather than considered or accepted.

Just as unsettling, aging parents feel thrust into an uncomfortable role of needing support. Parents struggle to maintain dignity and pride as adult children become involved in the daily lives of parents. Fear and loss are at the foundation of caregiving situations. Older adults, by the time care is needed, have suffered the loss of their parents, friends, and physical or cognitive abilities. Parents experience the slowing of thought processes including the ability once possessed to complete tasks, to plan, and to organize effectively. Projects that once were completed in a short period of time may now take an hour or more to complete with a greater level of effort and concentration than previously required, resulting in feelings of anxiety and frustration.

With age, the process of completing simple tasks becomes frustrating. The ability to bend over to tie a shoelace, to operate the buttons of a microwave, to possess the dexterity to push the buttons on a telephone, or to walk up a flight of stairs without huffing and puffing are threats to a successful and independent daily existence. While performing these activities may seem simple and automatic to those of us who are young, the day one experiences challenges with these activities is when confidence and self-esteem plummet, and a previously optimistic attitude changes to an attitude of paranoia, pessimism, or fear regarding an inability to manage.

Fear affects the willingness of older adults to accept help and support. Because of the experience with their parents or peers, older adults see their future. One of my clients lives in an independent retirement community. She talks about the day, with dread in her voice, when she will have to move "next door". Her husband, diagnosed with Alzheimer's, moved next door to assisted living and passed away within a month after the move. Her older sister, also living next door in assisted living, recently passed away. It is clear to me that my client views a move next door to assisted living as her next step toward death.

As abilities begin to fade, parents possess an unexpressed, silent knowing that life is coming to an end, and fear of change regarding daily routines exists. The time when abilities change or begin to decline is the day that life changes forever and a parent realizes they have become a care recipient.

Adult children experience similar feelings in situations of caregiving. On one hand children fear having to become more involved and responsible for the care of a parent. On the other hand, as time passes in the caregiving role, children fear losing a parent as health problems advance and become more significant. Conflicted feelings on the part of the caregiver and fear by the care recipient increase the stress of maintaining balanced interpersonal relationships.

By the time a parent needs support or care, the ticking clock toward the end of life is in motion. This is a concept rarely acknowledged by those involved because of all the realities and practicalities involved in the duties of caregiving. The realization that a parent is approaching the end of life, perhaps in the next several years, may be an important insight to add empathy and patience in situations of caregiving or family disagreement.

Few children grow up thinking they will take responsibility for the care of a parent or parents. When I was young, I watched my mother care for other family members in many different ways by visiting, delivering groceries, and on occasion bringing them into our home to provide care. Seeing this, it never occurred to me that I would one day change the diaper of an older adult or help with a shower as I did with my father when he became older. I now wonder if our brains catalog these early experiences and store the information until the experience becomes relevant and provide that "aha" moment that the provision or acceptance of care is a common life experience.

Because of my life experiences with loss—both of my parents, a sister, and a brother all dying before my fortieth birthday—I realize more than ever the importance of time, of visits with loved ones, and the value of balancing personal relationships and caregiving tasks. Time is more precious than we realize; the clock moves forward, never backward. The older we become, the more quickly time seems to pass and the greater the number of people that pass through our lives. Yet aspects of our daily lives complicate our ability to spend time with family.

The realization of end of life gave me the idea of translating "make a wish" from the young to the old. For many older adults nearing the last years of their life, it is my firm belief that if money exists, this money should be dedicated toward care and life enjoyment. Whether care is provided at home or in a care community there is always more that can be done to support quality of life. This care includes the extras: the ability to participate in favorite activities, to pamper with hair and nail appointments, to attend sporting events and to enjoy life as much as possible with whatever type of professional assistance that needs to be provided to support these "make a wish" activities. When this is possible, the stress of the caregiving situation upon family is greatly reduced, and it is possible to focus on the joy the relationship offer.

Caregiver Burden

Caregiver burden represents the emotional, physical, and financial aspects and responsibilities of providing care and support for an ailing family member. Real-life examples include meal preparation, medication reminding, bathing, dressing, housekeeping, grocery shopping, changing bed linens, laundry, maintaining the household, sorting mail, paying bills—the list of caregiving tasks is endless. For a short period of time providing a great amount of care is sustainable. For longer periods, realistic discussions and plans are necessary in order for caregivers to maintain physical and psychological well-being.

In situations of crises, when there are limited options, parents readily accept help and support from children. Many adult children begin by committing small amounts of time and quickly realize that any free time that existed has disappeared and been replaced with projects for parents. Parents experience no significant changes in their lives except that their lives are easier and more comfortable; projects and activities they were previously unable to complete are finally being accomplished by helpful adult children.

What a relief that groceries are in the refrigerator, the house is clean, bills are paid, and medications are placed in daily reminder boxes. The lawn is mowed, and snow is shoveled. Life could not be better for parents who exert minimal effort to manage their daily lives. Having the help of adult children in caregiving situations is like receiving assisted living support without leaving home, and better yet, the help is free. This situation represents the caregiving trap.

Adult children who allow their lives to become unbalanced in favor of nonstop caregiving activity rarely stop until experiencing some sort of physical or emotional breakdown. It is easy for caregivers to become overinvolved. Most important is to find balance between becoming overinvolved or detached, as these extremes result in the dysfunctional relationships experienced in many caregiving families.

Important if you are a caregiver is to listen and to hear the concerns of others regarding your well-being. Many caregivers are trapped in a self-created situation of providing care and later realize that this arrangement cannot continue, but the caregiver has no idea how to change the situation without conflict or disagreement, so they delay and delay and delay having a conversation with a parent. Not until the role of caregiving has become physically and emotionally draining, when family relationships are suffering, when projects at work are uncompleted and supervisors are commenting about poor job performance do caregivers realize that change is not optional but mandatory. A discussion must occur.

Caregivers attempt to discuss the situation through vague mentions of concern, hoping that parents will intuitively pick up on stated concerns; they do not. One day out of frustration, the caregiver's mouth engages before the brain and words are said that cannot be retracted. The parent responds with a verbal volcanic eruption, expressing a lack of appreciation for all that has been done, and turns the tables by saying, "I don't need your help. I'm fine living here by myself. I'll take care of myself." The caregiver feels rejected, angry and unappreciated.

Parallels exist in our approach to managing daily life as well as the responsibilities of caregiving situations. Challenges become a matter of perspective and attitude, often becoming overwhelming to caregivers who experience high levels of stress but have no idea how to resolve the situation. Surprising to caregivers is that care recipients experience the same range of emotions.

Caregiving is a revolving door where those involved become disgruntled with aspects of providing care because of repeated yet failed attempts to change unfavorable aspects: for example, an inability to receive appropriate treatment from a physician who seems never to listen to concerns or receipt of denial letters from an insurance company refusing to approve a long-term care insurance claim in spite of multiple requests for documented information.

These are events frequently experienced by overinvolved or frustrated caregivers whose behaviors or lack of detailed follow-through make situations more challenging because of a loss of objectivity and patience. Stubbornness and a lack of introspection occur on the part of the caregiver, resulting in an inability to see that the caregiver's own actions may be contributing to problems.

How does one avoid the burdens of the caregiving trap by achieving middle ground and the right balance? One suggestion is to gain awareness of the tug-of-war of emotions that occurs between the caregiver and the care recipient. This insight may provide a better understanding of the aspects common to aging not yet experienced by caregivers who are able and healthy.

Love and Hate Relationships

When relationships change as the result of caregiving and include expected or unexpected events, family members may be thrown emotionally off balance. The act of caregiving was not planned but is assumed to be a family responsibility. Uncertainty may exist by family members regarding a proper response to a request for caregiving. Because many family members have little or no experience in situations of caregiving, many are unsure how to respond to occasional or frequent requests. There are times when a response to a parent, thought to be appropriate, backfires.

The act of caregiving presents the idea of a love-hate relationship. Caregivers love the persons for whom care is provided yet have a strong dislike for the emotional, physical, and financial challenges presented by the caregiving situation. Many inexperienced caregivers feel as if they are sinking in quicksand because aspects of caregiving are unfamiliar and emotions run high.

It is reasonable that caregivers are uncertain about where to seek help or whom to trust for advice. Caregivers experience feelings of overwhelm and are pressured to evaluate information on short notice or to make immediate decisions. Mistakes occur because of heightened emotions and exhausted minds.

Skills of reasoning, critical thinking, and coping are important in care situations. Every situation is different, has its own set of complications and background, and involves a number of supporters helping or hindering. No one caregiving situation has a single solution or takes the same path.

Aging has a way of changing our abilities without consent. With aging, minds may react more slowly, as does the ability to solve problems or to cope in response to a difficult or challenging situation. Poor decisions may be made. Patience previously in abundance is now lacking.

Parents may ask for an opinion and then disagree with the response, not realizing that the response may have offended the caregiver providing the information. Aging may result in being less open minded and more opinionated. Some older adults drive family members away because of caustic behavior, unreasonable demands, or unwillingness to be flexible.

With age, previously large social worlds shrink. Some care recipients become homebound, rarely leaving the four walls of a bedroom. Changes in health, cognition or lifestyle may result in a sense of loss of control. In response to change, the care recipient may respond with what appears to be a tantrum—a negative reaction—spouting angry words and questioning why everyone else is so disagreeable and refuses to fulfill a desired request.

Think for a moment about this response and back to a time when anger was your response because an expected response or event did not occur. If we have grown emotionally since childhood, it may be possible to view this situation as the reaction of a child with little or no control over the circumstances of life. Similar to the reaction of a child who has no idea how to get what is desired without throwing a tantrum, a parent explodes like a volcano.

In some caregiving situations, aging parents revert to childlike behaviors because of compromised health or advancing cognitive issues. It is in these situations where a parent—feeling insecure or that their needs will not be met—finds a way (good or bad) to get attention to get what they want from a caregiver even though their action may not be the best course of action. These are challenging situations where caregivers may bear the responsibility of making decisions for parents who are unable to decide for themselves resulting from poor judgment and an inability to evaluate information or to make appropriate decisions due to cognitive impairment.

There are other situations where care recipients possess awareness and knowledge of a situation and feel unable to make decisions, or refuse to accept change. Care recipients also feel trapped in situations of care—trapped in ailing bodies, trapped by having to take a long list of prescription drugs, and trapped in a living situation that is less than ideal. In these situations helpful people or family caregivers feel as if they are also trapped or even held hostage because a willingness to help exists yet the person needing care continually refuses.

A good place to start, assuming a commitment of continued involvement, is to talk about the feelings of each side in the care situation so that neither individual feels trapped in a relationship of conflict or disagreement. The act of caregiving presents a "two sides of the coin" opportunity to gain perspective rarely considered prior to a need for care.

Caregivers become impatient with care recipients whose behaviors and demands seem impossible or unrealistic. Parents, having experienced loss, fail to comprehend the actions of adult children who refuse to be helpful and appear resistant or uncaring. In youth and middle years, there is little insight into events that progress to end of life. Until poor health arrives into our life, there is little comprehension of the daily challenges experienced by parents needing care, and when death occurs, we have little idea how to grieve our loss.

The act of caregiving truly presents a love-hate relationship that has the potential to result in caregivers who are involved or detached. A foundation must be set to develop a system of boundaries and alternatives that lay out a road map for the future. Successfully building this foundation begins with possessing an insight into the changes that occur in life as we age.

Aging and Change

If all of a sudden your spouse, family, or friends disappeared and you had to start all over again, how would you respond? Would you mourn the loss and immediately take practical steps to replace your previous social supports and daily routines? Would you feel excited and view this change as an opportunity to start all over again with a clean slate, minus past history and mental baggage? Knowing what you know today, how might you refashion your life to be more of what you want?

How you respond to the question of starting all over again is a combination of your lifelong experiences, abilities, interests, education, problem solving, personal values, and social connections. Rarely do individuals step back and examine the actions that resulted in the life experience of today. Even fewer have the insight to identify behavior patterns that may have resulted in poor health or poor family relationships. If you are unhappy with the present situation, do you keep repeating the same behaviors over and over and over again, hoping to experience a different result? Many people fall into this trap of repetition.

When life situations are not as we wish and we are in a rut of repetition, some type of catalyst must enter the situation to facilitate change. This catalyst is a change that we initiate or a change initiated from the outside. When unexpected events occur, how we react and the way in which we respond is within our personal choice and totally within our control. We are, in a sense, given the opportunity to respond positively or negatively to change. Acceptance of change is more readily accepted by younger adults and adult children caring for older parents than by the older parents.

For younger adults, the idea of starting all over again in response to a change may seem like a great adventure. Many younger adults frequently initiate change by changing jobs or relocating to another city for a fresh start. Others look forward to marriage and raising children.

As an adult child, your life may have existed in the safety of a protected bubble until you were thrust into a situation where parent care was needed—parents in poor health now needing care and who failed to save for retirement. While changes that must be made by your parents are crystal clear to you, these changes may be resisted or even denied by your parents.

For older adults in their sixties, seventies, or eighties, the idea of change may be intimidating or even frightening because of a declining ability to cope, problem solve, and manage change. For many older adults the first significant change relating to the aging process involves retirement. While many dream of golden retirement years, the real transition, voluntary or involuntary, significantly affects life satisfaction.

Even for individuals who plan retirement, there is a loss of identity as many individuals associate their identity with career responsibilities. For those who retire involuntarily, life transitions like health related declines or the loss of a spouse may be linked to the onset of depression. The experience of retirement, when one has a sense of control over the events has a significant effect on life satisfaction. "An organizational exit that occurs at the right time and on the basis of one's own volition represents the best case scenario when it comes to the prospect of experiencing late in life psychological well-being." [53]

Many factors in the lives of older adults change when daily work routines no longer exist. Retirement, although anticipated, brings its own routine of isolation and daily challenges and opportunities. Those who are successful establish new daily routines and activities to replace the routine of work. While it may be difficult to imagine the challenges of starting over at an advanced age, this type of transition will eventually become a reality for those of us who are caregivers. If we are able to examine the role of caregiving and the needs of loved ones we may be able to better prepare for our own retirement and care needs.

The act of retiring represents a significant life change. It is then reasonable to understand and empathize when more changes occur, such as advancing health concerns or an unexpected diagnosis like Alzheimer's disease. Parents experiencing multiple changes become stuck or remain in denial, allowing events to snowball and to create more complicated issues.

Older adults experience significant life changes due to poor health or loss of a spouse. Negotiating change is especially difficult when spouses shared responsibilities: for example, one spouse managed financial matters and the other managed the household. When fifty percent of a team is lost, this creates a high level of stress for the remaining partner. Unless lifelong coping and problem-solving skills have been a common experience, attempting to navigate life alone may be more difficult than anticipated. Aging brings familiarity and comfort with routines and a dislike for change. Loss and change may deliver stress, anxiety, loneliness, and depression.

In talking to caregivers who express frustration with parents, many mention witnessing lifelong behavior patterns of parents that were visible but not troubling at the time because the children were not directly involved on a day-to-day basis. When the care of parents becomes a daily concern or direct activity, problematic pasts of poor habits or undiagnosed disorders wreak havoc with family relationships.

Adult children become frustrated when parents fail or refuse to see logic relative to needed change or to the consequences of actions. When parents refuse change, some caregivers feel as if they are fighting a losing battle—and some are. If this is your situation, consider how you might respond to a parent you believe to be unreasonable or stubborn. Refuse to be pulled emotionally, and consider actions to set the tone for an ongoing relationship that promotes setting boundaries and achieving balance in the caregiving relationship. Remember, your offer of assistance should feel voluntary instead of mandatory.

Negotiating caregiving change involves managing situations where changes in health dictate timely responses. These changes will occur in the health of your parents or older family members. In order to maintain balance between being emotionally overinvested or detached, it is important to learn how to find middle ground in order to maintain positive health and well-being. Finding middle ground is accomplished by deciding how you and others involved in the care situation will participate prior to or in the middle of a care situation.

Into The Looking Glass

Any road will get you there if you don't know where you're going.[54]
—**Lewis Carroll**, Alice in Wonderland

In caregiving situations, it is important to know where you are going in order to arrive at a present situation with a roadmap. This process involves the idea of presenting change and negotiating levels of participation with a loved one to arrive at next steps and plans.

Presenting information or an idea that suggests any type of change to a parent feeling overwhelmed or hearing the news for the first time (even though it has likely been mentioned multiple times) is like igniting a stick of dynamite. How many times have you made what was believed to be an innocent comment to a parent about health or lifestyle choices and the discussion quickly went from bad to worse? You created the reaction with words, and now you are unsure how to respond to a person spewing angry words and accusations about your evil intentions.

A negative response by a parent as the result of suggested change is common. Caregivers want to help, efforts are refused, and ideas are disregarded. Caregivers feel powerless about a situation, not knowing what to do next because a first attempt at a suggestion failed miserably. How much easier might it be to throw yourself on a bed of hot coals rather than to make a second attempt at a conversation that might fail again?

For caregivers who are emotionally sensitive or who wish to act in a kind and considerate manner, starting difficult conversations certain to result in disagreement or conflict may seem like a formidable task. In these situations I recommend playing devil's advocate. Imagine the worst that might happen and then prepare accordingly. This involves the process of researching and identifying information and options, then anticipating a range of possible responses on the part of your parent. I find that when I over prepare for situations, the situation usually works out with ease.

Most caregivers are unsuccessful at holding initial discussions because pieces of information are presented in a disjointed fashion rather than a complete and well-considered plan. Some caregivers avoid having the discussion by withholding important information: for example, never telling a family member they have a diagnosis of Alzheimer's disease, by responding to a loved one who has questions about their memory by saying, "It's nothing to worry about; we'll take it a day at a time," and then never finishing the discussion. Delaying the discussion will not make the care situation easier at a later date or time and is certain to result in fewer options and greater complications.

Each person is responsible for making plans and provisions for his or her own care. A high percentage of individuals do not plan for care, which is exactly the reason caregiving situations become emotional and stress filled. Parents live in denial thinking the day-to-day situation will never get that bad and if issues do arise, that family will step in to take responsibility. Other parents prefer not to burden adult children or family but still take no action. Not knowing what to do or where to find reliable and trustworthy information, parents fail to plan or to take action.

In both situations where you might be the caregiver or the care recipient, professional advice is beneficial and saves money, time, and emotional distress. The initial hurdle is discussing the idea of care. Here are the more common arguments from those in denial or fear of the unknown:

- That will never happen to me (when attempting to discuss possible future events)
- I can take care of myself (when suggestions about not being able to care for oneself occur)
- That (type of help or service) is nothing I need
- I don't want to live with old people (when discussing retirement communities)
- I have nothing in common with those old people (when discussing participation at community centers or other activities)

These statements represent denial and fear about future changes. Individuals choose to believe that whatever is happening to someone else will surely never happen to them. Other people experience "*that*"— whether "*that*" is the experience of a job loss, a diagnosis of Alzheimer's disease, cancer, or another illness. Statements of "I'm only seventy-eight" occur in comparison to peers in their early eighties who may be in a better physical or mental state—as if the perception of a younger age is truly an indicator of ability.

This mental and verbal distancing is common in older adults who practice purposeful isolation by ending relationships with friends and acquaintances who become ill and those who use walkers or wheelchairs— bringing their own idea of mortality into the bright light of day. Some older adults believe that illness and death may be avoided if one distances from people who might be traveling down the path of aging and death. While one might believe that older adults would be more compassionate toward peers experiencing more significant health declines, distancing more often occurs because of the fear that death will occur sooner by association with others on this path.

Many older adults who supported their parents or grandparents by providing care are fearful of being in a similar situation. Those whose parent suffered from Alzheimer's may be in even greater denial that they have memory loss because they fear the experience of their parent. For others, the idea of preventative action to avoid a similar situation is a daily activity by way of taking vitamins, exercising, and remaining active.

While you may swear that you will never be like your parent, what steps are you taking today to make sure your later years in life will be different? What happens if at the end of life you find yourself in a situation you never imagined? Your parent also likely thought, "That will never happen to me." Married couples expect to sail into retirement together happy and healthy. A change in health or the death of a spouse derails these plans.

Look at your life today. Does your life mirror the habits, experiences, ethics, and morals of the individuals with whom you associate? If you are healthy, do you spend time with healthy friends, engaging in physical activity and healthy nutrition? If you smoke and regularly consume alcohol, do you spend time with others who engage in these activities, knowing that these actions fail to support health and longevity? Like older adults who may choose to disassociate with friends who are declining and near death, you might consider if associating with friends who embody health and well-being might be a better path to healthy aging.

In the caregiving experience, denial about care needs is a potent tactic to delay discussions and decisions. As older adults lose their peers to death this feeling translates to a loss of control over life. This loss of control and fear frequently exhibit themselves in behaviors that appear to others as obstinate, opinionated, and closed minded.

Not talking about care transitions will not avoid the inevitable. While these conversations may not be pleasant or comfortable, there is benefit to discussing the practicalities of care well before health issues occur or advance. Discussions are also better held at a time when potential family caregivers are logical and reasonable, rather than in the midst of serious issues when emotions are high and decisions must be made. Prior to a need for care, it is much easier to describe how you are able to help and in what increment of time. This discussion helps avoid unrealistic expectations on the part of a loved one and may actually support planning, especially if your ability to participate is limited. Unfortunately, discussions more commonly occur in the midst of serious issues, as most families do not hold care discussions until an event precipitates the discussion.

Exercise: Identifying Caregiving Traps

One key to successful caregiving relationships is finding ways to communicate that avoid common caregiving traps. First-time caregivers often make mistakes that involve time commitments and expectations that may be unrealistic.

Below are ten beliefs common to caregivers that foster disagreements and challenges. How many of the issues identified below are you experiencing? If you identify with three or more, developing a written plan to address these issues is a prudent next step.

1. Failing to have an initial conversation with a loved one to define care needs including discussion about caregiver availability, ability, and willingness to provide care.

2. Believing a caregiver has to do it all; that no one other person "cares" as much as you.

3. Failing to set boundaries because of concern of hurting a loved one's feelings.

4. Feeling so overwhelmed that decisions are delayed until a future date when an emergency forces the decision.

5. Failing to identify options for care as needs progress and intensify.

6. Refusing offers from family and friends willing and able to provide support.

7. Operating in continual crisis mode; time for planning is never a priority.

8. Focusing on tasks and busywork to the exclusion of creating an enjoyable experience with a care recipient.

9. Rarely taking breaks or time away from the care situation resulting in feelings of overwhelm, frustration, or anger.

10. Experiencing health problems due to the stress of the caregiving situation.

Are you a caregiver feeling out of control? Do you now realize that some of your actions have resulted in the current situation and you're not sure what steps to take next? You can change the current situation by making a realistic assessment of all aspects and then having a discussion with your loved one about practical aspects that include available time, assistance, financial matters and future planning.

If you are interested in accessing more tips and information about ideas presented in this chapter and about related subjects, visit http://www.thecaregivingtrapbook.com/store and select Family Ties.

Tales of the Caring Generation

George

George was the kid in high school that everyone teased. He appeared slower than most, was overweight, and somewhat shy. He lacked social skills to interact with large groups, yet he was highly intelligent. George was commonly seen eating lunch from a rumpled brown paper sack—alone. His clothes were plain black pants and a white shirt, his face covered with acne, his hair flecked with dandruff, greasy, and not always washed. How many of you had a George in your high school?

Looking back, even I thought George just a little bit odd. He and I shared math, chemistry, and eventually biology class. He helped any student struggling in these classes that most of us hated because we lacked skills or interest. He excelled in classes that were technical, requiring mathematical, calculus, and scientific skills.

In spite of his odd appearance, he had a nice smile and a pleasant laugh. Realizing that some of the boys had cruel intentions to play tricks on him, he somehow outfoxed them. He was musical, playing drums in the high school band, and wore those polyester band uniforms we all thought were just plain uncomfortable.

What most kids didn't know was that George had lost his father to cancer when he was five years old. His mother worked two jobs and did her best to raise George to make sure he had a good education. He was an only child.

George and I shared things in common. He, I, and another girl, Millie were the only students to ride the school bus all four years of high school. It was so uncool back in 1978 to be a high school senior without a car but there we were—the three of us riding the bus to and from school until the day we graduated. Our parents were barely able to pay our tuition, let alone buy us a car. We knew of our family's financial situations and knew not to complain; after all our tuition was the more important expense.

Then there was Lydia, my best friend in high school. I don't really remember how we met; it may have been in morning homeroom before classes started or in a dreadful algebra class taught by a teacher whose fast-talking explanations and chalkboard scribbles went right over my head. Lydia was good at algebra—I was NOT. What took her an hour took me three hours because I found it impossible to relate these numbers, equations, and theories to my life or to my future.

Did I mention I was different in my early high school years? After eight years in grade school, I was challenged to figure out what to do with my red, obnoxiously curly hair. I tried to straighten it, cut it off, let it grow, and was horrified that it would never look as perfect as the straight blonde hair of the beautiful cheerleader with whom I shared a locker. Why did school administrators match up students who were opposites in appearance and personality to share lockers? Doing so made the differences all the more painful. I was far from the cheerleader type; I was studious and little bit shy. I was definitely not part of the popular crowd.

I see students today stepping off school buses and I remember George, Millie, Lydia and myself. I can spot the students who are not popular—those others tease those with less self-confidence—their self-esteem diminished when other students call them names. I remember the name of my peer who wrote the word geek on one of my notebooks. I see the students who walk alone. I experience a sense of sadness when I recall my high school years, when all most of us wanted was to be accepted by our peers.

I meet students in high school today who find it difficult to imagine that life does change, that the things like nice clothes, having a car, and being accepted by others that seem so critically important in high school have a way of working themselves out in the years after high school.

Looking back, it was impossible to predict how we would change after graduation. In my imagination George became a cardiac surgeon, saving hundreds if not thousands of lives due to his early love for chemistry, math, and biology—all of those classes most of us dreaded. I imagine that Millie married and had a house filled with kids and that Lydia married, had children and today enjoys her grandchildren. And of course you know my story. I take care of disabled and older adults, many who have no one to speak up for them, and who might feel that they too do not fit in with their peer group.

The same desire to fit in when we are young continues as we age. If one belongs to a social group, cliques exist as they did in high school. If one lives in a retirement community, individuals become territorial about dining tables and table mates. There will be the groups that have the financial means to live in communities well beyond the means of many.

This does not mean that the right social group or community does not exist for a loved one. As with anything, investigation of groups, activities, and communities is important to ensure the right fit. Just as we are not right for every situation, every situation is not right for us. Be persistent in finding the right match of services and activities for a loved one and when in doubt, retain the services of a care navigator to provide support.

Chapter 7

The Next Chapter

Having "The Talk"

How many of you remember your parents having the "sex talk"—or if you are female the explanation of having periods or why a bra was not yet necessary even though all the other girls in school already wore bras? If you think these conversations were uncomfortable for your parents to initiate, the conversation about needing care and end of life is another uncomfortable conversation for adult children to initiate.

Why? Because caregiving is a conversation that adult children initiate with a parent who will likely deny a need to participate in the discussion. This conversation is not to be delayed, because similar to having periods, aging and needing care will happen; both are inevitable aspects of life that become more relevant when we reach middle age.

The best time to hold this conversation is when parents and loved ones are still generally healthy and do not require a significant amount of assistance. In reality this may not be the current situation. Maybe the care recipient has begun wandering out of the home, is incontinent, or is awake all night preventing the caregiver from sleeping.

Before having the talk it is best to formulate a plan to support the flow of the conversation. That being said, having an identified process and ground rules is helpful. To support the idea of having the talk, we will discuss shifting and defining roles, conversation starters, and talking points to support the conversation.

For now, consider the following points and keep this in mind as you think about ways to open the conversation with your loved one.

- Having an idea to open the conversation is helpful, whether the idea be something that recently happened in the news that relates to the subject or a friend whose parents are experiencing health concerns. You may also open the discussion with actions you are taking to plan for your retirement and costs of care.

- It is important to be able to discuss aspects of caregiving and end-of-life situations. Some families are very uncomfortable raising this subject matter. I have heard parents say, "I'll leave it up to God." What this really means is "I don't want to talk about my health issues; my children will take care of me when something happens." Some parents view children who are practical and desiring a plan as insensitive—"You can't possibly know what I'm going through." Understand that you may be faced with resistance to the idea of having this conversation.

- Initiate the conversation with questions of "what if?" "What would you want if xyz happened?" and "What do you expect from me or us?" You may be opening up a conversation with questions your loved one has not considered. Have a prepared list of questions in your mind that you can write down together to allow the thought process to begin. Your loved one may not be enthusiastic to talk about this subject, and it's unlikely you will be able to accomplish your list during a single conversation—be patient!
- It is helpful to formulate personal boundaries and to keep these in mind as the conversation progresses. I recommend that every caregiver give consideration to their personal boundary limit: "When [something specific] happens, I will no longer be able to provide care, and we'll have to look at other options."
- Accepting change in our lives is a given. All involved must acknowledge that the current situation will change with the passage of time and that alternatives must be identified and discussed.
- Include all interested parties. Rather than allowing opposing family members to avoid participation, schedule a meeting and invite them. Family members who are uninvolved become the most opinionated and demanding. This provides the opportunity for opposing family members to become involved. Those who fail to participate give up the opportunity to express their opinions at a later date.

When there are situations of potential or expected conflict, it is best to have a care navigator or an impartial individual with no skin in the game to lead the discussion. Examples of specific conversation openers are offered later in this chapter for you to use or to modify based on your individual situation. In extreme situations of conflict retaining a family mediator may also be beneficial.

By the time care is needed, change in some manner has already occurred. Situations are most successful when change is openly and directly discussed rather than attempting to hint or to talk around a situation hoping that a loved one will somehow absorb the information you are trying to relay—much like playing a trivia game and hinting hoping that the other person comes up with the right answer. Few individuals like change that is not self-initiated. In these conversations, consider whose life is changing. In caregiving situations major changes occur in the life of the care recipient. While the life of the caregiver also changes, this change is optional, not mandatory, if discussions occur and boundaries are set.

Changing the life of a care recipient is easy for the person suggesting change, but immensely difficult and complicated for the care recipient whose life and home situation may have been relatively stable for ten, twenty, or more years. Depending on the situation or the diagnosis, it may be the caregiver who also must change the approach to a care situation.

This is relevant especially in situations of memory loss where caregivers desire a loved one to remain as they were previously in mental and physical ability. Because of the disease progression, a loved one with memory loss is unable to retain prior abilities and may not seem to be the mom or dad that a child remembers. Even small things, like no longer being able to play a board game or an inability to participate socially at a family event, results in family caregivers feeling at a loss with how to communicate or spend time with a loved one.

While patterns previously existed that made it easy for communication and activity, new patterns and routines must be established. This is no different than parents reestablishing their lives when children leave and the nest is empty. The difference is that children have relied on parents to respond in a consistent manner and now this consistency has ended.

When health declines and care is needed, family caregivers must change their behaviors and responses to accommodate the care needs of a parent as the parent is unlikely—at this point in life—to change their behaviors to accommodate the needs of the caregiver. That being said, some situations require special tactics when the shifting of roles becomes a challenge.

Role Shift

When caregiving becomes a role, the roles of parent and child often reverse. Instead of being the child receiving care from a parent, the child becomes the caregiver for a parent. With caregiving arrives a loss of innocence about life, duty, and responsibility; lives are interrupted. Feelings of worry, anger, and frustration occur about having to make difficult choices and decisions relative to care for a loved one and how providing this care might change the daily life or future plans of the caregiver.

Caregiving represents a role shift that becomes necessary and at times complicated, depending on the family situation. The first complication is the existence of the "sandwich generation." Caregivers today find themselves sandwiched between raising young children and caring for aging parents. The second situation relates to single adult children sandwiched between careers, financial responsibilities, and caring for a parent. Any derailment in the career path or income stream of a single person has a negative effect on the ability to financially support lifestyle and care needs when older. The third situation represents grandparents caring for grandchildren because their children have proved to be less than ideal or responsible parents. All three situations, and variations of each, complicate the role shift.

Each situation bears an opportunity cost related to the role of caregiving. The missed opportunity may be personal time, financial investments, time in personal pursuits, or hobbies or the experience of a responsibility-free retirement. Whenever unexpected responsibilities enter, our lives something must "give" in order for us to devote time to the new responsibility.

Role shift is more difficult when the hierarchy of the parental relationship has been unwavering and long-standing with children taught to never question a parent. Care situations teeter totter when the balance shifts and parents become care recipients, no longer able to care for themselves or their home environment. It is difficult to predict how parents will respond to offers of assistance, especially when children view parents as wiser and more knowledgeable, and as individuals to whom children look to for direction, advice, or guidance. Many parents, on the other hand, see children—no matter the age—needing advice rather than being in a position of advising parents.

Many considerations should occur prior to accepting the role of caregiver. While many children see the role as mandatory, I prefer to say that the role is optional. Options exist relative to level of involvement, time commitment, financial commitment, duration of the commitment, and so on. Children who possess emotional intelligence fare better in situations of care. What this means is the ability to be aware, to control and to express one's emotions and opinions in a manner that is empathetic and thoughtful. Maintaining emotional intelligence in situations that are complex is a learned skill.

Many times—even though the child has accepted the role of caregiving for a parent—the parent remains highly resistant and prevents progress or necessary change. This resistance arises from a variety of situations. One is that the child will always be a child in the mind of a parent. Because of this belief, the parent hesitates to accept direction from a person not viewed as an equal and one who is generally unable to explain a plan supported by solid reasoning rather than emotional pleas.

Second, in many aspects and with age, the behavior of parents may mirror the behavior of young children. Think back. When you were young, how many times did your parents express concerns about the character of one of your friends or attempt to convince you of the importance of taking a particular action? Many of us refused, purposely ignoring the suggestions of our parents, and we did exactly the opposite.

Guess what? It is now your turn to be ignored and frustrated when your parents refuse to listen to your reasoning or logic. After all, *you* are the child, for heaven's sake; what could you possibly know about the physical aspects of aging including your parents' attitudes toward aging? In their opinion, you know absolutely nothing—you are simply trying to be mean and to control their life, of which you know nothing about.

Are these valid concerns? If you have been the adult child at a distance how well do you know your parents' preferences? Do you know their favorite color, foods, hobbies or music? Who are their closest friends? What do you know about their monthly income, personal saving habits, or financial ability to pay for care? Is their preference to remain at home or move to a retirement community? What do you know about their end-of-life wishes? These are all aspects of person-centered care, meaning knowing the personal preferences of an individual so that the care provided supports their desires and interests rather than the desires and interests of those providing the care.

When parents become care recipients, it is important to find a balance between reason and practicality versus reacting to the emotional challenges of the care situations. It is certainly much easier to make decisions about care rather than to ask parents about their personal preferences and desires however, making decisions without consulting parents rarely results in building a positive long-term relationship.

Take a step back and look at the care situation. If your parents are at a point in their lives where they need support, how did the situation arise? Was this a situation that evolved over time due to declines in health? Was this a situation your parents failed to address that now has resulted in a situation of crises where decisions must be made? Do current health issues dictate a change in care needs or living arrangement? Is the care situation at a point where options that previously existed are no longer available because the situation has progressed to a point of no return because of parental denial or stubbornness?

The realization that tough decisions must be made often results in a sinking feeling in the pit of a stomach or a feeling of panic and overwhelm. What decisions must be made? What are the options? How do we know if we as caregivers are making the right decision? Are we limited in options due to available finances? Decision making and living with the results—especially if plans do not turn out as expected, may lead to feelings of guilt or caregiver burden.

While it may be difficult to see yourself in the position of an aging parent, exercising compassion is beneficial to the overall situation. Rather than taking a no-holds-barred approach to decision making, a consultative approach should be attempted. As mentioned above, there is benefit to initiating formal discussions about care needs and planning including who will be involved in the care of a parent and how those involved agree to participate.

Defining Roles

Disagreement about roles and decision making is common among family members in care situations. A family meeting to discuss the needs of a loved one with focus on identifying caregiving roles is an important first step to help families arrive at a sense of cooperation and clarity prior to discussing care needs with a parent. It is important that family caregivers present a united front. Some parents will seek to split family apart and create warring sides if this has been part of the family history. Regardless of the disagreements that appear behind the scenes, family caregivers must commit to presenting information and to responding to parents in a consistent manner.

In defining caregiving roles and relationships, identifying by what method a family caregiver is able and willing to contribute in the way of time, effort, or money is critical. Some caregivers report that they are emotionally or financially unable to contribute—this type of honesty must be respected. Others, due to a present life situation, may or may not have available time to offer to a care situation. This is true in my own life. When my mother needed care I was young and generally available. If the same situation occurred today, the time I would personally be able to devote to her care would be significantly less. My participation would be in the form of overseeing caregivers or financially contributing to care costs.

Not every family member, no matter how much they might desire, is an appropriate caregiver. Many family caregivers accept the role because there is no one else available. If you are unsure or struggling with the responsibility, ask yourself if the role of caregiving is really for you. If you lack emotional intelligence, patience, and compassion your participation may have a negative effect on the situation rather than offering benefit.

The role of caregiving may be divided into 4 categories:

- The manager—organizes the care situation and identifies options and next steps
- The communicator—communicates changes and manages expectations
- The coordinator—ensures tasks are completed by family or professional paid caregivers
- The supporter—does not offer time or effort rather offers moral, emotional, or financial support

In the process of identifying roles, the following questions are helpful: Do your skills lend to the needed tasks? Do you have the emotional maturity to manage the situation? Do you have the patience? Do you really have the time? Are you able to make the caregiving experience positive for your loved one or will the experience be a constant battle of wills? Are there other interested people who may be able to provide support for tasks you find difficult? Should you hire outside professionals to provide support? What are the other options that have not been considered?

If you are a sole family caregiver, the entire responsibility of caregiving likely falls to you. It is extremely difficult for a single individual to act in all roles and to be able to maintain a loving relationship with the care recipient. In these situations, I recommend hiring a care navigator to help you identify options and to make a plan prior to having the care discussion with your loved one. In this situation it will be extremely important to be able to discuss how you feel because of the burden of care being solely on your shoulders. Many parents fail to see how their care or lack of participation in a care situation might affect an only child.

Even if family members are available and willing to participate, there are benefits to hiring a care navigator to provide support in identifying options and available services. A small investment in an hour consultation saves families hours of investigation and avoids potential hazards not obvious to inexperienced caregivers.

The process of identifying caregiving roles will identify responsibilities to ensure that everyone is contributing based on their level of expertise and personal comfort zone. Not all family members are comfortable performing tasks that relate to hygiene or personal care. It is even more important to recognize that allowing time for focus on the relationship with the care recipient must be a component of caregiving that receives great attention. This relationship balancing helps achieve the middle ground and avoids one individual becoming the overinvolved or detached caregiver.

While it is easy to get caught up in the task work, many caregivers tell me that their relationship with a parent or loved one is not as close as they wish. Some caregivers have forgotten how to talk or to interact with loved ones. Know that relationship building is a skill that can be relearned and that there is no time like the present when life is slipping away from your parent day by day. Sometimes the simple act of participation, for example working on a jigsaw puzzle or sorting family photos, helps build a relationship without a great deal of discussion. Other times it may be taking a walk, sitting together on a park bench, or participating in a Sunday afternoon drive.

The assignment of roles also allows the ability to review care options and to make plans with alternatives based on a situation guaranteed to change as the health of the care recipient changes. A revised plan may always be implemented and roles modified as needed. To support this idea, why not schedule a quarterly family dinner to serve as a progress check and as a reminder to all involved of the continuing commitment to the ongoing care of a parent? This also allows the parent to remain involved and provides the opportunity for all involved to express concerns and appreciation for family members involved in the care situation.

Appreciation in care situations is a significant and often overlooked factor. My grandmother Mary was one of the most appreciative and pleasant individuals I have had the privilege to know. When she was in her nineties she had horrible arthritis that crippled her hands, and she experienced back and knee pain—yet she rarely complained. On her worst day, all she would say is "It's no good to get old." Each time we visited, the moment just before we walked out the door, she said, "Thank you for coming to see me." I remember visiting her days before she died and her saying, "Thank you for coming to see me."

Thank your brothers, sisters, and family members who act in the role of caregiver. Make sure your parents and loved ones are aware of the positive effects of a simple "thank you." Appreciation joins people together for the common cause of caregiving. Discover new ways to celebrate and to give thanks.

Conversation Starters

The way in which the conversation is initiated sets the entire tone for the success of the conversation and the eventual outcome. Telling a parent that he or she is failing, mentioning past actions that were disastrous, or blaming the parent for the current situation will not ensure success. It is best to express concerns from the standpoint of love, concern, and practicality.

Initiating a discussion about needs, expectations, and roles is more difficult after you are a caregiver trapped in a routine where you have already given so much without discussion of a long-term plan. The difficulty is that you have established an expectation of care by your parent that now has to be changed because the time and effort involved is unsustainable. Your parent may perceive your change of heart to provide care by reacting with behaviors or responses supported by feelings of fear, rejection, or abandonment but may never directly tell you that this is how they feel.

Not having these discussions early or at all frequently results in caregivers feeling trapped. If you are feeling trapped, know that you are not alone. In these situations, caregivers benefit from opportunities to communicate, collaborate, and connect with other caregivers by way of in-person or online support groups. This supports gaining a greater perspective about care situations and receiving the support of others in similar situations. I highly recommend support groups, as participation offers a method to learn from the experiences of others especially in areas of unfamiliar territory.

Go back and take another look at the ground rules at the beginning of this chapter and then give thought to address the possibility of how you believe a parent might react to a conversation about care. The conversation will have a greater chance of success if you have a plan discussed by those involved prior to having the conversation with a parent or a loved one. It is important to present a system of boundaries and alternatives with a road map for the future. Having this conversation without a plan is sure to result in failure and repeated attempts to hold the same conversation.

As we discussed, asking "what if" questions and then developing a written plan is best so that your parent may read and reread ideas, options, and suggestions based on their initial responses to your questions. Have responses to questions that you anticipate your parent might ask. Never pressure a parent to make an immediate decision about your recommendations. These are discussions to initiate and to revisit, sometimes multiple times, so that all involved feel they have a voice and will be heard. That being said, it is helpful to agree on deadlines for decision making and to identify agreed-upon next steps.

How do we begin difficult caregiving conversations? As previously mentioned, starting the conversation by outlining the failings of a parent is rarely the road to success. You are still the child, and no matter how frail, feeble, or old your parent may be, your parent desires to remain or to appear to remain in control of his or her life. Remember the times when you were younger and you said to your mother or father, "I will never treat my children that way." Today your parent may exhibit childlike behaviors. Be mindful of your approach if you wish the conversation to succeed.

A conversation opener might be: *"Mom or Dad, I/we love you dearly. I/ we have been helping you for three years and feel that it is time to look at other options for support. It is not my/our intention to leave you without care or support (or to abandon you). It is my/our intention to make sure you have the care and support you need by agreeing upon options to replace the support I/ we have provided. My/our hope is that we can spend time together in mother-*

daughter or mother-son activities and conversations rather than time being
dedicated to caregiving duties."

The conversation opener will either be accepted with relief or responded
to with expression of anger or resistance. Some parents will deny the
benefit of or need for assistance by others who are not family members, or
parents will deny the need to move to a care community. Parents who have
had the experience of caring for their own parents may be more practical
and accepting of the progression of life and reality that it is not possible
for care to always be provided by family. Denial is more common with
individuals experiencing memory loss because they lack insight into the
consequences of their actions that require help from others.

If there is significant family disagreement over the care of a loved one,
a conversation opener may be: "*Mom or Dad, our goal is to ask and learn*
about your wishes because many of us have very different ideas about what you
might want for care when care is needed. Rather than having us disagree when
a situation arises, we'd like to talk about what you want today and have the
information documented and placed in writing." This is especially helpful
when adult children live at a distance or when there are blended families
resulting from second marriages.

The success of conversations with parents also depends on the
relationship that children and parents have developed over the
years. Habits become entrenched. Stubbornness turns into defiance.
Disagreeable personalities become more pronounced. Independence is
fiercely protected. Why should parents bathe, change clothing, eat healthy
foods, take medications, exercise, or go to the doctor? This represents the
experiences of many adult children when parents need care.

Know that these conversations may be initiated and shut down
quickly by the parent. If this is your experience, ongoing and repeated
attempts may be necessary to make progress. This may be accomplished
through frequent discussions. For example "*Mom or Dad, it seems this*
is not a conversation you are comfortable having right now. I feel it is an
important conversation as it involves your future care and my/our involvement
as caregivers. I/we plan to approach the subject every few weeks until you are

ready to participate in a discussion, as I/we have to arrive at a situation that is a good fit for both of us." The goal of this statement is to let your parent know that this discussion is important and that their refusals will not result in the discussion "going away."

In making plans for future care, many aspects of the care recipient and the caregiver's lifetime behaviors, personality and coping skills are involved. There may be times where parents continue to resist the conversation, and again the caregiver feels trapped in an unsustainable situation. When continued refusals occur, begin with introducing one small area of concern that is likely to develop into a serious issue. This may allow your parent to think about the concern and to prepare for a subsequent discussion. Also give consideration to your parent's feeling of being trapped in an aging body and in a situation where they feel forced to make decisions that they would rather not consider.

Talking Points: Tackling the Hot Potatoes

If you are at the point where it is time for the conversation, you likely have concerns about the care of a loved one. That being said, having the conversation involves extremely personal and sensitive issues that might include managing money, financial planning, responding to declines in health, cessation of driving, feelings of caregiver guilt, care recipient resentment, and cognitive decline. These are likely subjects that parents and children feel uncomfortable discussing. To admit help is needed in any of these areas may make a parent feel like they are failing at life and failing in the eyes of others, especially children who have looked up to them for a lifetime.

In starting these discussions, it is important to acknowledge and to say, "*We are all aging and at one point or another common issues will arise for which help and support are necessary. There is no need to feel embarrassed because you have family who love you and want to help. One day I will be in a similar situation and will have to accept that I will need the help of my children or others.*"

If a parent continues to deny that there are specific ongoing issues of concern, resolution may require time and effort—sometimes substantial time and effort with a high level of stress or frustration being experienced. You as a family member, brother, sister, child, or grandchild may not have available time to help your parent. You may not be in close physical proximity to provide help, or because of the present situation you may no longer feel the desire or have the patience to continue to attempt to help. In this situation temporarily stepping back to offer another option is a prudent strategy.

The option may be to allow your loved one to fail without help. While this may feel uncomfortable and plain wrong, sometimes allowing a parent to fail is necessary for Mom or Dad to admit that help is needed. This is no different from our parents stepping back when we were young children to allow us to fail. Lessons occur throughout our lifetimes that benefit repeating in different situations many years apart. Take a deep breath and allow whatever will happen with your parent to happen, knowing that you will step in to help when needed.

Another option is to retain a care navigator to provide support with the discussion and subsequent oversight and coordination—with the parent agreeing to pay for this assistance. The involvement of a care navigator may reduce the stress that occurs in the parent-child relationship by establishing a buffer or by offering an independent individual who can step in to establish sequential plans and checkpoints. Have the care navigator initially meet independently with your loved one to determine issues and concerns. The care navigator may then be able to reinstate family involvement in having a conversation of care, especially if the parent feels he or she has an advocate able to offer options and solutions.

Money is one of the most sensitive hot potato topics—including paying for the services of a care navigator and other supportive services. It often comes as a surprise to many children that parents did not financially prepare for retirement or the increased costs of healthcare, believing that social security or Medicare would be the answer. Few parents expect that health declines will complicate the ability to manage daily in a home environment.

Talking about money is one of the most personal and sensitive issues involved in having the conversation with parents, as the ability to pay for care (or not) is an eventual reality that is unavoidable. Many older adults, especially those who lived through the Great Depression, have difficulty paying for help whether help is a housekeeper or an in-home caregiver. They are saving their pennies for a rainy day or hope to leave an inheritance to children or grandchildren. This thinking is not always practical or possible.

A road map for care requires knowledge of available funds and making plans for how and where care will be provided. This includes understanding aspects of private payments, Medicare, and possible planning for Medicaid. A care navigator is able to explain care options for private pay and government assistance.

If you are uncertain about how to make a plan or a sequential plan, we'll look at a situation where a parent has been unable to keep up with financial matters like bill paying and managing a budget but may not require physical care. My first recommendation is to establish automatic deposits and withdrawals from a checking account to avoid missed payments and to establish a monthly budget. A trial period may be set to allow the parent continued access to accounts and the checkbook. If the parent is able to manage the budget and no adverse financial issues occur, then this situation can be monitored until additional attention is required. If the trial period proves unsuccessful, then the agreement is to implement Plan B involving increased assistance and oversight of financial matters. This plan supports change to occur sequentially and in steps, allowing parental participation by way of success or failure. If Plan A fails, Plan B will be implemented.

Poor and declining health is another hot potato. A similar plan may be put in place for physical or health issues. By the time a health crisis occurs, events have likely been progressing for some time with adverse effects. Prescription medications may have not been filled or taken as prescribed. Medical appointments were missed, recommendations for care not implemented. Now the health and well-being of a parent is at substantial risk. In this situation, Plan A, offering the support of family or a care navigator to arrange services and to provide oversight, offers benefit. If Plan A is unsuccessful, then Plan B may be implemented that involves moving a parent to a care community where similar supports are available.

The benefit of identifying concerns and making sequential plans allows a parent to participate in their own plan with the realization that their participation and choices have consequences. Next steps will be implemented if the progress required does not result. This method of trial and error, success and failure promotes dignity and participation.

Giving Up the Car Keys

The subject of driving is perhaps the "hottest potato" of all as for older adults the ability to drive equals independence. Few older adults, regardless of the number of car accidents or the frequency of becoming lost while driving, adamantly refuse to acknowledge that it may be time to give up the car keys.

When you are driving, you see them—the cars in the slow lane driving well below the speed limit or cars weaving to the left and right within the stripes of a single lane. While statistics show that teenage drivers represent a greater risk than older drivers, risks still exist for older drivers with physical disabilities and cognitive impairment. Giving up the car keys is often viewed as giving up the last remaining bit of independence for older adults.

George Weller is quoted as saying, "God almighty, those poor people. Poor, poor, tragic people. And what a tragic ending to their outing, and I contributed to it, which is just almost more than I can figure out." George's car stopped after veering out of control for nearly a thousand feet, leaving ten people dead and more than sixty injured on July 16, 2003, in Santa Monica, California. He also reported that "something" smashed into his windshield and he had no idea what "it" was; "it" was the body of an innocent human bystander colliding with his car.[55]

Weller was found guilty of ten counts of vehicular manslaughter and seriously injuring 63 others. The City of Santa Monica was slated to pay $21 million to settle dozens of civil lawsuits stemming from the case.[56] This presents a picture of what might happen when an older adult with multiple health conditions or a diagnosis of dementia continues to drive a motor vehicle. Very different from the humorous and heartfelt movie *Driving Miss Daisy,* older adults who choose not to give up the car keys have the potential of seriously harming themselves, other drivers, or pedestrians.

While some older adults willingly give up the keys, others, even after multiple car accidents, refuse saying, "I've been driving since I was a teenager." Lacking is the insight to realize that driving skills and physical and cognitive abilities change and decline over time. Older adults also fail to consider, like George Weller, that they may injure innocent people.

In situations where cognitive impairment exists, like a diagnosis of Alzheimer's disease, specialized driving tests exist to test reflexes, memory, and physical abilities related to the operation of a vehicle to determine whether a person is safe to drive. These tests are not administered by the DMV—who in my experience feel bad if they fail to renew the license of an older adult—but by special driving programs through the occupational departments of medical clinics and other health organizations.

When in question, begin by asking your physician to initiate cognitive testing or to make a referral to one of the specialized driving courses in your area. While your parent may resist, this is a wise course of action to prevent accidental injury or financial loss due to negligent driving.

But how do family members hold discussions about ending driving or about taking away the keys? What supports exist? Again, there is benefit to sequential consequences and a Plan A that involves testing and a Plan B that offers options for transportation.

Exercise: Forward Motion

Below are common situations that result in feelings of angst on the part of caregivers because of not knowing how to respond positively or the best way to offer support when parents begin to fail. The goal is to respond positively and to provide options without removing responsibility from a loved one who must take action and make decisions.

Below are three suggested responses to a variety of situations. Give consideration to how you might respond when these situations arise with your parent.

1. Your parent refuses care unless you are the caregiver. "*Mom or Dad, I really appreciate your confidence in me and your desire to have me help. I want to let you know that I am able to help on a temporary basis and I suggest that we start looking at other options to bring help into the home. Here are some of the resources I have identified so we can look at what you might prefer.*"

2. You are a long-distance caregiver for a parent living alone. The easy situation is to move your parent into a care community but your parent wants to remain in the family home. "*Mom or Dad, I know how important staying at home is to you, and I've given this some thought. In order to make this work for you, let's consider the following ideas.*"

3. Your parent recently caused a severe car accident by making a left turn in front of oncoming traffic; you are concerned about the driving ability of your parent. "*Mom or Dad, you were really lucky that you or someone else wasn't seriously injured. I think it might be beneficial if we schedule a checkup with your doctor to make sure something isn't going on with your health that caused the accident. I'd be happy to make the call right now.*"

Are you a caregiver who feels uncertain about the best way to have difficult conversations with your parent about care needs? Do you feel uncomfortable about expressing your true feelings or talking about what you are able and not able to provide in the way of assistance? You are not alone, difficult discussions are often avoided in family caregiving situations. Know that there is support and information available to help you have the conversation of care.

If you are interested in accessing more tips and information about ideas presented in this chapter and related about subjects, visit http://www.thecaregivingtrapbook.com/store and select The Next Chapter.

Tales of the Caring Generation

Harold's Lucky Day

Every day when the mail was delivered, Harold was filled with excitement. There were letters from psychics predicting a wonderful future if only he sent them a few dollars for his next report. There were offers to make $100,000 by mailing in only $10,000; there were sweepstakes offers for fabulous trips, cars, and other items. Then there were the sad letters—the children starving in Africa, the mistreated horses, the poor people with no water. Harold felt that by sending a dollar here and there he might help the entire world.

How much more fortunate could Harold be that his mailbox—and not the mailboxes of his neighbors—were filled every single day with these unbelievable offers? Harold's wife had passed away five years prior. They did everything together. Since her loss, Harold often found himself at odd ends with not much to do during the day. They had no children, only a niece, Marie, who called and stopped by occasionally.

Receiving the mail was the big event in Harold's day. He was certain—absolutely certain—that one day he would be the big winner of a new house, a car, a vacation home, or hundreds of thousands of dollars. He was so sure that he took out a first and a second mortgage on his already paid-off home. This provided money to send to the psychics who promised good fortune and the investors asking him to invest $10,000 to receive a return of $100,000. Then there was the acreage in Canada that he bought for a mere $50,000, but because of some complication, he had not yet received the deed to the property. These projects consumed Harold's entire day.

Harold served in the Army in World War II. One day he met a man offering all kinds of veterans benefits IF ONLY Harold would invest $50,000 with him in an annuity that would return a steady income and lock in a great interest rate for the next fifteen years. Harold was ninety, never considering that he might not live until 115, he wrote the check for $50,000.

He received postcards from realtors wanting to buy his home for cash. There were solicitations from retirement communities promising luxury living and help from FREE referral services. How much luckier could Harold be, with all these people sincerely wanting to help him?

There was even a man from Harold's church who offered to move in with him and help him around the house. Why not? His niece, Marie, expressed suspicion. Harold responded by saying that he was certain that someone from his church must certainly be an honest and kind person. Marie's suspicions were warranted. After calling for a few days with no answer, she visited her uncle's home to find him tied up, lying in bed covered in urine and feces and severely dehydrated. The church roommate had tied him up and escaped with his television, the cash in his wallet, and a few other items. The police were called and an investigation started, but the good church going man was long gone.

After further investigation, Marie discovered that Harold was unable to pay his mortgages because he had spent all of the money on psychics and get-rich-quick schemes. His monthly income was barely enough to pay the utilities and buy groceries. With Harold's agreement, Marie had his mail forwarded to her home so that she could pay his bills. Eventually Harold's home was sold, and he moved to live with Marie.

Looking back, the signs of potential financial harm were evident: piles of mail solicitations sitting on Harold's kitchen table, repeated mentions by Harold of winning the lottery or of good fortune coming his way. Harold spent hours alone with nothing to do but sort through and read piles of mail solicitations. Marie wondered how she might have stopped the situation earlier. After all, she did not want to interfere in her uncle's life, but there clearly were times she wondered about his well-being.

Is your parent in a similar situation—is he or she receiving solicitations in the mail from psychics, sweepstakes, lotteries, and Canadian companies offering land? All it takes is a single response to be placed on a list of solicitations that grows and grows. Offer to help before your loved one becomes involved in a scam.

Place a "do not solicit" message on your loved one's telephone and a "no solicitors" sign on their front door. Make sure that they do not purchase from door-to-door solicitors selling new roofs after a hailstorm or others selling magazines, light bulbs, or home improvements. Individuals who live alone are more vulnerable to solicitors because they see these individuals as someone offering companionship.

Just as children should be advised not to talk to strangers, older adults should be advised to ask for a second opinion regarding large purchases, financial investments, and solicitations. Speak with your parents about Internet, telephone, and mail scams so that they are aware and may be proactive in protecting their financial well-being.

Chapter 8
Self Preservation

- Teamwork, Collaboration, and Good Intentions
- Lifetime Behaviors and Coping Patterns
- It's All in Your Response
- Good People Make Poor Choices
- Exercise: Behavioral Modification
- Tales of the Caring Generation: Ceil and the Angels

Teamwork, Collaboration, and Good Intentions

When multiple caregivers contribute to the care of a loved one, a change in the ability to participate by one team member will change the entire dynamic of the situation. Life situations, career, and health are in constant flux and may result in a change in the type of care provided to a care recipient. If a caregiver is less able to visit this may mean making a decision that the time has arrived to consider an increase in time by paid caregivers or a move to a community of care.

An increase in the care needs of a parent may mean that a parent living at home has arrived at a care level where continued family involvement is no longer possible due to a need for around-the-clock care. The care recipient may be awake all night, incontinence may require constant clothing and bedding changes, and behaviors or agitation related to a diagnosis of dementia may be emotionally and physically exhausting for the caregiver.

When care situations begin, the hope is that the present situation will be maintained for a long time. In reality, what we hope for is not always the result. A move to a care community may be the next step, even though family members are experiencing a high level of guilt about making this decision.

Parents, because of their personal expectations, fail to realize that family caregiver support allows continued presence in a home environment by providing a level of care similar to the care provided in a traditional assisted living community. Spouses become natural twenty-four hour caregivers because they already live in the home. Adult children able to visit frequently or those who choose to give up their own home to move to a parent's home—or the reverse, those who invite a parent to live with them—provide an assisted living level of care.

For spouses who are twenty-four hour caregivers, giving up participation in enjoyable activities with friends will eventually result in compassion fatigue that includes a lack of patience and feelings of anger and resentment. Free time has all but disappeared; friends no longer call. This decision of the caregiver to opt out of life has placed their relationship with the care recipient at risk because both are now isolated and, in a sense, imprisoned in the caregiving home. It is not always obvious that caregiving becomes a role of isolation. Total focus on tasks and activities to care for another individual quickly become all consuming.

Conversations with care recipients may be infrequent, and the television or radio becomes a constant companion. Caregivers, rather than feeling connected to the care recipient, feel isolated, lonely, and at times depressed. Some care recipients are unable to carry on a conversation that tracks in a logical manner because of memory or cognitive diagnoses. As new mothers feel they have little access to intelligent conversation when caring for a newborn, caregivers of an individual with memory loss, also unable to have complex conversations, experience a similar feeling.

Some caregivers, especially spouses, believe that no one else will be as devoted to the care of a loved one. In my personal experience, the idea of "no one else will care like me" is especially evident with husbands who served in the military and have an extreme sense of duty to provide care for an ailing wife. Many military husbands go to great extremes to avoid accessing outside support because they feel they must do it all.

Being a sole caregiver who refuses assistance results in becoming physically and emotionally worn-out. While it may be true that the marital relationship is unique, the task work may be duplicated through the efforts of others allowing focus on the relationship rather than hours of daily work and tasks. The same may be said of children who are caregivers. These are situations where over involvement by the caregiver has the potential to create a dysfunctional and harmful situation.

In my opinion, all caregivers benefit from considering the idea of being temporarily displaced. This temporary displacement is called "respite," with the purpose of allowing time away from caregiving to minimize compassion fatigue. Respite is critical, even if this time is only several hours a week to play racquetball, go to an aerobics class, or to see a movie or have lunch with friends. This time, free of phone calls or worry about a loved one, provides a total break for the mind helping the caregiver realize the importance of small bits of away time.

Being with the same person day in and day out in a care situation leads to relationship burnout, especially when activity, physical or mental, is absent from the relationship. There are care communities that offer temporary respite from a single week up to a month to support caregiving situations that have become draining. This respite allows caregivers to take a much needed vacation knowing that their loved one is safe and receiving care.

Other twenty-four hour care situations involve children moving into a parent's home to provide care. As with spousal caregivers, it is likely that prior discussions did not occur between the parent and the caregiver about giving up activities or friends; this decision was made as caregiving responsibilities increased. The dedicated caregiver chose to reduce activities out of a sense of duty and responsibility, but did not realize the consequences of compassion fatigue. Other caregivers when looking back—years after becoming involved in a care situation—underestimated the personal effort involved to rebuild their life after the caregiving situation ended.

For parents, the factor of an adult child moving back home to provide care may feel like having a stranger or an intruder present in life and in home. The daily routines or habits of parents and children, when intertwined may be sufficient to lead to frustration for all involved especially if lifestyles and preferences are significantly different.

Another significant life change is the altruistic idea of moving a parent to live with an adult child and family. Parents living with adult children present a dual emotional and financial strain. The parent often feels out of place, as if they are living in a home where their presence is bothersome to their children. Adult children experience the opportunity cost of giving up their personal lives, privacy, and personal space while potentially being judged by a parent who has been absent from interaction in their daily lives for years. After a long day of work, adult children come home to a parent who has been home alone all day expecting to be entertained. Or more worrisome is a caregiver returning home from work to a parent who has forgotten to take medications and eat a prepared meal.

Good intentions notwithstanding, situations of twenty-four hour care sooner or later lead to high levels of stress, caregiver illness, and guilt due to feelings of caregiver burden. Eventually an event occurs that precipitates a move to a care community, and guilt may increase.

Caregivers for individuals with memory loss experience a different type of guilt when the time arrives to place a loved one in a care community. Persons with memory loss will adjust to a new environment and routine after a period of time. However, initially when family visits, there is often discussion including pleas from the care recipient asking to return home. This is common because of the familiar reminder of seeing family. The plea to return home tugs at the heartstrings of family members whose emotions may be highly sensitive. What begins as a wonderful visit ends as a guilt-filled event for the family member leaving a loved one behind in a care community.

As caregiving situations advance due to the complexity of the level of care or because of worn out emotions, it is common for caregivers to experience compassion fatigue. Memories of positive relationships from years prior keep caregivers involved, yet the day to day stresses results in dreams of ending the duty and responsibility of the care situation.

Lifetime Behaviors and Coping Patterns

In my role as a care navigator, it is common for adult children to experience stress and challenges interacting with parents when caregiving issues arise. Conflict arises from various aspects, including parental habits or behavioral patterns that have intensified and resulted in a need for assistance. Among these aspects are health conditions resulting in an inability to care for oneself or one's home, difficulty in managing routine bill paying and financial matters, accidents stemming from risky behaviors like driving a vehicle when driving is no longer safe, a decline in mental ability that places all aspects of managing daily life in question, or a fall placing mobility at risk.

When choices and decisions must be made about parental ability, managing finances, declining health, or changing living arrangements, turmoil results as children feel pulled emotionally. Children find themselves challenged to balance personal opinions and beliefs, the preferences and desires of parents, and a desire to take immediate action to fix the problem. We all have differences in responses, coping skills, and problem solving abilities. These differences result in positive interactions or promote negative family dynamics that complicate the ability and willingness of adult children to provide care.

Children caregivers feel uncertain because they have little control over the responses of parents to the idea of accepting care—even if discussions were held and plans agreed upon. Many caregivers are aware that the current situation will not sustain but at some point decline to a point of crisis. Some children believe that parents purposely act or speak in a certain manner to start an argument or disagreement in order to avoid care discussions.

Behaviors of parents, often viewed as maddening by children, may represent long-standing habits. These behaviors may also result from a diagnosis of memory loss evidenced by an inability to recall conversations and to remember information discussed. Children lacking the skill of emotional intelligence walk away from discussions without resolution and experience a looming dread that parental refusal will eventually result in children having to take action under less than ideal circumstances.

Parents, who may realize care and support are needed, feel threatened and fearful of change because there has been little change in their daily routine or life for many years. All of a sudden, children or other family members have identified imperfection in areas of a parent's life that the parent stubbornly denies there is any need or benefit to changing.

Rather than accepting the possibility that planning and preventative action might offer value, the resistant behavior of the parent to participate in agreed-upon strategies continues to stall progress. This same preventative stalling strategy by parents is beneficial to caregivers from a strategy that allows reflection and time and investigation that support plans for change.

Some parents have an innate ability to push the emotional buttons of their children with a single look, statement, or even the tone of voice. Over the years I have learned that reflection, otherwise known as biting your tongue and walking away, is a better response to refusals or perceived attacks than allowing the brain and mouth to react and respond with words or statements difficult to retract. Silence in a moment of stress can be golden.

How many times do we respond without much thought to what we perceive as a refusal or an attack and then later regret our response?

Delaying a verbal response for twenty-four hours or even several days allows caregivers to think more clearly about the situation and to develop a more appropriate response. The ability to delay and reflect, *"Mom, I hear your concerns. Before I respond, I want to give this matter more thought,"* is a mechanism to manage emotions in uncertain, complicated or volatile situations. Delaying a response also allows time for objective instead of emotional thought and time to investigate alternatives or options that might offer a new perspective to the situation.

While many of us become ingrained in our routines, behaviors and habits, when family rejoins in the effort of caregiving, it is important to be sensitive to how our behaviors and habits affect our siblings, parents and others involved in the caregiving effort. Common interests and goals are the foundation of collaborative caregiving relationships as well as a belief that the effort put forth will be appreciated and reciprocated in some manner by a parent.

For most caregiving relationships to succeed, expressions of appreciation must occur in equal presentation of demands by a parent stating "I want or I expect this from you." I participate in many situations where parents constantly and repeatedly complain about their health, their life situation, and a long list of other issues without accepting responsibility for their part in the current situation or being willing to take any action to change the situation. While we all have a need to vent from time to time, if complaints are the only form of conversation, these complaints will drive away helpful people and children with good intentions. Some level of appreciation or recognition of effort must be provided by care recipients to support balance in caregiving relationships.

There are other situations when a diagnosis of brain injury, dementia, or Alzheimer's disease prevents any type of appreciation being shown to the caregiver. Individuals with these diagnoses may be unable to shift focus away from their immediate needs due to faulty circuits in the brain and decreased memory skills. Caring for loved ones with memory impairment will be discussed in the chapter called "The Pleasantly Forgetful." In all caregiving situations the response of the caregiver is the secret to preserving physical and emotional well-being.

It's All In Your Response

Long-standing behaviors affect child-parent caregiving relationships. So many times I hear, "*Mom or Dad has always been like that,*" to which I ask, "Have you sought a diagnosis?" It is common that persistent negative behaviors may be the result of undiagnosed depression, chronic pain, or a personality or unknown disorder. Seeking and receiving a diagnosis may promote understanding of a behavior and allow treatment. On the other hand, the diagnosis may not promote acceptance of the behavior but may allow caregivers to modify their responses and to set boundaries regarding aspects of the relationship.

You may recognize some of these common unhealthy and inflexible behaviors:

- The helpless or avoidant:
  o Complain but are powerless to implement change
  o Prefer sympathy and empathy from others—oh "poor me"
  o May exaggerate situations to gain attention
  o Dependent on others to do things for them, they cling to relationships even though the relationships may not be positive
- The self-centered or narcissistic:
  o Believe that they are special, different, or more important than others
  o Fail to recognize the feelings of others
  o Desire constant praise or admiration
  o Have unreasonable expectations and will take advantage of people who lack good boundaries and an inability to say "no"
- The unmotivated:
  o Poor self-image, feel sorry for themselves
  o May be moody and sometimes act impulsively
  o Attempt to rationalize their choices

- o Lack belief that actions will result in any positive movement; they prefer to maintain the status quo
- o For every suggestion given, they provide reasons why your suggestion will fail
- The paranoid:
  - o Suspicious of others
  - o Perceive innocent remarks to be personal attacks or insults
  - o Hold grudges
  - o Believe that others are always doing something "behind their backs"
  - o Generally untrusting and believe that everyone is out to get them

In many of the above situations, especially if these behaviors have been long-standing, it is not likely the care recipient will be able to change his or her behaviors. These are emotionally draining situations where limiting time spent with parents may be the only way to manage the situation and still remain involved. Tips to responding and managing these types of caregiving situations vary case by case. Different tactics must be used depending on the situation. Behavioral specialists are able to evaluate situations and will offer specific recommendations for responding to the behaviors of a care recipient. The goal of behavior modification is to enable the caregiver to implement strategies and responses that will result in positive behaviors by the care recipient.

Acknowledging or empathizing—but not agreeing with difficulties—may open pathways of communication when disagreement exists. Continually dwelling on negatives, complaints, and reasons why solutions are not the answer is a poor use of time. Avoid phone calls and discussions that focus on the negative by attempting to change the subject. If the subject repeats, let your loved one know that you will end the phone call or discussion by walking away.

My advice for caregivers is not to remove responsibility from the care recipient but rather to focus on the idea of choice. For example, respond with, "*As long as you continue to make the choice to do nothing your situation will not change.*" Many caregivers default to making progress by their own action of doing, which is sometimes necessary but not a good long-term solution.

Do not complete tasks for the care recipient that they can do themselves but resist. If completing tasks that can be completed by the care recipient is the basis of caregiver interaction, the caregiver is enabling unhealthy and inflexible behaviors. Setting personal boundaries in these care situations is critical to allow the caregiver to maintain a sense of involvement minus feelings of frustration. Setting and maintaining boundaries is a cornerstone of success in challenging caregiving situations.

Individuals who are unmotivated to change habits represent a significant portion of the population. How many of us should exercise, lose weight or stop smoking? How many of us say, "I know I should, but?" We participate in behaviors that we know are not positive or conducive to our health or lifestyle, and we refuse to stop ourselves until an event beyond our own power forces us to stop and pay attention. This event may be a heart attack resulting in the discovery of blocked arteries and mandatory bypass surgery, a stroke that paralyzes one side of the body or an automobile accident resulting in injury because of "one more drink."

Crises or disasters will eventually force decision making. Making stress-based decisions as a result of a traumatic event usually results in a less than optimal outcome. As health and mental capabilities fail, higher levels of care are often necessary and are associated with greater expense. If preventative measures were taken or if planning preceded the crises, results will likely be different and less stressful.

Similar to care recipients who are inflexible and exhibit unhealthy habits, caregivers who feel stuck or trapped experience compassion fatigue when the act of caregiving becomes overwhelming, emotionally, and physically draining. Caregivers fail to investigate options for self-care or self-preservation for the same reasons care recipients delay—because effort is required and change must be accepted.

Compassion fatigue results from a variety of emotional states experienced by the caregiver that include denial, anger, fear of change, uncertainty about making decisions, and an inability to express empathy. There is a point where caregivers shut down emotionally and feel unable to accept information or take action. All of us have likely felt immobilized or frozen at one point in our lives as the result of an unexpected experience or a situation we felt was well beyond our control or ability.

When caregivers or care recipients feel that life or life situations are out of control, not taking action and not making decisions become a coping mechanism. When we feel forced to make a change or a decision, a common response is to resist. It is human nature to become angry and resistant when pushed to make a change we feel is unnecessary. We justify or rationalize not taking action through the actions of blame or hopelessness, "*He made me do this,*" "*I don't have a choice,*" "*I don't need any help,*" or "*That's just the way life is.*"

Compassion fatigue may result in irrational thinking that includes feelings of impending doom or incessant worry about unfortunate events that might occur rather than considering positive possibilities. Self-esteem is low because of the choice to ignore a situation that continues to advance in severity, and anxiety and depression result. Inaction becomes a self-fulfilling prophecy that leads to limited choices as time progresses rather than the availability of a greater number of choices. This is a key point lost to caregivers and to care recipients: waiting or not taking action is not a prudent choice. Each day good people make poor choices.

Good People Make Poor Choices
More choices exist early and in the beginning of caregiving situations. The longer caregivers or care recipients remain helpless, in denial, or resistant to change, the fewer choices exist because needs change and progress in severity. Financial expenses and care limitations result from ever-increasing health needs.

Instead of making decisions to promote choice, the decision *not* to act results in limited choices and stress-based decision making. By delaying decisions about care, control and choice are relinquished. Sticker shock regarding costs of care occurs when care is no longer optional but mandatory. The assumption that Medicare or health insurance pays for care as we age is faulty. As care needs increase fewer options exist to provide care.

An example of the consequence of choice or poor decision making is a person who refuses to take prescribed medications. Refusal results in a stroke, limiting mobility and resulting in memory loss. Previously the individual was independent and able to walk distances, climb stairs, and drive an automobile. After the stroke, the individual is no longer able to drive a car, struggles to walk from the bedroom to the kitchen, and lacks memory sufficient to organize and prepare meals and manage medications.

By refusing to take medications, this individual created an unfortunate event, a stroke, which eliminated the choice of living in a private residence. A decision must be made to move to a care community or choose to remain at home by hiring in-home caregivers at a rate of $300 or more per day, or approximately $10,000 a month if funds exist. This is an example of how situations turn catastrophic when ignored. If actions, choices, and consequences are not given consideration, choices will be forced by the consequences of an event.

It is easy to judge situations when one is looking in from the outside and has little or no experience with a caregiving situation. Personal relationships are destroyed when friends or others criticize a decision made by the caregiver—never having walked in the caregiver's shoes. In these situations I recommend inviting the judging party to spend a weekend or an entire week providing care. This level of participation will likely change the judging party's view of the care situation. If the person criticizing refuses to participate, refuse to have further discussions about the situation. It is clear the judging party lacks the experience, insight, and empathy to be supportive. Refuse to allow those who are negative or unsupportive to be a part of your life.

In situations of care, promises made are promises broken. Many spouses or caregivers promise never to place a loved one in a care community.

This promise, made with the best intentions, becomes impractical when the reality of being awake all night to provide care, changing a parent's Depends every two hours, or battling with a parent who refuses to bathe becomes a stressful and overwhelming responsibility. Life situations, when promises are made, change with the passage of time. What might have been practical and possible five years ago is not practical or possible today.

Also common are situations where an adult child becomes involved in the life of a parent and then becomes emotionally overinvolved by wanting to take control of every aspect of the care situation to prevent the situation from perceived disaster. The intention of the caregiver may be honorable and practical. The parent may strongly resist, even refuse to move or to comply with recommendations to take medications, monitor diet, etc. The consequences of not changing are crystal clear to the caregiver. The amount of change required in the habits of the parent needing care is overwhelming, resulting in refusals. The situation advances to a battleground.

In situations of denial or refusal, caregivers must examine their intentions, internal responses, and personal motivations. Is the caregiver reacting to a personal experience, or is the caregiver able to remain objective and examine the facts? How much easier might it be for a caregiver—emotionally and from a time perspective—to place a parent in a care community? This move may reduce caregiver worry, including the time involved in coordinating activities and overseeing care required to allow the parent to live in their home.

Is moving a parent in the best interest of the parent or in the best interest of the caregiver? Ask yourself these questions:

1. Have you as the caregiver become personally judgmental and angry that the care recipient is unable to provide self-care?
2. Have you taken an all-or-nothing attitude toward helping the care recipient, meaning he or she must do as you demand?
3. Are you frustrated with the amount of time devoted to providing care?

4. Are you looking for the easiest solution to removing responsibility and time commitment?

If your response is yes to any one of these questions, retaining a care navigator may be beneficial to provide support to ensure that plans for care are balanced and well considered. Making decisions in anger or frustration results in poor outcomes. Parents, even though relationships may currently be experiencing a significant degree of stress, are still individuals deserving of kindness, compassion, and dignity.

Attention to how we respond to stressful situations as a caregiver is indicative of our level of compassion. If our first response is one of a desire to take control, feeling we are the only one able to solve the problem or that others' opinions and ideas have no value, we are too far down the path of becoming overly involved and potentially abusive in the situation. Many caregivers, too close to the situation, lose perspective, become overly controlling and make poor decisions on behalf of a parent.

When one feels that being a caregiver is a personal identity rather than a role in life, the actions of the caregiver become damaging to the care relationship. Overinvolved and controlling caregivers lose perspective and the ability to positively cope with the demands of the care situation. Caregivers become angry and depressed rather than beneficial to the caregiving relationship. Caregiving actions become detrimental to the life of the care recipient.

Overinvolved caregivers lack the insight to see the negative effects of their behaviors. Similar to an alcoholic being unable to admit that alcohol has become an addiction, an overinvolved caregiver is unable to see that their actions cause harm rather than benefit the care situation. Attending personal counseling or support groups may offer beneficial support.

Working through this type of conflict when many individuals are involved may present a challenge. Caregiving is a role of trial and error. What works in one family will not work in another. The relationships of parents and children differ. What works in one situation will fail in another.

The progression of disease, especially related to memory conditions, is never the same.

In situations of stress, caregivers fall into the trap of a single-sided perspective. It is easy to forget that the art of maintaining successful relationships relates to the way one interacts and responds to others, and that doing so under stress rarely has a positive outcome. In few other life situations are positive interactions more important as in the role of caregiving. Sensitivity to changes in the life of the care recipient and to their desires and wishes is critical to the success of the caregiving relationship.

This sensitivity supports the idea of "person-centered care" that is embraced by many care communities. Person-centered care means considering the history, preferences, and values of a care recipient and incorporating these into all aspects of care including relationships with family caregivers.

There will be times when caregivers, regardless of the response of the care recipient, will have no choice but to change roles to become the decision maker if they have been designated as the power of attorney. These are uncomfortable situations for caregivers because of the concern that they may permanently damage the relationship with a parent, especially if situations that have been apparent for some time have quickly advanced and decisions can no longer be delayed.

I support many families in these situations: for example, by implementing the decision to move a parent to a care community. By intervening, I am able to separate the child who made the necessary decision from the action of the physical move. While the parent may be angry at the child, at least during the process of the move time is allowed for emotions to subside and to allow the parent time to succeed in a new environment without the immediate involvement of the child.

In many of these situations, children may live at a distance and intervene when care or support is needed. It is possible parents were invited to move to be nearer to children years earlier and today this is no longer an option or a prudent decision. In these situations my company provides care oversight and ongoing communication for families at a distance. This type of situation is becoming more common as families move apart.

Exercise: Behavioral Modification

As we age, the habits and behaviors of our youth age with us. For many individuals, this means that lifelong patterns relating to communication, social activity, maintaining health, managing the household, or managing money become more noticeable when family caregivers become involved again in daily care. This also means that these behaviors may be challenging or upsetting to those providing care.

A term called "behavioral modification" may be helpful in explaining a method that caregivers might use to avoid emotional upset. In simple terms this means that as caregivers, we must change the way we respond to care recipients because it is unlikely that the care recipient will be able to or will be willing to change their behavior.

The following gives a three-step example of how behavior modification might be implemented in a situation of complaint and refusal to change.

1. A parent complains constantly but is unwilling to make a change that may improve a situation. If a caregiver allows a parent to complain about the same subject day after day without attempting to change the focus of the conversation, the caregiver appears to agree with the action of the parent to complain without making any plan to change the situation.

2. A better response is to ask the parent what a better situation might look like and then to discuss changes to arrive at this situation. If the parent prefers to complain rather than participate in a solution, the caregiver might say, "We've already discussed this. When you have a plan to change the situation, I will help, until then I will not listen to you complain." The corresponding physical response is to walk away making it clear to the parent that this is a closed conversation.

3. While this verbal and physical action may initially be uncomfortable, this is a good method to end unproductive behaviors and to protect the well-being of the caregiver. Eventually the care recipient may

realize that repeated negative behaviors are having an ill effect on family relationships.

Many times we fail to understand how our responses or actions complicate care situations. Sometimes by saying nothing, our response is perceived as agreement. Other times, by expressing a different opinion, we may be perceived as unsympathetic or cold. How can we be supportive when participating in difficult or uncomfortable conversations with loved ones?

If you are interested in accessing more tips and information about ideas presented in this chapter and about related subjects, visit http://www.thecaregivingtrapbook.com/store and select Self Preservation.

THE CARING GENERATION®

Tales of the Caring Generation

Ceil and the Angels

I grew up in a small Polish neighborhood in Omaha, Nebraska surrounded by the stockyards and industry. On the corner, in a whitewashed house, lived the Strudowski family with four children—John, Julianne, Ceil and Chester—whose parents immigrated to the United States from Poland in the early 1900s. The Strudowskis were probably not an unusual family according to standards of the "old country," Poland, but to me as a young child and then later as a young adult, they were a curiosity. True to the traditions of the old country, the four Strudowski children took care of both parents at home until they passed away. What was unusual was that the four children—John, Julianne, Ceil and Chester—never moved from their childhood home, and none of them married.

John was the cook and the caretaker of the immaculate yard surrounded by a picket fence overflowing in the summer with blooming red and pink roses. He had a green thumb and worked each day in the vegetable garden planted in the backyard. Julianne was the financial person; she had a job at the local telephone company and was always dressed to the nines. Ceil, the third born, was the caregiver, the family mediator responsible for care of Chester, the baby, born with a learning disability—he was happy-go-lucky but a bit slow in thought. I had the sense that Ceil felt obligated to work to make sure that Chester had everything he needed or wanted. He was the closest person to a child she would ever have.

The Strudowskis never owned a car. They walked to their destination or took the city bus. I remember seeing them come and go, walking alone or in pairs—always John with Julianne and Ceil with Chester. To arrive at the bus stop they had to walk by our house, so I saw one or all of them daily. My mom said that the girls were night and day different, and even though she never said, I suspected Ceil was her favorite.

Ceil was my favorite too, always smiling, happy, and wearing flowery print blouses and bottoms that I called pedal pushers. She also wore large floppy hats of all colors and designs. The other thing I remember is that she always carried a large black purse. I often wondered what exactly she kept in the large bag. My mom, when going to the store, would always call to ask Ceil if she needed a ride. More often than not, Ceil declined as she preferred to walk.

On many occasions Mom dropped Ceil off for errands or to shop in south Omaha. Ceil disappeared quickly to the post office, to the library, and other locations not to be seen until hours later. I was always very curious about her errands and activities and had a sense that she had a mysterious life. Ceil talked to Mom about how she wished to have married and had children, but that she had to be the one to care for Chester. Ceil did not believe that a husband would want a wife and her brother.

The years passed and I moved away from home. In the forty years after I was born the neighborhood seemed to stand still. I still remember the names of every family on the three blocks leading to the bus stop. Families were born and stayed—that is, until they went to St. John's, the Polish

Cemetery on South Thirty-Sixth Street. I kept up with the neighborhood goings on through my parents, my brother, and my sister.

I was always curious about the Strudowski family. John, experiencing heart problems, passed away first. Julianne took his death particularly hard and was the second to pass away. Ceil kept up with the care of the household, likely feeling that she needed to outlast her brothers and sisters so that Chester would not be left alone with no one to care for him. True to form, Chester was the third to pass away, leaving Ceil in her late eighties to care for herself.

One day when talking to my mom, I asked about Ceil. To my amazement, she said that Ceil had three young adults living with her—taking care of her. This shocked me since I knew that Ceil had never married.

You see, after all these years, Ceil did have a secret. All the times we dropped Ceil in South Omaha when she disappeared to the post office and to the library, Ceil was writing letters and sending money. She had adopted three orphaned Polish babies, a boy and two girls, who lived in an orphanage managed by nuns. Over the years Ceil supported the care of the babies, making sure, like with Chester, that they had the best care, needing nothing, and that they had good educations.

She kept in touch with the children, sending and receiving letters and photographs she hid in boxes underneath her bed. When the time arrived that she grew old and needed care, the three baby angels she helped raise came home to the whitewashed house with the picket fence overflowing with roses to care for her until she passed away. A quote from Claudia Quigg: "There are angels that pass on from one generation to another, but they are seldom noticed or talked about." Ceil Strudowski was one of those angels.

PART THREE

DANGER AHEAD— THE UNEXPECTED

Life is filled with hope and possibility. Little do we realize, until the bubble of good health bursts and we become a caregiver or a care recipient, that no one escapes this world unless by accident without becoming physically old or frail.

Chapter 9

Managing The Unpredictable and The Unexpected

- Importance of Relationships During Retirement Years
- Why Care Recipients Refuse Change
- Identifying Advocates and Responsible Parties
- Caregivers at a Distance: The Benefits of Communication and Technology
- Exercise: Gaining A Perspective On Aging
- Tales of The Caring Generation: Arnie and Mary Two Sides of Caregiving

Importance of Relationships During Retirement Years

Prior to retirement, making friends and maintaining relationships occur naturally because of the situational aspects of attending school or being with co-workers on a daily basis. The ability to be present in groups of people at school or at work makes it easier to meet and to establish relationships with others. Participation in social networks, like churches and interest groups, supports engagement in common interests, hobbies, and lifestyles that provide benefits that extend far into the future. Making friends, maintaining relationships, and remaining socially engaged support the ability to connect with others versus the inherent risks of isolation.

After retirement, individuals tend to become less socially active and spend more time at home. While connections through technology are supportive, connections by way of direct person-to-person contact are most beneficial with age. Individuals still physically able to engage in activities and groups fare better socially, emotionally, and physically. Participation in activities offered by community groups, including activity centers is extremely beneficial. For those who experience cognitive impairment, day programs exist to provide activities with associated physical care and support.

"The benefits of social-network size on health are robust. Older adults with larger networks show higher levels of health and well-being in many areas, including executive function, episodic memory, cognitive decline and allostatic load." [57] In simple terms, allostatic load is a term that means the wear and tear that occurs to the body and mind as a result of chronic stress and adapting to changes and transitions in life. The transition of retirement is an event resulting in a high allostatic load due to greater levels of stress experienced as the result of experiencing a significant life change.

Our social networks are comprised of others with similar interests. Just as this peer behavior promotes friendships in earlier years, peer behavior has an equally important impact with age and one's perception of being in a group of individuals in good health or in poor health. Perceptions of our health shape our day-to-day lives and our futures. "Studies have indicated that poor self-rated health is a reliable predictor of disability and mortality." [58] As in many aspects of our life, our self-perception becomes our reality.

Physical disability and chronic illness are limiting factors in the ability to maintain and support social ties and emotional connections with friends and family. Many older adults who become socially isolated experience feelings of loneliness and subsequent health declines. We benefit from having a reason to get up in the morning, whether the activity be taking a dog for a walk, meeting a friend for coffee, or looking forward to participation in an event. Poor self-esteem and worry related to physical disability or chronic illness make daily life a challenge.

Difficulties experienced on a daily basis resulting from chronic and disabling diagnoses generally remain behind closed doors because these individuals have low levels of participation in public activities; they are rarely seen in public. Individuals with chronic fatigue syndrome—for which there is currently no diagnosis or cure—have difficulty with the physical act of getting out of bed or the physical exertion required to stand in front of a stove to heat breakfast. These are actions that most of us perform without even thinking. Others diagnosed with chronic fatigue syndrome plan to participate in events with family or friends and decline at the last minute because they are unable to muster the energy required to leave home. The cycle of a disabling diagnosis combined with isolation results in a high level of emotional distress and depression for adults of all ages, but especially older adults.

"Social isolation may have a negative effect on intellectual abilities as well as emotional well-being."[59] Participation in solo activities, like playing solitaire on the computer, or going to the movies alone, may become a habit that results in a decreased desire to interact with others who may—unknown to us—be someone with whom we may have many things in common. Neuroscience research provides compelling evidence that participating in new activities benefits the brain through the creation of neurons. These include activities that are new and establish learning and thinking patterns for example, learning a foreign language or learning needlepoint or knitting.

A lack of ability or desire to connect with the outer world has significant negative effects on the quality of life experienced by isolated older adults. This lack of contact may result from a lack of connections: for example, everyone this person knew is either living at a distance or deceased, or an individual has a physical disability that makes going outside the home extremely difficult. For others, a decline in cognitive ability or memory loss results in decreased ability to plan, to organize, and maintain a household and results in a decreased ability to maintain relationships with friends and family.

Individuals who are isolated commonly experience depression and anxiety. "The rate of severe depression rises with age. Severe depression is evident in about 20 percent of people aged eighty-five and older compared with 15 percent among people age 84 or younger.[60] Older adults hesitate to talk about depression, as if being depressed carries a stigma.

Many older adults feel hopeless based on a faulty belief that nothing they do will change the current situation. The emotional aspect of feeling that life is worthwhile and has meaning makes a significant difference in daily attitudes, performing self-care, and interactions with others. Older adults who feel as if life has no meaning, become apathetic and lack motivation to participate in life; they isolate themselves from others and from the outside world.

Coping skills are an important component of responding to difficult situations presented by the environment. The ways that individuals view stress and the sources that result in stress allow identification of methods of appropriate response. Feelings of frustration and experiences of conflict are very common in caregiving situations. Many times caregivers respond with anger or harsh words. In practical terms, positive coping behavior includes searching for information or methods to support managing stressful situations—and our reactions—including evaluating options in order to make a plan. Care recipients, because of physical and emotional challenges, often feel unable to explore options and evaluate information. Developing coping skills is an important aspect of the role of caregiving to allow forward motion.

After my mother's death, my father experienced significant depression. He talked about committing suicide. One day he reported sitting in his car in the garage with the motor running and the garage door down. Rational thinking stopped him from remaining in the car with the motor running. He did not want his children to find him dead in the seat of his car. Other than recognizing his feelings, my father had no idea that he was experiencing depression or what actions to take to improve his situation.

My father was evaluated, diagnosed with depression, and was prescribed medication. When my sister visited, or when his children called to speak with him we reminded him to take his happy pill. This single change in my father's daily routine greatly improved his mood and his outlook on life. He became more physically active. He was able to enjoy travel to Hawaii and Alaska that he was unable to do when my mother was alive because of her health limitations and her fear of leaving home to travel.

Why Care Recipients Refuse Change

Feelings of apathy and lack of motivation on the part of an aging parent result in refusals to plan, to participate in discussions, or to change a current situation. This lack of action is supported by the ideas of motivation and risk. Understanding this concept may help caregivers relate better to the challenges and experiences of care recipients, and to acknowledge that the idea of motivation relates to the pros and cons of perceived risk no matter one's age.

Perceived ideas about risk and the unknown affect the level to which aging parents will participate with adult children and family caregivers in plans or efforts that involve change. Loneliness and social isolation are aspects of aging. The idea of loss and negative experiences may be supported by the idea of prevention. Any one of us has experienced the benefits of preventative action, whether the action is to have the oil changed in our car to keep it running or to take a daily multi-vitamin to feel better. Not taking preventative action usually results in expensive outlays for repairs or the expense of missing work because we do not feel well. As with the experience of my father and the diagnosis of his depression after my mother's death, many older adults have difficulty identifying and understanding the benefit of preventative services, including the aspect of understanding the cost and benefit of these services.

Older adults resist change, whether the change be accepting in-home care or moving to a retirement community. Forced change occurs because of a lack of belief that any effort put forth to make a change will result in a substantial positive result or gain; why try when no good will come of the effort? For others who may be ill or physically disabled, the ability to "just get by" is important because of the absence of emotional or physical stamina to support change. There comes a point where individuals become complacent and have no desire to put forth effort to improve their physical or nutritional states. Many clients tell me that they have no desire to lose weight, to improve their diet, or to exercise because these actions require effort that they are no longer willing to put forth.

The concept of loss and gain applies to all individuals. Patterns we learn when young and throughout our life affect decision making and choice. The act of being proactive and planning for changes related to aging offers the best hope that we will be participative and proactive care recipients. For those desiring better than average care, it is important to ensure that one has an advocate or a responsible party. The same applies to individuals who just want to "make it through the day" and who may be surviving in situations of isolation or loneliness where self-neglect commonly occurs.

Identifying Advocates and Responsible Parties

"Living alone has become more widespread as the rising number of one-person households offset the shrinking number of married households with children. In 1970, the number of households with men and women living alone represented 17.4 percent of the population. In 2012 this same segment represented 27.5 percent of the population."[61] These statistics characterize a current society with an increasing number of persons living alone and a society where the importance of planning for care needs and associated costs of care is becoming increasingly important.

Regardless of age, possessing the foresight to identify an advocate or responsible party is practical. What is a responsible party? A responsible party is an individual with a legal relationship with the care recipient by the title of financial power of attorney, medical power of attorney, guardian or conservator, personal representative, trustee or executor. If a power of attorney exists and if the requirements of the power of attorney have been met—which usually means that one or more physicians agree that the care recipient can no longer make good decisions—the responsible party [caregiver] has the power to do whatever is necessary as identified in the legal documents to provide care and support.

In other situations when the power of attorney is immediate and the power of attorney is making decisions contradictory to the wishes of the grantor the grantor may immediately revoke the power of attorney. This occurs most frequently when adult children are appointed as power of attorney and begin taking immediate financial advantage of a parent. There are also similar situations where a power of attorney is immediate and the care recipient continually makes poor decisions relative to money or health that places him or her at risk: in this situation the power of attorney may become guardian or conservator.

If a caregiver is already a guardian or conservator appointed through a court process, consideration has already been given as to whether the care recipient is able to make appropriate decisions. The appointment of a guardian or conservator provides full power to the individual designated to make decisions in the best interest of the care recipient.

In situations where a guardian or conservator is appointed, it is common for families to appoint a professional to serve in these roles because actions taken by adult children in the best interest of the parent may be in opposition to the parent's wishes. In order to support an ongoing relationship with a parent, adult children prefer not to place themselves in a situation that may be contentious or highly emotional. It is preferable that an impartial party provide support than to permanently damage family relationships. There are also situations where adult children are unable to agree on care for a parent because of feelings of hostility or disagreement; in this situation a professional guardian and conservator may be appointed.

A personal representative or executor is an individual who ensures that postlife wishes are executed by way of a will or a trust. These situations can also be highly contentious if family members have an interest in receiving money or property. I have been involved in situations where new wills were completed within days of an individual's death. In this situation the will was significantly changed from the wishes of the prior will and instead granted property and money to a single individual—the individual initiating the new will. Stipulations may be put in place in current documents to avoid the possibility of this type of abuse.

How does one decide whom to appoint as a responsible party? Some parents—not wishing to burden their children—make their own plans to appoint professionals. It is more common that parents have concerns about appointing children to act in the role of a legally responsible party when they witness adult children behaving irresponsibly in managing their own lives. Concerns exist by parents whether children would be an appropriate caregiver of a parent's well-being or financial matters, especially when adult children no longer share the same morals, values, and character as parents.

More frequently parents and middle-age adults are choosing to retain the services of professionals to act as responsible parties. This action guarantees that adult children will not have the power to make decisions or have the authority to become involved in physical care or financial matters, other than visitation. Singles are also among those who are excluding family members from having control over care and financial matters. While appointing a professional may shock family and seem like a harsh decision, in many cases appointing a professional is a prudent decision.

I am contacted by many parents who painfully acknowledge that their adult children lack the degree of moral character and responsibility they desire of someone to be responsible for their care. I am commonly appointed by older adults as what I call a "power of attorney in waiting." These adults are healthy today but recognize the importance of preparing for an unexpected event and knowing a responsible party will step in when necessary. While parents may initially feel apprehension about having to make alternate plans for care, appointing a professional has become more common and routine.

Similar situations exist where single adults realize that their ex-spouse, brother, sister, or children may not be an appropriate choice for a responsible party. Also common are situations where wording is placed in legal documents to prevent family members—who may have a financial or personal interest in belongings—from contesting the appointment and responsibilities of a responsible party. Preparing these documents is similar to drafting a prenuptial agreement to avoid potential issues at a later date. Taking this action is practical and avoids family disagreements. While family relationships are thought to be predictable, it is surprising how family members respond when health, money, and property become relative factors.

Let's not forget the elephant in the room—the fact that family members do not always have the best interests of loved ones in mind, especially when it becomes clear that health or memory is deteriorating. The temptation to take control of a vulnerable care recipient's money and property can be overpowering for a caregiver who has never been skilled at managing money or saving for the future. Individuals planning for the future are wise to look realistically at persons considered for the role of responsible party to determine the best person to carry out wishes.

Too often this responsibility defaults to the eldest child or the one who lives closest despite the child's history of poor money management and decision making. The default choice can be disastrous for the parent when inadequate care results from emotional or financial abuse and desire exists by the parent to change legal documents and appoint a different responsible party. A child already appointed the responsible party will do everything in his or her power to paint a picture of a parent who has "lost their mind" or "has no idea" about a desire to issue new documents and appoint a successor responsible party. These situations place a parent at risk of abuse from an angry child whose inheritance is at risk.

Rather than wonder who might take advantage of situations at the end of life, individuals who decide in advance to choose professional support for powers of attorney and personal representative are in the best position to ensure that their wishes will be implemented—and to live their final days with peace of mind. In my professional role as an advocate, I serve as guardian, medical and financial power of attorney, and as a personal representative. I have no doubt that the appointment of professionals will increase in demand as the population ages, due in part to geographically scattered families and relationships that have suffered over time due to differences in personal character and morals.

Caregivers at a Distance:
The Benefits of Communication and Technology

Isolation and distance may be barriers for family caregivers. For adult children with family members who live alone or who are isolated, discovering ways and supports to monitor the situation from afar may offer peace of mind. Isolation is cause for heightened awareness of the quality of living situations. Uncharacteristic behaviors should not be ignored. These include the more obvious behaviors of poor hygiene, body odor, appearance-appropriate hygiene, wearing the same clothing day after day, and forgotten or repeated behaviors.

A previously meticulous home now filled with stacks of mail, piles of newspapers, collections of plastic grocery bags or rubber bands because the Great Depression might happen again is a sign of a potential lack of ability to manage daily life. Letters arriving in the mail threatening electricity, gas, or water shutoff are proof that intervention is needed. Letters from the IRS appear when tax returns have not been filed. Prescription bottles dated from prior years sit on the counter while a parent swears she faithfully takes her medication every day. These behaviors indicate a loss of executive function and the ability to plan and to manage daily life.

Expressions of paranoia—or conversations that repeat and repeat and repeat from one visit to the next—indicate a possible cognitive or mental health concern that would benefit from a medical evaluation. While a primary care physician may be able to complete simple memory testing, a neurologist or a neuropsychologist evaluation is important to identify and diagnose conditions and to recommend treatment.

Technology is available to support peace of mind for family at a distance. Communicating is easier through use of the Internet, social networks, cell phones, texting, and email. While these advances have helped technologically savvy older adults find new ways to communicate with family members at a distance, the use of new technology is beyond the learning skills and interest of many other older adults.

Technology, including automated medication machines, personal alert systems to document falls and motion, and video technology exist to support independence in the home. While some of these may seem like Big Brother watching, this technology offers benefits to evaluating situations for care planning purposes.

Ensuring that care recipients take medications daily and on schedule through the use of technology may offer a significant improvement in health for an individual previously experiencing difficulty organizing, arranging, and remembering to take prescribed medications. If balance or recent falls have been an issue, the ability to press a button to call family or 911 may offer peace of mind. Motion sensors and video type camera equipment offer the ability to document waking and sleeping times and other activities, including no activity which might indicate a health emergency.

While technology and equipment offer support, in-person supervision is also important. The activity of care planning and providing care oversight may become another task on a long list of projects for family caregivers. If possible, investigate this type of assistance from a care navigator who is well versed in all of the options to provide care and oversight, including the use of technology. In challenging as well as in routine care situations, taking the initiative to seek information, to talk with experts, to take action and to make plans, including backup plans is important to prevent unexpected events and crises. Family members often express concern about their ability to manage their own lives as well as the life of a parent, especially when families live at a distance.

Societal changes are affecting family relationships, careers, and end-of-life care. Families are mobile, marriages end in divorce, and outside influences threaten values, morals, and individual character. A changing society and the corresponding pressures identified that "84 percent of American adults called 'pressures to make ends meet' a serious problem. By comparison 63 percent said that about the rise of single parent households, 55 percent about 'the declining role of religion', 54 percent about violence, entertainment programs, and games and 51 percent about 'putting career ahead of family'."[62]

While independence is valued, maintaining independence may result in a point of disagreement when a parent needs care and adult children become involved in daily care. As discussed previously, when family members become caregivers, an entirely new set of relationship parameters, boundary setting, and communication skills is required because parents and caregivers are establishing a new relationship. This is the relationship between a care recipient and a caregiver, a relationship of give-and-take and compromise, and a relationship of concessions and ongoing negotiation, for which there is little preparation.

Exercise: Gaining A Perspective on Aging
Many individuals have unrealistic fears about aging; others deny that aging will occur. Have you asked your parents or grandparents about the benefits of being an advanced age?

When thinking about aging, below is a list of twelve questions to consider that might support changes in lifestyle or identify insights today that might bring about positive change in later life.

1. What changes have you experienced through various decades of your life? Have your life experiences become easier or more challenging?
2. What experiences do you recall with great joy?
3. What experiences do you recall with great sadness?
4. If you could write yourself a letter of advice, what would the letter say? Are you willing to take action today on any of this advice?
5. What changes might you make today to avoid experiencing regret at the end of your life?
6. How are your parents aging? Are they in good or poor health?
7. Do you have positive and supportive family relationships?
8. Has your family held discussions about caregiving for your parents?
9. How do you feel about aging?
10. How do you feel about being a caregiver for family members?
11. What do you want for your care when the need arises? Who do you want to care for you?
12. What discussions and plans have you made for your care? Have you initiated discussions with your children or other family members?

What is your perspective about aging? Does the idea of aging make you fearful or are you looking forward to your retirement years as the time to participate in hobbies and travel? What plans have you made to ensure that you will receive the care important to your well-being? What is your plan for the unexpected?

If you are interested in accessing more tips and information ideas presented in this chapter and about related subjects, visit http:// www. thecaregivingtrapbook.com/store and select Managing the Unpredictable and the Unexpected.

THE CARING GENERATION®

Tales of the Caring Generation

Arnie and Mary
Two Sides of Caregiving

Arnie woke up one morning exhausted and decided he had had enough—he had reached his breaking point; he was finished giving and giving and giving even more. No more patience, no more waiting hand and foot on his wife diagnosed with memory loss. Their marriage had not been great to begin with and after two years of caregiving, Arnie wanted to walk out the door to never return.

His wife had received her diagnosis several years earlier, but for a period of time she was able to care for herself. Arnie decided against recommended medications for his wife. To him, a diagnosis of Alzheimer's disease was a death sentence. It was his opinion that she may as well die now and die quickly rather than take any medications that might prolong her life and his time as a caregiver.

207

Arnie's plan did not quite work out the way he expected. He lacked knowledge about Alzheimer's disease. He watched his mother care for her mother with Alzheimer's disease and told himself he would never be a willing participant in a similar experience. Arnie refused to do any research. He refused to attend support groups: he decided Clare's demise would be quick. No medications, no special treatments—certainly his wife would be dead soon.

Instead years and years passed after the diagnosis. His wife Clare was now unable to remember conversations, instructions, and other general information. She needed reminders and assistance with dressing and using the bathroom. Arnie felt as if he was chained to the house with Clare because it was not safe to leave her home alone. Their home had become a prison, and this woman whom he had married had become more of a penance than he could have ever imagined.

Arnie couldn't even remember what he had seen in Clare to make him love her, let alone marry her in the first place. The only thought that carried him through each day was that he might wake up the next morning to find Clare dead. His daily existence was miserable, and he had no friends or family who offered to help. He refused to retain paid assistance to come into the home or to place Clare in a community, as he was adamant about not spending their savings on her care.

One day a social worker from Adult Protective Services came to his home. Someone had reported that he might be abusing his wife by neglecting her care. The social worker discovered Clare, whose appearance was disheveled. It appeared that she had not bathed in some time, her clothing was soiled and she paced repeatedly throughout the house, muttering to herself words that could not be understood. Professionals were appointed to act in Clare's best interests. She was removed from the home and placed in a care community where she was able to receive the care that she needed and deserved. Arnie was free to go on with his life and never saw Clare after the day she was removed from their home.

Mary loved Al. They had met in their twenties and now in their seventies, they were still in love. Some days Al didn't know who Mary was, but that was okay. Mary hired caregivers to come to their home several days a week so she might visit friends, attend a bridge group, and grocery shop. Al sat in the living room chair and enjoyed listening to classical music most of the time, so he did not require significant effort for his care. The caregivers who came to the home doted on Al because of his kind and sweet demeanor.

Mary made sure he had the best medical care—a neurologist and geriatric physician and medications to slow the progression of the disease. Mary couldn't imagine living without Al. They spent evenings reminiscing about how they met, raising their children, and the vacations they took together, when Al's long-term memory was still relatively good. Their children visited and provided support.

For Mary, while the diagnosis of Alzheimer's disease was a shock, she did not feel it was a challenge that their marriage could not withstand. Their children felt the same and were able to provide support financially and in the way of spending time with their father. Al would always be the love of Mary's life until the very end.

A diagnosis of dementia and Alzheimer's disease tests all relationships including adult children, married spouses, and friends. Your response to the disease—to the constant repeating, the behaviors, the refusals to bathe or to change clothing or to eat or take medications—depends on the quality of your relationship before the diagnosis and upon your willingness to understand the disease process. All individuals diagnosed with memory loss deserve dignity and kindness. If you are unfamiliar with the disease and the disease process, becoming more educated will allow you to cope and respond in a positive manner.

Chapter 10

The Tip of The Iceberg

- The Titanic
- Scorched Earth and Toxic Relationships
- Older Adults and Self Neglect
- Pray or Prey
- Broken Promises and Consuming Guilt
- Reflect versus React
- Exercise: Identifying the Dangers of Isolation
- Tales of The Caring Generation: The Kindness of Mrs. Fyson

The Titanic

There are times when I compare the act of caregiving to a floating iceberg. Small icebergs bob up and down synchronistically with the waves of the ocean. As we know, the small portion of ice floating above the water is insignificant in size as compared to the remaining 80 percent of the iceberg lurking below the water and waiting to sink the ship. The act of caregiving is similar because responsibilities begin as small projects that grow over time. Caregivers have little awareness of how a time commitment of 5 percent quickly becomes all-consuming with 80-100 percent of one's free time devoted to caregiving. This time commitment, rarely predicted at the beginning of caregiving, places relationships on unsteady footing because of feelings of anger, impatience, or resentment.

Because of great demands on time, some caregivers seek to control situations to reduce stress. Some adult children step in to manage the day-to-day situation regardless of the opinions and desires of the parent. From the outside looking in, this behavior may appear insensitive and overreaching. From the viewpoint of the adult children involved in providing care, taking over and taking control is expeditious because of feelings of forced— rather than willing or voluntary—involvement.

Many family caregivers do not have available time or the desire to become significantly involved in the life of a parent needing care, especially when relationships have grown distant or are challenging because of personality or differences in opinion, character, or lifestyle. As a result, any solution that makes the role of a caregiver easier and less time-consuming is seen by the caregiver as the right solution. While this may be the right solution for the adult child, the solution may negatively affect the parent and result in overall decline. Similar to rearranging the deck chairs on the *Titanic*, easy solutions are sometimes a like a bandage that unravels when the severity of situations advances.

Years ago, I was involved in the care of a man whose wife had recently passed away. Joe had a number of chronic health conditions that required constant monitoring. Without telling his father, Joe's son completed paperwork to move him into an assisted living community over a long holiday weekend. Joe discovered his son's intentions, called his attorney, and rescinded the power of attorney documents, negating his son's ability to make decisions on his behalf. Joe made it clear to his son that he was not leaving home until absolutely necessary, as he was determined to maintain his lifestyle and independence by retaining supportive care at home. He succeeded in fulfilling his desire to remain at home until several days prior to his death.

For Joe, this was the ideal situation. For his son, wishing to reduce worry and time involved in caregiving, the ideal situation was to place Joe in an assisted living community. The compromise position was hiring a care navigator to develop a plan of care, who then provided oversight of medical care and in-home caregivers. This compromise allowed Joe to remain at home. His son was given freedom from the responsibilities of caregiving to be a son who visited and took his father out to enjoy events and social activities.

While taking control of day-to-day situations may offer a sense of relief for family caregivers, compromising by retaining professionals to support the care and well-being of a loved one offers the most positive solution. Preserving family relationships and supporting the desires of a loved one—even if it means compromising and giving up control—ease difficult situations where family involvement may not always mandate the best or most appropriate care.

Involving professionals outside the family may be a difficult concept if the care recipient has staunch beliefs about family duty or preserving money for inheritance. In situations where care is needed and family is not locally available or able to devote a significant amount of time to the provision of care, paying for professional involvement represents a compromise to allow options that are least restrictive. This means that the desires of the care recipient may be honored in the most pleasant setting: for example, the family home, rather than requiring a move to a care community. Compromise also supports the desire of family caregivers who do not wish to become excessively involved or burdened by the care of a loved one. Compromise offers the potential to ward off aspects of care relationships that may become unintentionally toxic over time.

Scorched Earth and Toxic Relationships

For many of us, the idea of an adult child abusing a frail, vulnerable parent may be shocking. Elder abuse is common and significantly under reported. Research from Statistic Brain offers a startling reality.[63]

- In 2010, 9.5 percent of the elderly population (age 60 or older) experienced some type of abuse
- Of reported elder abuse cases, neglect was greatest at 58.5 percent
- Sixty six percent of all abuse is committed by adult children or a spouse
- Research reports that 91 percent of nursing homes lack adequate staff to properly care for patients; insufficient numbers of staff results in inadequate care and potential neglect

Adult children who become caregivers, unwillingly or willingly, are the primary abusers—physically, emotionally, and financially—of care recipient parents. Adult children or any one person in the role of a caregiver possesses a great deal of influence on the care situation because individuals who need care may not be able to identify options for care other than family members.

This is similar to spousal abuse when the ill spouse is totally dependent on the well spouse for care. Spousal abuse, including relationship manipulation that has been ongoing for years, becomes more pronounced when care needs arise. The abuse may be as simple as a controlling spouse who refuses to retain outside care because of the expense or because the spouse holds the belief that only he or she is suitable to provide care. These are potentially dangerous and abusive situations for the care recipient, who may be fearful or unable to express concerns. Many care recipients become prisoners in their own homes.

I have been involved in many situations where relationship issues grow challenging, especially in spousal situations of care. The well spouse feels caught between the idea of duty and care versus enjoying what they might see as the rest of their life with a limited time frame. These situations are particularly difficult in second marriages where the health of one spouse significantly changes within a year or two of the marriage. Second marriages where care needs arise early often end in divorce.

If family members have attempted and are unable to intervene in a situation where abuse is suspected or where a parent is clearly not safe at home (and is refusing help) there are other options for support. County Adult Protective Services departments exist to investigate potential situations of abuse. Some families fear involving government or county departments because they feel they may lose total control of the situation. My experience is that Adult Protective Services is very supportive and able to offer resources and options when a loved one may be at risk of abuse from a spouse, family members, or helpful friends.

Because many abuse cases go unreported, many states are implementing elder abuse statutes requiring individuals to report to police any suspicious activities toward older adults. It is best that families or friends with knowledge of the situation report the case along with attempts to solve the issue. Many situations arise where family members may be suspected of abuse because they were aware of a situation, they did nothing, and substantial harm resulted.

If you are a family member, ignoring the situation is not the solution. Know that when you stop visiting, calling, or checking in on a loved one, someone else might take your place. This outwardly appearing well-intended person may be more interested in money or property than having a sincere interest in helping your loved one.

Over the years, I recall client care situations where I suspected something was amiss, but I lacked hard proof. In one particular situation, I coordinated in-home care for a married couple whom I met because of calls from concerned neighbors. John and Mary were childless; no extended family was available or willing to help. When I first met Mary, she was in a nursing home recovering from a hip fracture. She was a small woman, with a strong desire to return home. Mary and John were in their late eighties and in my opinion were barely getting along in their home, which was kept curiously dark with the shades always pulled shut. The nursing home physician and care staff expressed great concern about Mary returning home without some type of daily assistance.

The first time I met Mary's husband, John, he was resistant to the idea of having caregivers whom he viewed as strangers in the home. Because of the recommendations of the nursing home staff, he did acknowledge that if his wife were to return home, he would have no choice but to retain assistance for her care. The ability to pay for care in this situation was not an issue.

The neighbors supported the idea of caregivers by telling John that while they wanted to continue helping, the situation had advanced beyond a grocery trip here and there. They explained and supported the need for more assistance with housekeeping and personal care for Mary. John's own health was poor; he was nearly blind. Arthritis made it difficult for him to stand and walk. Reluctantly, he agreed to the assistance of in-home caregivers.

Mary returned home and care began. She pulled the caregivers aside in private and said "Don't cross him or he'll bonk you on the head." There were also times when she asked the caregivers not to leave because she was afraid of being alone with John. When they asked Mary a question, John would respond for her. While helping Mary bathe and dress, the caregivers noticed bruises on her back and her arms. Mary said she could not remember how the bruises occurred. It became clear to me and to the caregivers that this was a toxic relationship.

I contacted Adult Protective Services because of concerns for Mary's physical safety and well-being. The caregivers witnessed signs of anger, agitation, and impatience by John toward Mary. He was verbally abusive at times, yelling at Mary for moving too slowly or being unable to perform household tasks.

Before an investigation was initiated, Mary had another fall. She broke a hip and an arm and was hospitalized; she passed away several weeks later. The details of the fall were never confirmed; however, all involved suspected that John had a hand in the accident. Mary was becoming more vocal with the caregivers about John's abuse and he was not the type to want outside interference in their relationship.

According to research statistics on the subject of domestic violence, "85 percent of domestic violence victims are women and three to four million women in the United States are beaten each year by husbands, x-husbands or male lovers."[64] Further research indicated that abuse by non-intimate family members significantly increased from 35.5 to 65.2 percent as older women victims reach sixty years or older. The suspects of the latter abuse included sons (46.2 percent), daughters (26.9 percent), and grandsons (8.6 percent). The abuse does not necessarily relate to caregiver stress.[65]

I have been appointed guardian for spouses who have been abused by a husband or wife on the basis of financial abuse or neglect—failure to provide care. I have also been appointed when a spouse feels he or she may be unable to provide care and do not wish that their children have legal responsibility. Family relationships are complex. There are times when a spouse or adult child is not the best person to provide care.

Older Adults and Self-Neglect

In some situations older adults age, live alone, and neglect their needs. These include nutrition, medications, personal care, and maintaining an appropriate or safe living environment. Self-abuse and neglect represent the most common form of elder abuse. In many of these situations, the older adult is adamant that he or she is equal to the task of preserving independence and daily life. Absent is an understanding of why others—observing the situation from the outside—might view the situation differently.

The suspicion of elder self-abuse and neglect reported by neighbors or other concerned individuals in the community represents the majority of referrals to county Adult Protective Service departments. These good Samaritans, who might feel guilty about reporting concerns, often save older adults from further abuse and self-neglect.

While some older adults are purposely isolated from contact with others by their caregivers, some older adults rarely invite family or friends into their homes. One day, a phone call comes from the hospital emergency room reporting that a friend had a heart attack. A request is made by the hospital staff to visit the apartment to pick up clothing. When the apartment door is opened, the discovery of items—clothing, trash, furniture—is made, stacked from floor to ceiling in tall piles. Small, narrow paths lead from the front door to the kitchen, from the kitchen to the bedroom, and from the bedroom to the bathroom.

This description represents a situation of hoarding of items and in some situations hoarding of animals. Hoarding is associated with obsessive-compulsive behavior and personality disorders but is rarely diagnosed. Most hoarders are women. Hoarding is one of the most difficult situations to resolve, unless the individual's home truly presents a risk that the health department or other regulatory agency finds dangerous. While therapy may be supportive, many individuals who are hoarders refuse to acknowledge that a problem exists and will continue to hoard even after a home is cleaned of contents.

Other contributors of self-abuse and neglect include health conditions and physical disability. Without available family or friend caregivers, older adults experience challenges in caring for themselves. Isolation, cognitive impairment, depression, mental disorders, and poverty are contributing factors. As is common when a need for care is unidentified or denied over time, an event like the loss of a spouse, a heart attack, stroke, or broken hip elevates the requirement for care to a more critical and pressing level.

Some older adults lack appropriate coping mechanisms to respond to personal losses; others are unable to organize and implement systems to receive care. Some lack the motivation or desire to respond appropriately when there is no one in their life who expresses interest. Others, having poor judgment, allow helpful people into their lives who take advantage of them emotionally and financially.

Situations of self-neglect also occur when older adults experience mild cognitive impairment that advances into episodes of paranoia, hoarding behaviors, poor hygiene, refusing to comply with medical recommendations, and allowing helpful people into their lives whose intentions are not honorable but selfish. Situations of memory loss, mental health, and self-neglect occur more often with isolated individuals.

These situations require the intervention of friends and family. When family or friends live at a distance or do not visit frequently, these issues are easily hidden by phone conversations that may at times seem a bit odd but at other times perfectly normal. Rather than waiting to visit to confirm suspicions, it is best to take action to investigate the situation by contacting a local professional.

Caregiving—when situations of denial, self-abuse, or neglect exist—benefits from the goodness, integrity, and personal interest of observers who view the situation and intervene either personally or by contacting professionals. There are situations where the personal and emotional drain of attempting to resolve these situations becomes too overwhelming for caregivers. Many caregivers feel their skills are inadequate when repeated attempts toward resolution have failed.

These may be situations where care recipients are emotionally abusive and threatening to any person attempting to change their routine. This often represents an impossible situation for family caregivers who respond poorly to threats, anger, and emotional abuse when they are attempting to be helpful. Because these situations are so complex, I recommend contacting a care navigator who has worked in similar situations and is able to offer support and a path to resolution.

Pray or Prey

Human beings are social beings. While some people enjoy occasional solitude, many of us feel better in the presence of others who share similar feelings, interests, or activities. The older we become, the more effort required to establish and maintain friendships.

Those who are married spend time with spouses, children, and extended family. Having family provides a built-in social network, diminishing the perceived need or benefit of establishing and maintaining outside friendships. Having a family consumes and requires time and dedication, especially if children are involved. Those who are single likely have peers and friends who are single. Regardless of whether we are married, partnered, or single, we arrive into this world alone and we depart alone, unless we take steps to change this route.

Our degree of sociability and ability to maintain and develop new relationships has a significant impact on daily lifestyle. Acquaintances and friends support emotional connections and enjoyment of life, which brings us feelings of contentment and happiness. At the point care is needed, our prior ability to be self-sufficient and to maintain relationships significantly contributes to our future lifestyle and quality of life.

When health fails or other challenges in life arise, many individuals wait, hoping for some event or superhero to fall from the heavens to change the situation for the better. This is unrealistic thinking. Some people look at others' lives and think that they "have it all" yet know nothing of their daily struggles or earlier life experiences.

Prayer is comforting; however prayer without taking specific steps or actions to change a situation rarely results in the outcome we desire. Prayer minus action results in our becoming prey to all types of situations by which we feel trapped. Daily and ongoing effort to make a life worthwhile is important to quality of life as we age. By the time we need care, it is difficult to initiate social relationships and build friendships because of health, mental, or physical challenges, and those we come in contact with may not have our best interests at heart.

Appreciation of all aspects of life is valuable. The act of appreciation supports positive relationships. An example of this is a situation where an older adult has become isolated due to certain circumstances: for example, the loss of a spouse where care is provided by a single individual due to the absence of family or friends. While it is appropriate to be thankful for the care provided, appreciation may quickly turn into overreliance and dependence, resulting in vulnerability on the part of the care recipient.

When a single family member or individual is the sole source of caregiving support, the caregiver may, over time, feel trapped and express frustration about care demands. If a caregiver even hints at leaving a care situation, the result is a fearful care recipient. These discussions, rather than being managed successfully by the caregiver, may tend to be unintentionally abusive. Abandoning a care situation without having other options to present to the care recipient is never a good idea.

In situations where older adults live alone and experience infrequent outside contact, the arrival of a helpful person, with good or bad intentions, is a welcome sight. This helpful person, unless thoroughly checked out and transparent in intention, should be of great concern to friends or family at a distance. There are other situations where contact is made and professionals become involved to provide support. Not all similar situations have a positive ending.

Several years ago, I met a woman who was physically able, yet she had not ventured outside of her apartment building in three years. Fear and refusal to leave her apartment were the results of a traumatic incident. She was carrying groceries home from the store and was attacked by a man who unsuccessfully attempted to steal her purse. After this incident this woman who later became my client refused to leave her apartment building.

A cousin living in another state organized weekly grocery delivery. Besides the staff of the apartment building, her only human contact with other people was infrequent hellos with other residents of the building leaving for work or returning home every day. Residents of the building would have never imagined that this woman previously had a successful career and many friends.

As she grew older, visits from friends became more infrequent; she became more isolated, alone, and fearful. Through a contact at her apartment building, I was able to contact her cousin, and through a series of events, I became the woman's power of attorney. Our journey was one of my client's initially resisting help to eventually accepting that living in an assisted living community was the best choice.

As one might imagine in situations of isolation—whether the isolation is self-imposed or because of a physical disability or chronic disease—various factors contribute to a need for support or assistance. There are times when self-care and maintaining a home become difficult and challenging. Behavioral patterns ingrained during a lifetime grow more significant with age, for example, purposely avoiding bad news about health conditions until health advances and a decision is forced about receiving medical care.

What happens in situations where individuals lack the social support of friends or family? What happens when one lives alone and is not aware of choices for support? If no plans were previously made, and the individual is unable to take steps to manage the situation, a situation of "prey" often occurs. The result of isolation places individuals at risk to phone solicitors, sweepstakes offers, psychics, and others who appear to be friendly but have bad intentions.

After becoming involved again in the lives of parents, many adult children discover situations of financial abuse and exploitation. Discovered are situations where helpful neighbors provided assistance and feel owed in some manner, taking personal property or money in return for their time and assistance. Many voluntary caregivers who may have been housekeepers, friends from church, or neighbors eventually feel entitled and the relationship becomes potentially abusive.

On the other hand, statistics indicate that family members and adult children more commonly exploit parents. Many parents in these situations become reliant on the abuser whether a stranger or family, and fear being abandoned. Poor decisions are made. Helpers take advantage of money or property in return for the provision of ongoing support and care.

Caregivers threaten care recipients into providing access to bank accounts and signing property deeds over to the caregiver in return for care provided. The care situation may continue with the caregiver making sure that the individual remains isolated so that information regarding provision of money or financial transactions remains secret. When friends call, the caregiver listens on the telephone to make sure that the care recipient does not express concern or distress over the situation. When friends visit, the caregiver looms nearby to ensure that the care recipient is unable to alert the visitor to the threats made by the caregiver. Caregivers in these situations threaten to leave if the care recipient makes derogatory comments to an outside party. These situations are similar to spousal abuse where the abused party feels like a prisoner in the relationship, lacks financial resources, and feels unable to leave.

Care situations that turn abusive may begin as well intended or selfless acts that over a period of time turn the caregiver and care recipient's lives upside down. Spouses, out of a sense of duty, scale back activities and life involvement to accommodate the care needs of a husband or wife. Caregivers over time become as isolated, as alone, and as frustrated as the care recipient. Adult children live and care for parents with parents being the sole financial support. Aspects of these situations have the potential of becoming abusive.

An innocent desire to help backfires as caregivers—who made the choice to accept the role of caregiver—find that their patience and tolerance have disappeared. Positive feelings are replaced by feelings of resentment and malicious intent. Some caregivers realize they are failing miserably in managing their own life and the life of a parent. Desire exists to extract some form of payment or revenge for the way their life has been ruined by a parent's need for care.

The caregiver develops a sense of entitlement: "Here I am, the martyr, the caregiver, doing all this work. I deserve money, personal belongings, an inheritance, and my parents' home in return for giving up my life to provide care." Resentment leads the caregiver to justifying actions that in any other circumstance would be considered reprehensible. I have witnessed care situations involving theft or emotional and physical abuse by family members who see nothing wrong with their actions. Because older adults in these situations are often isolated, there are no peers to question the behaviors or intentions of family members.

These situations occur because of long-standing care needs and emerging situations that require immediate attention. Caregivers rush in to rescue in a variety of ways, from providing financial support to completing tasks, and then feel powerless to leave when the caregiving situation becomes so demanding on their personal lives that they reach a boiling point.

Parents who believe that their children must provide support for them may become demanding when caregivers begin to pull back because they are exhausted. Changing the rules in a care situation is difficult when there was no previous discussion about the type of support that would be offered, for what period of time, a plan for when care needs increase, and what changes might become necessary.

Broken Promises and Consuming Guilt

Promises made are not always promises kept. My sister promised my mother that when Mom needed care my sister would return home. When my mother became ill, it was impractical for my sister to give up her job and move across country to provide care. This is an example of one well-intended promise that was impractical to honor.

Other times promises are made to keep a parent at home. This promise cannot always be kept when the care of the parent surpasses the caregiver's ability to provide care. In situations of care, a promise made is most commonly a promise broken. Better to avoid promises and to plan for the practicalities and realities of care needs because it is impossible to anticipate future needs and the ability of family to provide care as life situations are constantly changing.

Guilt—especially when adult children cannot keep a promise they made to their parents—is an aspect of all caregiving situations. Family members, whether they live nearby or far away, often experience guilt for any number of reasons. Guilt clouds good judgment and becomes a heavy burden when difficult decisions are required.

Caregivers feel guilty for being angry about making a sacrifice, a choice, to take care of a parent. The placement of guilt is rampant in care situations. Adult children place guilt on a parent, who serves as a caregiver for a spouse, and who might express exhaustion or a desire to be rid of caregiving responsibilities. Individuals with no experience with caregiving place guilt on friends who provide care. Feelings of guilt result from an inability to provide support, from not being present when an accident occurs, or from being on the receiving end of a parent's request for a child to take time off work to visit and provide care. Even if prior discussions were held about a caregiver's ability and availability to provide care, parents forget these discussions when emergencies arise and demand immediate support.

The important aspect for caregivers to recognize is that parents, like everyone else, have the right to make poor decisions and choices about their care and lifestyle. In caregiving relationships, one person gives and another receives. Caregivers often forget that while they made the choice to caregive, they can also make the choice not to caregive.

The time may arrive to discuss options for paid care and assistance. When this occurs, the parent may feel rejected and balk at the idea of anyone else providing care. They may insist that they can take care of themselves and don't need help, when it's obvious that they can no longer manage their lives without some type of care or support.

The mere mention of needing help bruises egos and dignity, resulting in the parent responding in a resistant and negative manner to the caregiver, who then feels the parent is ungrateful and insensitive to the time and effort he or she demanded of the caregiver. These early struggles are often the precursor to a parent needing a higher level of care or more time-consuming care, resulting in even greater feelings of guilt on the part of the caregiver.

Caregivers suffer high levels of stress, depression, and physical illness resulting from the act of caregiving. Parents resistant to the provision of care negatively affect the health of the caregiver through their attitudes, verbal comments, and potentially abusive behaviors. Avoiding manipulation by a care recipient is critical to the health, life, well-being, and emotional survival of the caregiver.

On the other hand, caregivers experience emotional struggles that include a need to be needed or to foster a codependent relationship. Remembering not to allow caregiving to become your personal identity may help you retain perspective when situations become difficult. This may also help you transition more easily out of the role when your work ends. This is no different from allowing your profession to become your identity and is why when older adults retire, some feel no purpose in life because their work was their life.

Setting boundaries is necessary in all caregiving situations, especially in situations that quickly spiral out of control. For example, you stop by your father's home every evening to make dinner, and one day you decide that this is counterproductive, leaving you exhausted and ineffective at work the next day. Options include delivery of meals by Meals on Wheels or hiring a caregiver to prepare meals. Your father resists both suggestions. You know that he will not eat or take medications without some type of support, and you plead with him to accept outside assistance. Your father refuses. You feel guilty about your decision to end evening visits because you suspect that without this type of support his health will decline; however, you hold steadfast to making this choice.

While it may seem like tough love, I recommend holding your ground. Allow your father—or mother—to make a choice and experience the consequences. Nothing adverse may happen. Your parent may continue to live successfully. Or the opposite may occur; your parent may end up hospitalized and may be told by doctors he or she should no longer live alone. Your parent made a choice that resulted in a consequence, and decisions regarding other care choices must now be made because of his or her prior refusal to consider other options.

The reality is that the provision of care by you allowed your parent to live at home longer than would have been possible without your involvement. You did nothing wrong in realizing that preparing dinner every evening was detrimental to your life. In the end, your parent will likely be in a better care situation, although you may be blamed for the results. Any anger from the situation belongs to your parent, not you. Caregiving is not your identity; caregiving was a role you played and included the support you provided.

If, on the other hand, your parent is suffering from memory loss or a similar cognitive impairment, making choices for them is incumbent upon the caregiver, especially if the caregiver is the legal power of attorney. The choice to accept Meals on Wheels or a paid caregiver is not optional.

This type of support is in the best interest of the situation because the parent is unable to choose between options or understand consequences. Resisting the need for care will result in other consequences that may include moving a parent to a care community against his or her wishes. The decisions one makes as a responsible party are not easy when the decisions conflict with the wishes of a parent. It takes an emotionally strong caregiver to take the right action and to make the best choices.

Many times issues and concerns related to caregiving stem from a place of ignorance. Someone's parent had this or that—did this or that—and this was the result. On the outside, your situation may appear similar. From the inside, the circumstances could not be more different.

A common thread in caregiving is family disagreement about decisions that must be made. Many assumptions are based on incorrect information. Facts are not considered, and as a result, family members are at odds because no one truly knows all the circumstances related to the care situation. Family members may not know what happens on a daily basis in the life and care of a parent. Making caregiving decisions without information is unwise. Sometimes facts are foggy or information is not available because parents refuse to provide the information—or they intentionally hide information.

I prefer to look at the idea of accepting help to be the action of a wise person who knows and understands the value of prevention. A closed mind results in limited choices. An open mind results in many choices. Having a discussion today with your loved one about choices may make a difference in the long-term outcome of the care situation. Examining choices about your own care, if you are the care recipient, will make a difference.

Reflect Versus React

In caregiving, the ability to reflect versus reacting immediately to persons and situations is crucial to the overall best interest of the care situation. For caregivers able to balance personal and caregiving demands, situations rarely veer out of control. This is not to say that occasional periods of feeling emotionally overwhelmed will not occur. However if you are able to reflect rather than to immediately react, you will be better able to manage care situations including those that require pragmatic planning.

Caregivers who react experience a very different result. When caregivers react, brains run haywire, assuming the worst and believing that the care recipient has a malicious intent. Caregivers make intractable choices and otherwise experience an emotional meltdown that turns the situation into a mountain rather than a molehill. Reactors raise the tenor of situations to constant high drama, the reaction being always more about the caregiver rather than the person in question. Reactors fail to consider the facts and reality of the situation.

As care situations advance, the number of professional providers increases. Physicians, healthcare providers, care staff at communities, and others are often involved in the care of a loved one. For caregivers unable to manage their emotions in a positive manner, the creation of adversarial relationships occurs that places the care a loved one receives at risk. Family members may be perceived to be abusive if angry or emotional outbursts have occurred during interactions with professional providers.

Caregiving reactors are hooked on emotional drama rather than arriving at solutions. Generally unable to view situations from an opposite perspective, they are attention seekers who want control over situations and people. Caregiving reactors are crushed by disagreement or rejection. They may be polite in person for as long as their personalities allow and then become backstabbing and vicious in an attempt to destroy relationships between family members and caregivers.

Caregivers playing the martyr role are commonly reactors. We hear, "Oh poor me,—no one will help me," "I deserve more respect," or "This mean person did this or that to me." We hear more about what others are doing to the reactor but never any reports about the reactor's responsibility in creating the negative situation. Reactors rarely believe they have done anything wrong to make day-to-day caregiving situations more difficult. In these situations, the parent may truly be on the receiving end of emotional abuse because the reactor's behaviors are unpredictable and unstable.

Feeling emotionally torn is one of the main reasons caregivers feel overwhelmed and trapped by caregiving situations. We all possess the ability to control our behaviors and reactions to situations. Each thought that enters our mind and each action we take will create an outcome or a result. Setting boundaries with parents that are not malicious or manipulative but based on honest feelings allows the caregiver and care receiver to achieve emotional equity.

Caregivers will remember the relationship with a parent when he or she is gone. Not remembered, will be the times you scrubbed the urine from a bathroom floor or cleaned toilets. Family caregiving should not solely be about tasks it should be about relationships and making memories that will remain when the care recipient is gone.

As our life experience grows, we eventually realize that communication in relationships is at best imperfect. Intentions are easily misinterpreted, perceptions vary, and miscommunication becomes the norm rather than the exception. Through trial and error, we learn that flexibility, understanding, communication, and patience are the keys to supporting relationships.

We also learn that there are some relationships from which it is simply better to walk away; these include impossible caregiving relationships where expectations are unrealistic or the person involved continues to practice self-harm or neglect. These include relationships with family members who are consistently negative or toxic.

If we choose to bear the responsibility of the care of loved ones or parents, we must do our best to participate with love, compassion, and understanding. How can we do our best to consider what our loved ones want and desire when their wishes compete with our own desires? It is possible to achieve relationship equity through reflection and honest conversations about care situations.

Exercise: Identifying the Dangers of Isolation

Are you at risk of the effects of social isolation? Both caregivers and care recipients suffer the effects of isolation and depression. Isolation has a negative impact on health, well-being, and longevity.

Below are ten questions to identify the potentially negative present and future risks of limited social contact:

1. On how many days are you generally alone, meaning by yourself at home with absolutely no human contact except for the television, the radio, or the computer and a day when you do not leave the house?
2. On how many days are you generally alone except for being with your care recipient?
3. On days when you are generally alone in the situations above (1, 2), how do you feel mentally?
4. On days when you are generally alone in the situations above (1, 2), how do you feel physically?
5. How many contacts with others do you have on a daily basis, whether the contact is in person, on the telephone or through the Internet?
6. How motivated are you to bathe, dress, and participate in some type of physical activity on a daily basis?
7. How often do you take a break from your caregiving situation?
8. In what hobbies do you participate on a regular basis?
9. How often do you see family or friends?
10. How often do you participate in social groups or group activities?

If you struggled to respond positively to three or more of the above questions, I highly recommend speaking to your physician or therapist about methods to reduce feelings of isolation and possible depression. If you or a loved one is isolated, what steps might you take to preserve your well-being? What plans might you make to increase participation in social activities?

If you are interested in accessing more tips and information about ideas presented in this chapter and about related subjects, visit <u>http://www.thecaregivingtrapbook.com/store</u> and select The Tip of the Iceberg.

Tales of the Caring Generation

The Kindness of Mrs. Fyson

My grade school teacher, Mrs. Fyson, was old. I'm not sure how old she really was, but as grade school children, we all imagined her to be ancient—at least in her fifties. She was tall and towered over us as seven- or eight-year olds. While we called her Mrs. Fyson, we never saw or knew if there was a Mr. Fyson. She was kind, bringing candies and baked goods to class as a reward when we spelled a word correctly or completed a mathematical equation on the board in front of class.

My grade school was in a small neighborhood. Most of us walked to school. It was a Catholic school and Mrs. Fyson was the only lay teacher; the rest were nuns wearing black habits and cardboard hats covering their hair and most of their faces. In bad weather Mrs. Fyson wore boots that she called rubbers. Now you can imagine the immaturity of children, especially the boys, when Mrs. Fyson instructed us to take our rubbers off before entering the classroom or to put them on before leaving for the day. I think back and often wonder how she put up with us; we were only in the second or third grade and already causing trouble due to a high level of immaturity. I believe she had the patience of a saint.

Another curious thing about Mrs. Fyson, at least to us, was that she left a pair of shoes in the class room closet, wrapped in a brown paper bag. These shoes became a great curiosity; they were the old heavy granny shoes with lace-ups, a tongue in front and a big clunky heel you probably know the type of shoe I am describing. When she removed the shoes or returned the shoes to the bag, the sound of crinkling paper filled the room.

Wearing these shoes resulted in her hobbling and stepping from side to side, favoring arthritic feet, knees, or hips. If you remember Lurch from The Addams Family TV show, you might get the picture of how she walked. One day the boys hid her shoes. When she arrived, she put her rubbers on the carpet outside the room, proceeded to open the closet door, and found no brown paper bag containing shoes. She turned to the class, walked over and looked under her desk where she sometimes left her shoes, looked up and began to cry, saying that she didn't know how much longer she could put up with a class of such careless, thoughtless children.

Imagine a class of seven- or eight-year olds who then began to cry because of being chastised so strongly. Seconds later the door opened, and the principal, Sister Emery—whose presence alone instilled the fear of God in small children—walked into the classroom and discovered the teacher and a room filled with crying children.

The room immediately became silent—one could hear the drop of a pin. It seemed an eternity that everyone held their breath, waiting for someone to speak. Mrs. Fyson, true to form, said to the principal, "I was sharing a sad story and we all decided to have a good cry." The principal shook her head, turned, and left the room, rosary beads clicking at her side. Whew!

Breathing began again and relief was experienced by the children who feared their act of cruelty might have been revealed to the principal. It was this day that a small room of children grew to respect the ancient Mrs.

Fyson. Her students spoke up for her when other children, who might see her as an old woman or comment negatively on her unusual habit of wearing rubbers, made fun of her. Those in her class survived grade school and graduated. Mrs. Fyson proudly attended our eighth grade graduation. Most of us went on to high school and to college.

My parents lived across the street from Mrs. Fyson and I saw her on occasion outside working in her yard. She had a husband, children and grandchildren, a life outside of school to balance the craziness of teaching classes of immature and at times not so nice children.

How many of you have teachers that you remember? How many of you had role models growing up? In many life situations, having someone to provide support or someone to look up to as an expert is beneficial. There is no school for caregiving. Seek support through others in similar situations and from experts who are able to provide recommendations and guidance.

Chapter 11

The Pleasantly Forgetful

- "I Got Lost"
- How Will I Know?
- Memory Loss and Diagnosis
- Memory Loss and Emotional Stress
- The Forgotten
- Exercise: Choosing a Care Navigator
- Tales of the Caring Generation: Bernice and the Black Cat

"I Got Lost"

"You will know what a sore knee or ankle is or something like that but what goes on in your head doesn't necessarily give you any indication yourself, does it?"[66] George, an individual diagnosed with Alzheimer's disease, attempts to explain that he is aware that he may not be able to assess his own abilities. It is common that many individuals diagnosed with dementia or Alzheimer's disease lack insight into the progression of their disease, the impact on daily life, and the impact on their caregivers.

Driving a car, waiting in a line at the grocery store, walking down the street, or sitting in the seat next to you at the movie theatre, the slightly forgetful are everywhere but are rarely noticed. How might they be recognized? Many go on day after day and are not acknowledged until the pleasantly forgetful become part of our lives.

You return to your parent's home for the holidays. Something is different, but you are unsure what has changed. Similar to seeing an old friend and wondering if their hairstyle is different or if they have lost weight, you are hesitant to pose the question out of embarrassment. Something is definitely amiss. Your parent seems distracted or unable to concentrate. There are times when information has to be repeated, sometimes multiple times. You brush this aside as the response of a parent who is just getting old, absent-minded, and forgetful. You return home to the hustle and bustle of career, family and day-to-day life.

The holidays pass. During telephone conversations you promise to visit again soon. You forget about the nagging thoughts that bothered you when you visited that are now long forgotten.

The ringing of the phone at 2 a.m. wakes you. The police report that your father is at a truck stop in a city a thousand miles from home with no recollection of how he arrived or where he lives. A cashier called the police because Dad did not have money or a credit card to pay for gas. A business card with your home telephone written on the back was in your father's wallet. The police offer to put Dad up in a local motel for the night rather than arresting him—but only if you promise to be on a plane the next morning to pick up Dad and drive him home. You think about the phone conversation with Dad yesterday when he was getting ready to leave for the grocery store; everything seemed fine. How on earth did he end up a thousand miles from home?

Mom—surprised to see you on the family doorstep—was expecting the police to arrive instead of you. She called them moments before to report that her car was stolen from the garage. The next-door neighbors, noticing an out-of-state car parked in the driveway, rush over, gushing with relief that you have finally arrived to help your mother. Neighbors are unsure how she arrived home after the car accident. You learn that her car is several blocks away, buried in mud in a ditch.

Neighbors speak in hushed voices while Mom is in the bathroom. She has become more confused during the past several months. Not wanting to anger your mother by contacting you, they tried to do their best to check on her daily to make sure nothing serious happened. Whew! What a relief to know that you will now take over the responsibility of watching over and caring for your parent.

You work in a bank, at a beauty shop, at the grocery store, or at the mall. Regular clientele of an advanced age come and go each day. It's not as if you keep track, but you admit relief when you see them return every few days, sometimes even multiple times in a single day not remembering they visited there an hour ago.

You say a prayer when they leave, concerned for their safety. They need help counting change. Arthritic hands struggle to write a check, and sometimes you are asked to write in the amount which is concerning as someone else might not be as honest. You can be trusted to help with check writing since you work at their bank, but not everyone can be trusted. Sometimes they forget why they came. Darn it! They left their grocery list at home and came to withdraw cash so they might purchase a gallon of milk.

You watch them wander through the parking lot, searching for their car. Their clothing is dirty and their hair is unwashed. Some stumble even with the use of a walker or cane. You do your best to be welcoming, polite, and helpful. You try to ask questions about family; they reply that they have no family. You are not sure whether they remember if family exists or not. What else can you do? These dear, sweet older people that you see daily represent a failing boxcar in a train wreck waiting to happen. Welcome to the stranger-than-fiction surreal world of the pleasantly forgetful that you as a daily observer—not a family member—do your best to support.

Alzheimer's disease, Pick's, Lewy body disease, and mild cognitive impairment all represent words to describe a loss of memory that affects millions of persons around the world. Years ago we called people who were forgetful or who exhibited strange behaviors senile. How little did we realize that senility would become a progressive illness falling under a broad term representing memory loss called *dementia*.

The more research that is completed about our brains, the more we realize that cognitive impairment is the result of many factors: injuries to the head, heart disease resulting in circulatory problems, diabetes, and stroke or winning the lottery of life to live beyond the age of eighty-five. "Mortality from Alzheimer's disease has steadily increased during the last 30 years. Alzheimer's disease is the sixth leading cause of death in the United States and the fifth leading cause for people aged 65 years and older."[67] If we are fortunate enough to reach the age of eighty-six or older, 50 percent of us will experience some type of memory loss. Is aging really something to look forward to? Perhaps only something to look forward to if we are in the other 50 percent who experience no memory loss and who are reasonably physically healthy.

What about the lives of those who are younger and pleasantly forgetful? The athletic world has finally acknowledged the effects of head injuries and concussions. This was brought to light again in May 2012 when the death of football player Junior Seau, age forty-three was ruled a suicide. He suffered from depression as a result of the concussions he sustained as a pro football player.[68] Another sports legend Muhammad Ali is today cared for by his wife Lonnie who has been his caregiver since his diagnosis in 1974. "In Muhammad Ali's case his Parkinson's Syndrome was likely caused as the result of repeated blows to the head which irreversibly damaged his brain stem.[69] Ali, philanthropist Jimmy Walker and Dr. Abraham Lieberman established the Muhammad Ali Parkinson's Center in Phoenix, Arizona in 1997.[70]

Alzheimer's is now being diagnosed at younger ages. There are incidences of memory loss, called early onset dementia, in individuals under the age of sixty-five that are not likely trauma related. Early onset dementia usually progresses to a diagnosis of Alzheimer's disease.

There are other types of memory loss related to changes in the frontal and temporal lobes of the brain. Terms for this type of memory loss are fronto-temporal lobar degeneration or FTLD. "FTLD is a common cause of dementia in a younger population and is frequently diagnosed in the 45-64 age group. Many individuals with this diagnosis experience mental rigidity and inflexibility and perseverative behavior."[71]

Changes in personality and behavior occur in individuals with memory loss and in those experiencing brain injuries. These changes include inappropriate social behaviors, repetitive behavior, circling conversations often called perseveration, paranoia, a lack of attention to personal hygiene, the inability to organize and plan, and mentally losing or forgetting words. In most cases, the individual has little or no insight into changes in their day-to-day ability. This lack of insight results in memory loss that remains highly undiagnosed until the condition is well advanced and problematic if the person lives alone and has limited contact with others.

For caregivers of persons diagnosed with brain injuries, the role of caregiving is even more challenging. Brain-injured individuals experience forgetfulness, exhibit anger, speak in circles, and are sometimes so demanding in their behaviors and words that family caregivers throw up their hands in frustration because positive interactions are few and far between. The only reasoning that the brain-injured person understands is their own. They want what they want regardless of the situation or the involvement of others and pursue their desires to the exasperation of others.

What if you are reading this and suspect you might be experiencing short-term memory loss? What if you met someone yesterday that you are unable to remember today when they show up at your house for tea? The most significant challenge with individuals who have memory loss is that they think caregivers or friends purposely make up stories about their inability to recall information. Paranoia and distrust of family and friends take root.

The pleasantly forgetful proceed to ask the same question again. Eventually frustration rises, and the caregiver directs the forgetful to stop repeating information or to stop asking the same question. These circular conversations are frustrating for family members who would benefit from learning about the concept of redirection that will be discussed later in the chapter. Some adult children, unaware of the circling conversations of memory loss, purposely believe that a parent is trying to be difficult.

Unless an interrupt occurs in these conversations they will continue to repeat. For example, I participated in circular questioning with a client and purposely allowed the questioning to continue to see if there was any point where the question would change. This did not occur. In the span of ten minutes, the client asked the same question eight times, and I answered the same question eight times in exactly the same manner. This is a situation where a simple redirection of the question to another subject allows the conversation to continue without becoming frustrating to the family caregiver.

How Will I Know?

When changes in behavior or memory loss begin to occur, many general physicians lack the observation skills to diagnose memory loss. This relates in part, to a factor I call the "fifteen minute medical appointment." Insurance companies allow physicians a limited amount of time to complete a medical appointment. The goal of insurance companies is to move patients in and out of medical offices in the least amount of time possible.

For most people, it takes fifteen minutes to warm up to having a conversation with a physician. Some patients write a list of concerns that is too lengthy for the physician to cover in a brief period of time and are asked to make another appointment. No wonder that rushed appointments fail to diagnose health or memory issues. A short time frame for a medical appointment adds to the complications of diagnosing a person experiencing memory loss who is unable to self-report concerns. In many individuals, memory loss remains undiagnosed until well advanced.

Another complicating factor in receiving proper medical care as we age is that most individuals continue to see the same family practice physician for years and years not realizing that healthcare needs change as we near the age of sixty. Patients often ignore poor treatment by office staff or a physician when visits are infrequent. A medical office is different from a restaurant where you might receive poor service and refuse to tip or return. A medical office is not like a bank where the tellers bend over backwards to serve because they know you can take your money elsewhere.

The hassle factor in changing doctors and the issues in dealing with insurance companies result in patients remaining with their current physician for years longer than beneficial, even if the relationship is not a good fit. Doctors rarely fire patients, even though they see patients they dread almost every day because they are considered difficult patients.

When we are comfortable, we resist the idea of changing to a new physician whom we may not like. Children see pediatricians and older adults benefit from geriatricians, physicians who specialize in the process of aging. Many older adults attend the annual physical; nothing is wrong except for a few ongoing aches and pains of which the doctor is already familiar. Others fail to mention potentially important information to the doctor because of being unsure of what information should be mentioned, or they intend to provide information and totally forget the concern they wished to relay.

How many of you have accompanied a parent to a medical appointment? Older adults show up for medical appointments dressed to impress and on their best behavior. If parents have problems with memory, the issue is not mentioned, and if recognized by the doctor, the individual will go to great extents to hide any problems for fear of a diagnosis. Many of the forgetful grasp every remaining ounce of independence, fearing that their life will change significantly if anyone discovers their secret.

Prescriptions written by physicians to treat serious issues like heart disease, stroke, arthritis, or diabetes remain in wallets or purses. Prescriptions are unfilled due to memory loss and unfilled at other times because older adults refuse to take a large number of prescription drugs. Others simply cannot afford the cost.

Do you ever consider what your doctor might say to you if he or she could? "I think you should find a new doctor. I feel dread the moment I see your name on my appointment list." According to Laura Landro you might be surprised to learn that:"[72]

- Doctors consider 15 to 25 percent of their patient encounters difficult.
- Doctors with relatively high numbers of problematic patients were 12 times as likely to report burnout.
- Doctors weary of dealing with tiresome patients were more likely to report that they had provided suboptimal care or they expected to make future errors in their practice.

Medical teaching institutions are challenged to find time to focus on communicating the value of compassion relative to treatment of older adults who require more patience and time. Who would you rather see—a nice doctor with good social skills or a qualified, skilled doctor who is less likeable? Patients want a combination of the two. Patients want to feel that their doctor takes a personal interest, even though visits may occur once or twice a year.

Unless a medical professional or a family member is very familiar with the indicators of memory loss, the diagnosis is easily missed because the signs are varied and subtle. Family members notice changes in parents. They have no idea if the occurring events are significant, or they assume that if anything serious were to occur the physician would certainly recognize the condition. No concerns are mentioned by family at the medical appointment; life goes on.

A support to diagnosing memory loss is the ability of the physician to receive information from family members who spend time with a forgetful parent. If a person lives alone, information about memory loss will rarely if ever be reported because of a lack of self-insight. Many times it takes a child, family member, or friend to express concern to a physician before testing or a diagnosis is made. The challenge then becomes the physician directly addressing the individual with memory loss at the appointments versus holding a side conversation with the family caregiver. These side conversations by physicians usually anger the person with memory loss by making them feel insignificant and unimportant.

Another challenge in diagnosing memory loss is that many diagnosed with "moderate cognitive impairment" appear to perform well in social situations. They are able to carry on appropriate conversations, perhaps forgetting bits of information here and there. The forgetful commonly laugh at jokes, are moderately well groomed, and seem to be doing as well as others of a similar age. The weaknesses, the little chinks in the armor here and there, are the ones that result in the greatest self-harm. The abilities that are most challenged include the ability to learn and to process new information, to evaluate information and to make appropriate judgments.

For example, the ability to judge a person to be trustworthy by asking questions to confirm reliability or credibility is important, as older adults are often abused by helpful people. The ability to evaluate and to respond to recommendations, like those of a physician, is important to self-care. The risks of financial exploitation, unpaid bills, automobile accidents, missed medications, and similar aspects of life are concerns that are hidden or barely noticeable in social situations but that indicate support is needed for the pleasantly forgetful.

Some individuals with early memory loss lose their entire financial savings to scams or financial abuse. Others lose medical care because they forget to pay insurance premiums. Others become involved in car accidents and not only seriously injure others, but also seriously injure themselves. Others forget to take medications or take medications inappropriately, ending up in hospital emergency rooms on a regular basis. If an individual has children who visit frequently or friends or neighbors who are involved in their lives, the signs may be more easily identified and reported to the physician.

I have worked with older adults professionally since 2000. To me, the telltale signs are easily recognized. These include sticky notes all over the house, repeated questions in the span of minutes, poor hygiene, wearing the same clothing day after day, piles of disorganization, forgotten conversations, missed appointments, and confusion over information provided—all of which are representative of not normal aging.

I find that there is great fear by family members about diagnosing memory loss because of the unknown. Some adult children are aware of the experiences of friends who describe parents diagnosed with the disease to be challenging or disruptive. Hearing this information is frightening for those with little experience of the disease who might be on the verge of having a family member receive a similar diagnosis.

Below is a checklist of signs indicating that it may be time to act responsibly for a parent, family member, or friend who may be struggling to manage day-to-day affairs by reporting any of the following to their physician or to a family caregiver.

- When you visit the home, are there piles of mail, newspapers and notes everywhere? This may indicate unpaid bills and mismanaged finances.
- Is the home dirty? Is there an unidentifiable odor?
- Do you see a repairman or handyman constantly coming and going from their home? This may represent financial exploitation.
- Have other neighbors or friends expressed concern about an ability to manage day to day?
- Has the individual lost weight or appear to have health issues that are worsening?
- Does the individual have hearing loss or poor eyesight and report that others are stealing from them, poisoning their food, or performing other difficult-to-believe activities?
- Do you see the individual driving erratically and you worry for their and others safety?
- Does the individual wear the same clothing day after day?
- If you are helping the individual, are they relying more and more on you for daily tasks?

- Do you notice that the individual repeats information, asks the same questions, or forgets that you spoke to them about a particular subject?
- Is the person becoming paranoid regarding forgotten conversations?
- Does the individual appear generally confused about information or conversations?
- Are they able to speak in complete sentences or do they only respond using single words?
- Are there medication bottles throughout the home but no system of taking medications? Do the bottles show dates that are months or years old?
- Has someone moved into the home to help out, but the situation seems to be getting worse instead of better? This may indicate abuse by a family member or friend.
- Does the individual express fear of a family member or friend?

If you are seeing one or more of these signs, it is best to bring up concerns in a compassionate manner. The challenge of this conversation is that no one likes to be singled out for behaviors or for making decisions that might seem inappropriate. Your concern may be met with anger. A conversation starter may be to offer support with projects and see if the person responds with a comment like, I sure do need help with this as it seems to be getting more difficult for me to complete. This opens the door for further conversation.

Many of my clients are unable to remember events of their daily lives. I have clients who were the cause of automobile accidents with no recollection of the event. Other clients threatened to jump out of my car while I was driving because they did not want to see the "mean doctor" who diagnosed their memory loss. "There's nothing wrong with my memory. I don't have Alzheimer's" are statements often repeated. Other clients swear they take medications daily only to be presented with untouched med minders full of pills. Many of the pleasantly forgetful are in disbelief that they cannot remember information so significant, yet there is little benefit to reminding people with memory loss that they forget or simply don't remember.

Memory Loss and Diagnosis

Why is diagnosing memory loss important? Why does denial exist on the part of the individual with memory loss and family or friends? Is it possible to diagnose memory loss, dementia, or Alzheimer's disease? Would you really want to know? How would life change?

The answer to questions about the value of diagnosing memory loss raises controversy among healthcare providers and family members. Some believe that a diagnosis is not helpful when there is nothing that can be done anyway. "It's just something that, I surmised, that it will never get better, will it? I mean I might get up in the morning and I might not know where I am."[73]

Trying to do something about a diagnosis of memory loss may appear to some a futile effort, as one day life will end. Others believe that a diagnosis should be made so that treatment, even though not curative, and a plan for care can be developed, especially if one is single with little or no family support.

Is there a surefire way to diagnose memory loss? Not yet. There are various forms of tests that support a diagnosis. The most commonly and easily used in many physician offices are the MMSE (mini-mental state exam) and the SLUMS (St. Louis University Mental Status examination) that ask simple questions like the day of the week, the year, recall of five objects or a short story along with simple mathematical and drawing equations. Individuals who are highly educated, have maintained pursuit of occupational activities, and continued education after retirement, even though they have memory loss, may score higher on these tests. These individuals are said to possess cognitive reserve.

Further examinations include MRIs and CT or PET scans that look for white matter deterioration in the brain and attempt to rule out other conditions but may not affirmatively confirm memory loss.

Blood tests are available to identify the ApoE4 gene that indicates risk of Alzheimer's disease but may not indicate a true diagnosis. Examinations by a neurologist and neuropsychologist are beneficial, in my opinion, to establish a baseline by which to monitor the degree of advancement of future memory loss.

The only accurate method of detecting Alzheimer's disease is an autopsy after death. There are many research centers in the United States offering autopsies at no charge to program participants. Information is provided to families within months of the autopsy. Many families find that receiving final diagnostic information provides closure to their caregiving experience and information for future generations of the family to promote awareness of the disease.

Knowing the diagnosis, in the opinion of some, is better than not knowing because at least there is an explanation for the unusual and sometimes odd behavior that is experienced. For example, when Mom or Dad shows up wearing a winter coat in the heat of the summer, children can explain to those concerned that Mom or Dad has Alzheimer's. Other experiences like a parent undressing while standing in the line at the grocery store or squatting to urinate in public while still embarrassing are at least explainable.

For others, the idea of receiving a formal diagnosis brings a stark reality to the present day and to the future that they hope to avoid. If a diagnosis was known, some believe that the life they previously knew would be over. They would be forced to confront the reality and fear of the disease, including difficult decisions. For some, not knowing is preferable. Individuals making this choice have likely denied issues most of their lives, resulting in crises when family members or others pick up the pieces and come to the rescue.

The choice to avoid knowledge of a diagnosis is certain to result in crises that will force decision making and eliminate choices. Not knowing places a burden on family members who one day will be called to provide care and support both personally and financially. If there is no family, not knowing places the individual at the hands of neighbors, property owners, and others who, if knowledgeable, will report to county Adult Protective Services if the situation becomes noticeably dangerous and unmanageable.

To promote individual understanding, a diagnosis is helpful if the diagnosis is made early enough to allow the care recipient to comprehend the diagnosis and attempt to understand consequences of the disease. Many individuals experiencing memory loss deny the experience of memory loss and become angry when approached by family members or friends.

When one can no longer manage day-to-day needs, the insight to recognize this fact has disappeared. The forgetful will deny difficulty and will become angry with family or close friends who mention the benefit of care and support. Liken this to an individual who is hard of hearing and family continually repeats information in a loud voice. Until a hearing exam occurs, the idea of having hearing loss is usually met with disbelief. I have witnessed spouses and family members agree not to tell a family member they were diagnosed with Alzheimer's disease for fear the news would be upsetting.

On the other hand, knowing may bring relief to the diagnosed, who may have been concerned about behaviors or symptoms experienced that are now explainable by virtue of the diagnosis. Knowing also allows the ability to have conversations about fears, concerns, and planning for the future. Caregivers and those diagnosed have the option of attending support groups to share experiences with others in similar situations. As difficult as the process may be, planning provides peace of mind that the caregiver is doing all he or she can for a loved one and is able to plan for care needs.

What if, long before a time of needing care, you were able to record a video or draft a document to record your wishes relative to an eventual need for care? What if you were able to prepare an instruction manual for your care including likes, dislikes, things never to do to you, your favorite foods, your favorite hobbies and more? If you are diagnosed with memory loss, how might this information be valuable to your care?

At the time you can no longer manage your day-to-day needs, this video or document would be helpful to those caring for you, especially if there are few family or friends remaining to tell your personal story. Many communities providing care attempt to put together a social history, including preferences so that caregivers may support individual wishes. When there is no one to provide this information, care staff is left to make guesses and hope that they are providing appropriate care.

For those diagnosed when memory loss has already progressed, an understanding of the condition is impossible regardless of how many times a discussion occurs. Provided that family relationships are positive and that care and support are available, lacking understanding of the disease is not viewed as negative. Many individuals with memory loss appear to live in a world of their own making. Who are we to say that their world is not a fascinating place to live? Many family members choose never to mention the diagnosis to loved ones after the initial conversation for fear of upsetting a loved one. In my opinion, ongoing discussions are helpful to allow caregivers to accept the diagnosis and to foster ongoing and open communication.

Maintaining Emotional Balance

What about situations of memory loss that have gone beyond diagnosis to a need for care intervention? Advanced cognitive impairment is more common with older adults living alone whose diagnosis has gone undetected for years. By the time family becomes involved, the situation is adversarial, either because of denial of the diagnosis or because of feelings of emotional overwhelm on the part of a caregiver who feels incapable of caring for a parent with a combination of advanced memory loss and behaviors. Due to refusals and unreasonable behaviors, caregivers throw up their hands in disbelief and frustration that parents refuse to accept care.

Situations of care result in emotions that are conflicting and range from feelings of love to hate to guilt. Caregiving in situations where conflict occurs represents a love-hate relationship. Caring individuals feel most vulnerable and rejected when someone they care about refuses their help. Caregivers also experience stress when care needs exceed their personal ability to provide care.

In other situations, there may be a combination of a diagnosis of memory loss and the identification of a long-standing personality disorder. If you find yourself in this situation seek additional support so that you may learn how to respond appropriately knowing that the behaviors of the individual will not change.

Maintaining an appropriate emotional balance is important in caregiving situations. Here are five tips:

1. Eliminate judgment. Realize that the care recipient has a right to their own life and the choices they make—even if their choices are different from your personal standards. Accept that the standards, ideals, and personal practices of the care recipient are different. Accept that their concept of a relationship may be different from your expectation. If you are unable to maintain this acceptance and you arrive at a place of judgment or anger, remove yourself from the caregiving situation and hire professionals who are able to act impartially to support your loved one.

2. Eliminate the tendency to rescue. Remember that the care recipient has lived for many years without your help. They were once independent. Help care recipients to do as much as possible so that they remain independent and do not need more assistance prematurely. Independence fosters self-esteem and self-respect.

3. Eliminate control and offer choice. Ask the care recipient HOW you might help. Explain what you are able to give in terms of time or financial support. Then be willing to do what the care recipient asks within the boundaries of what you are able to offer. Understand that we are all different and may arrive at the same ending or conclusion, but the journey taken is different.

4. Eliminate the possibility of harsh words. In tense situations, think before you speak. When you become frustrated with words or

actions of a care recipient, walk away, take a break. Realize that frustration solves nothing and may only make the situation worse. Attempt to gain a new perspective by acknowledging the difficulty of the situation. Seek counseling or join a support group.

5. Eliminate regret. Remember that the care recipient may be near the end of his or her life. They may be in pain or suffering and may have horrible behaviors. Think about the end of your life and the people you hope will care for you. Do what you can to provide support, but not so much that you allow yourself to feel angry due to your level of participation or not so much that you compromise your own health and well-being. As caregivers, all we can do is our own personal best and at times our personal best may not be enough based on the expectations of others. Accept what you can do and let go of all that is not within your control.

The Forgotten

With memory loss, the day will come when a parent no longer recognizes a child or recognizes himself or herself. A parent may believe a son to be their husband or a daughter to be their wife or a sister. For a spouse or child caregiver, this lack of recognition is a heartbreaking experience. Confusion is made more difficult by a desire to console or correct a parent for their lack of memory or to explain the personal relationship: for example, saying, "Mom, I'm your daughter."

My first experience of being "the forgotten" was with a client I had been involved with for about six months before she moved to a memory care community. She was an accomplished orchestra pianist. I often sat with her at the piano in her home while she played. Mrs. B. was a tiny woman with beautiful long silver hair who often spoke about how difficult it was to be a woman pianist performing in a male symphony orchestra. While I did not know her prior to being involved in her care, I imagined she could hold her own in any group, even with males who may have viewed her female presence in the orchestra as intrusive.

It became necessary for Mrs. B. to move to a care community because of increasing physical care needs: she required two people to assist her with mobility. After she was moved, I popped in for a brief visit. When I entered the room, Mrs. B. was sitting in front of the television watching one of her favorite programs, Animal Planet. I introduced myself as a friend coming to visit. In perfect form, Mrs. B. apologized that she did not recognize me, yet thanked me for coming to visit.

In that split second, I felt my heart break into a thousand tiny pieces as I became one of the forgotten; tears welled up in my eyes. Instead of making any further explanations, I picked up her silver brush and sat in conversation while I brushed her hair, an activity she always appreciated. When I left, her attention was distracted by another program on television. She stopped for a moment, looked up, and thanked me for visiting. I knew that within a few seconds after my leaving, she would not recall my visit.

In another similar situation, I dropped in on a client, Ellen, who had a caregiver visit her several times during the week so her son could have an afternoon away from caregiving responsibilities. The caregiver was the type that any family would be fortunate to have; she was kind, compassionate, patient, and had a wonderful sense of humor and play. When I arrived for my visit, the caregiver and Ellen were sitting on the couch paging through a photo album from Ellen's wedding years earlier. I watched as the caregiver marveled at how beautiful Ellen appeared in her wedding dress. Ellen asked how the caregiver knew that it was she in the photo. The caregiver paused a moment and responded, "Because I was there and danced with you at your wedding." This small therapeutic fib resulted in a huge smile of relief on Ellen's face, confirming that it was truly she in the wedding photos.

By accepting the day to day reality of the forgotten, rather than reverting into a long explanation about the relationship, or in the telling of a small tale to help one who has forgotten feel better, we offer the kindness of being present offering comfort and dignity rather than focusing on our feelings of loss. Opportunities to reminisce are comforting for older adults who may have reverted to times of living with parents or discussing others who are no longer living. Rather than correct memories, by participating without correction, we offer comfort and joy and live in the present moment of the care recipient rather than attempting to orient them to facts they no longer recall.

Because care needs and tasks are often overwhelming, family caregivers forget that memorable experiences with parents may be small snippets in time. Whether watching a television program, brushing hair, or looking through a family photo album, these activities are the moments caregivers remember, when family transcends into another world where memories fade and the caregiver is recognized as a kind visitor who stops by from time to time. There is no substitution for making memories with a loved, one even when days seem fictitious.

Living in an Altered Reality

Being a caregiver for a loved one with memory loss requires a great deal of additional effort, time, and patience. Many times the act of caregiving involves attempts of trial and error as one never knows what action will achieve a desired result in the present day. As one becomes more experienced in communicating with loved ones who have memory loss, the ability to understand that short and simple responses—rather than lengthy or detailed descriptions or discussions—support communication that is more successful and comforting.

Caregiving for an older adult requires equal if not more patience than caring for a child because the behaviors of a loved one may not be rational and may require investigation. A list of common behaviors includes depression, wandering, resistance to daily care, physical aggression, sexually inappropriate behaviors, repetitive questioning, sleep disturbances, anxiety, rummaging or hoarding, social withdrawal, disruptive statements, sundowning, demanding or verbally aggressive behavior, urinating or defecating in places other than the bathroom, and refusing to eat, drink, or take medications.

There are documented, researched, and proven interventions for responding to many of these behaviors as the result of the Cache County

Memory Study and the Kansas Bridge Project.[74] Ongoing education and support is an important aspect for caregivers of loved ones diagnosed with memory loss. While behaviors may seem extreme or unusual, many of the behaviors that occur are common, with no need to be alarmed or embarrassed.

For a caregiver, learning how to respond appropriately to an individual diagnosed with memory loss offers great success. In some situations, the act of redirecting or changing the present activity or subject offers benefit. For example, if an individual stands at the front door repeating that he or she wishes to go home, a caregiver may say, "Let's have lunch before you leave," or "Let's do laundry so that we can make sure you have clean clothing for your trip." These suggestions will offer an activity to distract from a potential focus on another single activity.

That being said, many family caregivers are somewhat naïve about behaviors that are disruptive, physically or verbally aggressive, or behaviors that might harm others. It is important not to ignore these behaviors, as they may be a result of the behaviors of a caregiver toward the care recipient. Additionally environmental factors such as too much noise or commotion may result in disruptive behaviors.

I frequently receive calls from adult children or spouses who are concerned that a loved one has become violent or dangerous. In these situations medication management is an option that should be strongly considered. Depending on the situation, medication management in an adult in-patient geriatric-psychiatric unit may be most beneficial.

While families are taken aback by the word *psychiatric*, it often takes a skilled geriatric psychiatrist to determine what medications may work best to resolve aggressive behaviors. This does not mean that the goal of medication management is to prescribe medications to make an individual incoherent or appear drugged. The goal of medication management is to find a balance that eliminates aggressive behaviors and allows caregivers to successfully provide care without threats of verbal or physical harm. In many cases, after a period of time, medications may be reduced and eliminated as behaviors adjust or subside.

There are as many responses to the behaviors of individuals experiencing memory loss as there are different types of behaviors. Becoming more educated and engaging in efforts of trial and error supports caregivers in knowing that they are supporting a loved one's needs. It is also important to realize that frequent breaks are necessary to support the ongoing patience required in caring for a loved one with memory loss.

Exercise: Choosing a Care Navigator

Prior to contacting a care navigator, or care management provider, visit the company website to determine how much information is readily available to answer the questions below. This activity will help improve the detail of the questions you ask when you contact the agency to make an appointment. Below are ten starter questions to evaluate a company's background on their website before you make a phone call:

1. Is the website appealing, friendly, and easy to navigate; is it easy to locate information?
2. Does the website explain the services provided by the company; does the company focus on a single area of business i.e. care navigation or do they also offer caregivers (which may represent conflict of interest).
3. Is information readily available relative to the background of the owner featuring a resume or background page on the website; does the owner have certifications or belong to associations supporting healthcare and care oversight?
4. Does the website offer an easy way to make contact? If so, make contact through the website, and request a phone call or a meeting.
5. How long has the company been in business? Longevity is an important factor.
6. Is the company's service profile and rate sheet available on the website?
7. Is there a list of Frequently Asked Questions?
8. Does the company offer educational information for caregivers?
9. Does the company specialize in a particular type of client; disabled adults, older adults, developmentally disabled children, or others?
10. Are legal services of guardian or medical power of attorney offered; this usually means the company has a greater degree of responsibility, accountability and oversight.

If you are comfortable with the information presented on the website, I recommend making an hour-long appointment to meet the staff of the company you are considering. In most cases, you will pay an hourly consultation rate; however your time and money will be well spent if the appointment helps you determine if this care navigator has the skills and experience to help in your particular situation.

The challenge in navigating the healthcare system is the unknown. Do you feel comfortable that your knowledge will result in the outcome desired? Do you feel that you know enough to make informed decisions? Providing care for a loved one with memory loss can be challenging if you are new to the experience. What options exist for care and support for your loved one and for you as a caregiver?

If you are interested in accessing more tips and information about ideas presented in this chapter and about related subjects, visit http:// www. thecaregivingtrapbook.com/store and select The Pleasantly Forgetful.

Bernice and the Black Cat

Bernice lived in a whitewashed house, the paint beginning to peel, shrouded behind a tall thicket that surrounded her yard. The main entrance was a narrow walk leading to a small gap in the thicket where an old rusty gate sat waiting for someone, anyone to stop by. The gate, silent until opened, creaked as if it were experiencing pain and served as an alarm calling to let Bernice knew someone approached. There were few visitors except for the mailman and the newspaper delivery person.

During the autumn, leaves falling from the maple trees in the yard danced circles on the front porch. In winter the porch was buried in snow; a few footprints visible were the only sign of Bernice coming and going down the stairs. In spring the sparrows built nests and had their babies under the safety and shade of her porch, and in summer wild roses climbed the trellis. Hers was a quiet existence, more comfortable with aspects of nature than with people.

No one really knew Bernice except a neighbor, Betty, who lived a few blocks over from her home in the small neighborhood. Bernice's parents had died years ago, leaving the house to her and her brother David. David followed in his father's footsteps working at the local packing house, never marrying and drinking heavily, which ended his life while young in his sixties— leaving Bernice alone.

Bernice never married and seemed to be a lost soul to those who saw her outdoors while walking. She still dressed in her seventies more like a young girl, wearing pastel-colored ankle-length calico-print dresses, white ankle socks, and black laced shoes. She wore her silver hair back in a ponytail clasped by a barrette; her face never saw a touch of makeup. She was amazingly beautiful in a sorrowful sort of way.

Betty, a neighbor, took it upon herself to check in on Bernice. She would bring an occasional casserole or leftovers and share a meal with Bernice. Betty was the only one, other than the mailman or newspaper delivery person, who visited and was allowed inside Bernice's home. The inside of her home looked like a museum, filled with antiques dating back at least a hundred years. There were stuffed pheasants, an old piano that Bernice played in the evening, china cabinets filled with crystal, an old phonograph with records of classical music. The house including her parent's bedroom had not changed with time. Bernice kept the home immaculate, housekeeping likely occupying the majority of her day. There was no television, only an old radio that received a signal strong enough to receive local stations.

Not many people knew that Bernice's parents had emigrated from Austria or that she had inherited money from a grandmother never having a need to become employed. This was a curiosity to the entire neighborhood. Betty and Bernice had a comfortable, trusting friendship. They talked about the weather year-round. In summer they watched birds and squirrels running through the yard. In the fall they baked apple and plum pies that Betty took to church bake sales. In winter they read books together by the roaring fireplace in Bernie's living room.

Betty believed that Bernice's family even though passed on, somehow kept her company and watched over her as she continued to live in the house alone. There were occasional warm gusts of air gently blowing doors open or closed when it was evident the windows in the house were closed tight. Other times Betty smelled lilacs in the dead of winter or heard a few chords of music when no one sat at the piano. She asked Bernice about this once, and Bernice replied with an "Oh that happens occasionally; I just think nothing of it," although Betty suspected it happened quite frequently and Bernice was just trying to keep her secrets just that— secret.

Bernice had a black cat that lived in the barn behind her yard and kept watch on the front stairs of her home at night, scaring away anyone who dared come near, including adventurous neighborhood children. As she grew older, she preferred to stay inside, listening to music or playing the piano. One particularly warm Halloween day, Bernice invited Betty to an early supper, letting her know that she'd leave the back door open like she had so many times before. When Betty arrived, she found the black cat circling around the back door and immediately knew something was amiss. Inside she found Bernice, who appeared to be asleep on the couch, but she knew better. In Bernice's hand was a note:

Dear Betty—Sorry to surprise you this way. I knew it was my time, and I didn't want just anyone to find me. Your friendship over the years meant more to me than you'll ever know. I know most of the neighbors saw me as the crazy old lady living in the haunted house who rarely made an appearance in public. The house was never haunted, just filled with the memories of my parents and my brother, and I found myself more comfortable with them than with anyone except for you. Tom at the bank has my will: most everything I've left to charity, except for my diary, which has been left for you so that my life and the life of my parents will somehow live on. Feel free to donate it after reading it to a preservation society or another group who might have an interest in the town's history. All the best to you. Your friend in this lifetime and in the next— Bernice.

PART FOUR

CLOSURE

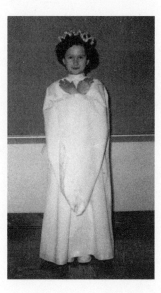

With the role of caregiving arrives a loss of innocence about life, duty, and responsibility. There are times when caregiving—rather than feeling like a blessing—feels like a trap. Difficult relationships offer hidden lessons that we may not appreciate or recognize until many years down the road of life.

Chapter 12

Dying Changes Everything

- The Kiss of Death
- "I Don't Do Funerals"
- The Wisdom of Planning
- Life Goes On

The Kiss of Death
The way in which caregivers respond to poor health, advancing illness, caregiving roles, and to death are framed by life experiences. Mention of the impact of serious health issues and death is not discussed as a part of daily life until we read the news, watch television, or experience a personal family situation. By bringing these subjects into family discussions when children are young, parents may be able to change societal views that aging and death are experiences to be feared.

Ageism, meaning prejudice or discrimination based on a person's age, is prevalent in society. If you are middle aged, you may not be aware that ageism exists. Research reviewing Facebook group category postings indicate that ageism is widespread. "statistics related to negative aging stereotypes found in postings reported that "74 percent criticized; 'old people do not contribute to modern society at all', 29 percent related their actions to those of children and 37 percent advocated banning them (older adults) from public activities such as shopping."[75]

In my opinion, many of these ideas and behaviors occur because of limited contact with healthy and active adults of an older age and those of advanced age. Supporting intergenerational activities by visiting grandparents or participating in volunteer activities where older adults are present bring generations together and have the potential to decrease negative attitudes toward aging.

The idea of birth and death being removed from the public eye resulted from an interview with a centenarian of 104. Anna told me that in the early 1900s hospitals treated only sick people. A birthing mother wasn't sick—babies were born at home, not in the hospital. Family members died at home and their bodies remained for viewing by friends and family until burial. This is the way in which families honored their dead at the turn of the century and before. It has been only in the past one hundred years that the beginning and end of life—birth and death—have been removed from the home and hidden behind hospital walls.

Death is a mystery, an event rarely discussed until death becomes a part of our present reality. Early experiences like the loss of a pet may occur, but it is not until death becomes personal that we realize the true effect. How many of you are familiar with the term "the kiss of death"? How many times do we hear this statement and others related to negative subjects, "the nail in the coffin" or "waiting for the other shoe to drop"?

The first funeral I remember attending was in 1967; I had just turned six. My mind still runs a reel of photos of St. Francis of Assisi Church, me standing on the kneeler and leaning over to peek at Grandpa Lawrence resting peacefully in his casket. He was dressed handsomely in a suit and tie. That stern look he flashed, when we knew we were in trouble, was absent from his face, as was the brown-wrapped cigar he held in his hand and lifted to his mouth to expel puffy circles of smoke.

Seeing Grandpa lying in the casket was not frightening; he appeared to be sleeping. If Mom had no fear of standing next to him or touching him, I guessed that I should feel as she did, not showing any great distress except for the tears running down her cheeks. I ran my fingers across his folded hands; they were cold to the touch. The skin on his hand was wrinkled and of a texture that seemed waxy because the skin wasn't soft or movable when touched like the soft skin on the hand of a living person. There were so many details I noticed. It was new knowledge to me that dead bodies were cold and rigid.

Mom talked to Grandpa as if he could hear every word. She said her good-byes, and much to my surprise, she kissed him on the lips. The vision of that final kiss served as an example to me of something one did to show love and respect for a parent who had died. I realize today that through her actions—and many actions I witnessed as a child—that she was setting an example for me.

I remember seeing tears and sadness on my mother's face and thinking that death must be a sad experience. Nearly thirty years later, I followed her example. I kissed my mother on her lips one last time as she lay in her casket moments before the cover was closed. I paid the same respect to my father prior to his casket being closed.

Today when I remember these experiences, tears still well up in my eyes. I don't know that most children can say this, but I had parents who were role models, setting examples by which I live today. They were strict, honest, loving, kind and hardworking. I hit the parent lottery.

"I Don't Do Funerals"

After my parents and several other family members passed, there was a time in my life when I joined the ranks of those who say "I don't do funerals." Today I feel differently. When I was young, I feared death and the sadness associated with loss because the experiences were so frequent. I recall family members dying and having to attend their funerals in my early years. At my young age I had no idea of the process of grieving or of resolving feelings of sadness or loss. This is likely why some parents shield children from sickness and death of family members.

People who say "I don't do funerals" are expressing an understandable desire to avoid feelings of grief. The emotional experience of losing a friend or a parent can be incredibly heartrending and painful. When I hear "I don't do funerals" from others, I empathize and understand their feelings. Rather than being a statement to be judged, "I don't do funerals" is the statement of a person unsure how to respond to feelings of loss or how to grieve. These feelings are a lesson and an opportunity to learn appreciation of life and ways to cope and grieve losses that are inevitable.

Attending the funeral or memorial service of a loved one offers the opportunity for closure, one last time to see or remember the person in the presence of family and friends. Memorial services comfort and allow closure for those of us who remain. How many of us see distant family members and friends at a memorial service and feel comforted by their presence? Attending a memorial service is similar to attending a family reunion to get together and share memories. If one is wise, advance planning lessens the stress experienced by family members rushing to plan a service in a matter of days.

Today in my career, death is a frequent visitor, and proof that facing my fears has reduced my belief that death is a part of life to be feared. The process of dying is no longer a great unknown but a normal progression and part of life. I have witnessed my clients die peacefully and without pain.

When I visit clients for whom I oversee care at the end of life, many report they are ready to go home to see their mother or father who has gone before them. Many individuals near death express appreciation for the life they have lived. Others, without belief about the afterlife, express fear or concern about the journey. For those who have had little experience with death, the very idea of dying is filled with fear.

The importance of visits with the dying and the act of providing reassurances should not be underestimated. This was proven to me as the result of a personal experience. It was a warm summer evening, a Tuesday, when I visited Ann at the hospice she had entered two days earlier because the pain of cancer could not be appropriately managed at home. Ann was sleeping peacefully. I held her hand and talked to her in the same manner as I did when I visited her at home. I let her know that all her bills were paid and that a good home was found for her cat, which was of great concern. When I left, I kissed her cheek, and I told her I would see her again.

I drove home, and as I slid my key into the lock of the front door of my home—less than thirty minutes after sitting by Ann's side—my cell phone rang. It was the hospice nurse calling to tell me that Ann had passed away moments earlier. I believe she waited for my visit. The news I delivered gave Ann peace of mind that I had carried out her wishes and she was comfortable in moving on to a better place. It is likely that some of you have had a similar experience.

Many older adults still in good health question the continuation of their lives and ask, "Why am I still here?" Death may be a blessing for a person who is physically suffering because of health issues. Other times death is regrettable because of situations involving neglect or poor care. For others death comes at the right time, according to their wishes and desire to be with long-lost loved ones.

No matter how many times a person experiences the loss of a life, sadness occurs because of the loss of an emotional and personal connection. Accepting and realizing that life is finite has the potential to support caregivers through even the most difficult and trying times with patience and grace.

The emotional experience of losing a parent or any loved one is challenging to navigate especially today when people are living longer but not necessarily healthier lives. Many individuals at the age of fifty have not experienced the death of an immediate family member. The benefits of an advanced medical system have resulted in life extensions that sustain life in spite of chronic disease and terminal diagnosis.

The time will come in all our lives for an event that I refer to as the "last call." This last call is not the last drink served before the bar closes but the last phone call, conversation or visit with a loved one before death occurs. Sometimes the experience is expected, if a loved one has been ill or has lived with complicated health concerns. Other times the phone call comes as a complete and unexpected shock. I clearly remember saying goodnight to my sister Becky the night before she was killed in a car accident, seeing and saying "see you again" to my mother at St. Joseph's Hospital before her death, and the enjoyable evening phone call with my father prior to his death the next morning.

The Wisdom of Planning

Because of my personal experience, I advocate the idea of detailed planning regarding all later-in-life issues with my clients. In situations where I am a court-appointed guardian or have power of attorney, I make sure that burial or cremation plans are purchased well in advance of the need. My mother preplanned for her and my father's funerals—I thought her crazy at the time—yet at the time of death she could not have given us a better gift. We did not have to rush about while grieving our loss like she likely did when her close family members passed away.

If wishes for cremation, burial, or a memorial service are not expressed or placed in writing, there may be a great deal of family interpretation and disagreement about what a loved one would have wanted. The time of death is not the time for disagreement over end-of-life wishes. The rush to plan a memorial service in a matter of days pulls those involved into a planning and organizing sequence to make sure everything goes well, and it is not until after the event that the planner is able to take the time to process loss and grief.

I hear older adults say that when they're gone, they're gone. Some do not care what occurs with their body after death whether or not they have a service. One client suggested I throw his ashes on the grounds of a parking lot. So that I might fulfill his wish, I found a beautiful lookout above a valley adjacent to a parking lot, and deposited his ashes on the edge of the parking lot overlooking an incredible view. I pass by this area frequently and always say hello to my friend, who has a great view of the valley in one direction and, according to his wish, a parking lot in the opposite direction. The evening of the same day that I laid his ashes to rest, my husband and I were eating in an Italian restaurant, and above my husband's head was a plaque listing the name of a town in Italy that was the last name of my client. I knew I had made the right decision.

If you are ambivalent about having a memorial service and have extended family, consider prearranging your funeral. Give a gift to your family by hosting in absentia a family reunion they might not otherwise have the opportunity to plan themselves. A colleague of mine who works at one of the few family-owned memorial companies put this idea into perspective. When most people marry, the event is anticipated and planned for months, similar to the expected birth of a baby. We are so focused on celebrating happy events, why is it that we rush to prepare for a celebration of life in three days or less?

Preplanning a memorial service ensures that wishes are carried out. Planning provides an opportunity for reuniting family and friends allowing closure. This may be unimportant to the person who died, but very important to the survivors.

Life Goes On

I know many families today who place table settings and recognize empty seats at holiday celebrations to remember family members no longer present. When I was young, our family did not celebrate Thanksgiving and Christmas for several years because my parents were grieving the loss of my sister Becky.

Moving forward after loss is different for each individual and family member depending on age and lifestyle. I recently spoke to a family member of a client, who in response to my call advising that her cousin had passed away expressed relief that her cousin was no longer suffering, but sadness in the recognition that she was the only family member of her generation now living.

Caregiving has become complicated by the mobility of society and the lost art of sitting on the front porch visiting with family or friends.

Porches and porch swings have been lost to architectural design and space constraints. Children, rather than playing outside, are immersed in video gaming, computers, cell phones, iPads, and other technology. Every day another gadget is invented that one simply must have.

Grandparents, who years ago lived in the same neighborhood, are today miles, cities, states, or even continents apart. The opportunity to imprint happy childhood memories by sitting in Grandma's lap or helping Grandma with hands-on projects like baking cookies has all but vanished. There is a mystique and a depth in the old black-and-white photos of family members that today's digital photos cannot duplicate.

Young adults and children lack exposure to products and experiences that those of us now in our forties, fifties, and even older remember with fond admiration. How many of you remember the hand towels that were free gifts inside boxes of laundry detergent? Dial telephones? Gasoline selling for twenty-five cents a gallon? When going to the penny candy store with a quarter resulted in coming out with a brown paper bag brimming to the top with candy buttons on long rolls of paper, edible red wax lips, Pixy Stix, bubble gum cigars, Cherry Mash, and wax bottles filled with fruit juice? What about SPAM sandwiches and Jell-O cake? The value of reminiscing with aging loved ones should not be under estimated as this activity provides comfort and the opportunity to focus on relationships and to document family history.

Publications are changing to digital access at an alarming rate. Years from now the library my mom took me to on Saturday mornings for story time when I was a child will exist in a very different form from a stand-alone building. People purchase books, like this one, in bookstores but also through the Internet. Books appear instantly on digital readers and by way of audio CDs. The progression of technology has fast-forwarded life.

The world today, as did the world of our past, will affect our ability to relate and to communicate with others. If we wish to change our future, we must work to instill knowledge and responsibility. We must embrace establishing roles by teaching children the value of parental and caregiving relationships and by providing examples of interactions with grandparents and other aging family members.

Many people who care for their aging parents tell me their children are off at college, working, or hanging out with friends. Young children and adults have very little interest in the experiences of Grandma or Grandpa. Many young adults have no idea of the level of involvement of their parents in caring for grandparents, which yields many surprises years later when their own parents need care.

While this may be the current state of affairs in grandparent, child, and grandchild relationships, conversations with young children that describe the role of caregiving as a potential future role will reduce the element of surprise. If understanding exists when young that issues related to aging are part of life, conversations about aging and care will occur throughout life and will ease conversations of care between parents and children when the time comes that care is needed. Ageism and negative attitudes toward aging will be reduced.

In reflective moments I realize how different life was a hundred years ago from the stories told to me by my grandmother, parents, and clients—and how different life will be in another hundred years for those born after us. The aspect that I believe will not change is that time passes in the blink of an eye. We exist one day and are gone the next. What difference have we made? Whose lives have we touched? What do we leave behind for future generations?

Today is the time to make connections with your parents and loved ones. It is also time to have conversations about care—years before care is needed. If you are already a caregiver, your parent is passing into the next world little by little each day. Be patient and kind. Help if you have available time. Retain the services of professionals who are able to support the situation rather than falling into the caregiving trap. Hire caregivers who are able to care for your parents. Make your caregiving experience and the care of your loved one the best it can possibly be—with the help of others

I expect that I will react like many of my clients when my health becomes frail. I hope that I will follow their examples and age with grace and appreciation. I hope that I will maintain friendships and social connections to support me when loss overcomes my life and I am alone. I hope that I will pass through this world peacefully and without pain. I wish the same for you.

Afterword

Writing this book has led me through a journey of examining my life purpose, goals, and beliefs. Like many caregivers I have experienced the ups and downs that pass through all of our lives. Further exploration and research have led me to many unexpected but welcome insights, some common sense and some that others would view as a bit out of the ordinary.

I believe that universal principles exist and guide us through life. One is the idea of balance, which many caregivers—family and professional—fail to experience. The same idea of balance is challenging for many other individuals who are not yet caregivers. Finding ways to achieve balance in life is more about how we think about our lives and achieving balance—than about how the outside world affects us. We are not as powerless as we sometimes think.

The other universal principle is the idea of cause and effect. As I researched aspects of health, both good and bad, I recently became aware of a belief held by individuals in the nursing profession. A "badge of honor" exists in this profession with the idea that giving up good health and mental well-being to care for others is an honor. I researched and discovered the following:

"This view that "good nurses" deprive themselves of even the basic necessities of life, such as sleep, to care for their patients, is pervasive within the nursing profession and establishes a dangerous and unhealthy environment for patients and nurses."[76]

Working in the aging and healthcare field, I meet physicians, nurses, healthcare workers, and others in the profession whose health and well-being suffer. Because these individuals are challenged to promote balance and to set boundaries, they are unsuccessful at practicing self-care, subsequently leaving a profession that they initially loved to become a care recipient. Family caregivers experience similar aspects of burnout, depression, and poor health as a result of the role of caregiving.

In my opinion, "badge of honor" thinking increases the need for healthcare and related costs by establishing a spiral that never ends. Caring for another person makes it acceptable to neglect self-care which results in a need for care by others who then neglect their own care. What about this thought process is faulty?

What makes caregivers believe that giving up good health for poor health is a positive action? Is there more to the story? Does the act of caregiving make it easier for caregivers—family and professional to have an excuse not to take responsibility for their own well-being—as if to say, "I care for my mother, and she is the reason I am sick, overweight, depressed, and generally miserable."

Many caregivers tell me that their lives are out of control because of caring for a loved one and that little balance exists in their lives. I understand these statements and feelings because I was and I am a caregiver. However, over the years I have learned the benefit of taking responsibility for my actions because of the principle of cause and effect. I have learned the importance of paying attention to my health through nutrition and exercise.

Feeling overwhelmed and at the mercy of situations is a direct result of cause and effect. Our outer world reflects the inner world of our mind.

Our thoughts and actions create our everyday reality. If a caregiver feels that everything is happening to him or her and is feeling powerless over aspects of life, then the caregiver has chosen to remain affected by life rather than to take action to effect change. The same back and forth, up and down, feeling powerful and then powerless relates to the life of the care recipient.

The Caregiving Trap represents our thoughts—positive or negative—and our beliefs that it is possible to change situations through our actions. Many caregivers fall into ruts of negative thinking feeling, powerless to change situations. Others caregivers are plain stubborn and refuse to believe that a situation might be otherwise. Both caregivers and care recipients become trapped in thoughts and habits that increase the severity of situations making daily existence challenging.

The role of caregiving can be positive *if* caregivers make choices to support personal well-being, to become educated about health, and to learn to advocate. In a healthcare system dominated by varying beliefs and systems of care—including alternative therapies—personal responsibility and advocacy will support changing the future of caregiving, aging, and healthcare.

The death of my parents and many of my family members prior to my reaching the age of forty was life changing. I experienced the effects of poor health in relation to the life and care of my mother in addition to an imperfect healthcare system that resulted in her diagnosis of Hepatitis C. I was raised in a family with siblings I considered to be intelligent at the time we were navigating the care of my parents. Today I realize how much we did not know and the questions we did not think to ask of physicians and other healthcare providers—because we did not know any better.

Becoming more educated and learning to advocate is important as well as taking personal responsibility for achieving good health. When in doubt, seek education and support and utilize professionals who have expertise to support you and your loved ones.

About the Author

Pamela D. Wilson, MS, BS/BA, CSA, NCG is an expert in the field of caregiving. Since 2000 in her career as an advocate, a care navigator, and a caregiving educator she has supported family and professional caregivers. Pamela's experience has a professional and personal foundation. By the time Pamela was forty years old, fifty percent of her immediate family, including both of her parents, had died. Part of her life story is told in this book in the section titled Tales of The Caring Generation: The Baby.

Some view Pamela's life experience as a tragedy, Pamela views the events as multiple defining moments supporting her passion to raise awareness of the importance of advocacy on behalf of the caregivers and care recipients she helps through her company, The Care Navigator. She has personally experienced the challenges and frustrations of the caregivers and the care recipients that she serves. Her professional experience allows her to provide support for clients in extremely complex situations.

Pamela educates and speaks to family and professional caregivers with an openness and authenticity about caregiving that warms and inspires. She developed and produced *The Caring Generation* an educational radio program which has transformed into an educational website for caregivers and is the foundation for the book, The Caregiving Trap. She chairs a local Healthcare Ethics Committee in Denver, Colorado. Active in many professional organizations, Pamela has a firm belief that minimum standards of care in the healthcare and aging industries must be raised through advocacy and education.

Meet Pamela, and subscribe to receive free articles, videos and podcasts on the subject of caregiving at http://www.TheCaringGeneration.com.

Pamela D. Wilson, "The Baby"

Endnotes

1   Katja Pynnonen, Timo Tormakangas, Riitta-Liisa Heikkinen, Taina
    Rantanen and Tiina-Mari Lyyra, "Does Social Activity Decrease Risk
    for Institutionalization and Mortality in Older People?" *The Journals
    of Gerontology, Series B: Psychological Sciences and Social Sciences,*
    67(6), (2012) 765-774.doi 10:1093/geronb/gbs076.
2   The Bible, Hebrews 13:2.
3   Karen Windle, Jennifer Francis and Caroline Coomber, "Preventing
    Loneliness and Social Isolation: Interventions and Outcomes," *Social
    Care Institute for Excellence,* Research Briefing 39 (2011): 1-16.
    http://www.scie.org.uk/publications/briefings/files/briefing39.pdf
4   Aaron Smith, "Older Adults and Technology Use," *PEW Research
    Center,* 4/3/2014, http://www.pewreserach.org
5   Krames StayWell, "Older Adults and the Importance of Social
    Interaction," Krames Stawell, www.kramesstaywell.com
6   Tineke Fokkema and Kees Knipscheer, "Escape Loneliness by Going
    Digital: A Quantitative and Qualitative Evaluation of a Dutch
    Experiment Using Electronic Communication Tools to Overcome

Loneliness Among Older Adults," *Aging & Mental Health*, 11:5, (2007) 496-504, doi: 10.1080/13607860701366129.

7   Edel Mannion, "Alzheimer's Disease: The Psychological and Physical Effects of the Caregiver's Role. Part 2, *Nursing Older People*, May, Vol. 20, No 4 (2008):34.

8   Alzheimer's Association, "2014 Alzheimer's Disease Facts and Figures," *Alzheimer's and Dementia,* Volume 10, Issue 2(2014) 57, 61.

9   Drew DeSilver, "As Population Ages, More Americans Becoming Caregivers," *PEW Research Center*, 7/18/2013, accessed February 15, 2014 http://www.pewresearch.org/fact-tank/2013/07/18/as-population-ages-more-americans-becoming-caregivers/

10 Susan C. Reinhart, RN, PhD, FAAN, Senior Vice President and Director AARP, Carol Levine, MA Director, Families and Health Care Project, United Hospital Fund and Sarah Samis, MPA, Senior Health Policy Analyst, United Hospital Fund, "Home Alone: Family Caregivers Providing Complex Chronic Care," *AARP Public Policy Institute.* October 2012, accessed 2/15/2014 http://www.aarp.org/home-family/caregiving/info-10-2012/home-alone-family-caregivers-providing-complex-chronic-care.print.html

11 Lynn Feinberg, Susan Reinhart, Ari Houser and Rita Choula, "Valuing the Invaluable: 2011 Update the Growing Contributions and Costs of Family Caregiving," AARP *Public Policy Institute.* Caregiving in the U.S.: Executive Summary. (2009). *National Alliance for Caregiving in collaboration with AARP.* Funded by MetLife Foundation. accessed http://www.caregiving.org/data/CaregivingUSAllAgesExecSum.pdf

12 Federal Interagency Forum on Aging-Related Statistics, *Older Americans 2012: Key Indicators of Well-Being*, accessed October 13, 2012, http://www.aging.stats.gov

13 U.S. Census Population Statistics, http://www.census.gov

14 David E. Bloom, David Canning and Gunther Fink, "Implications of Population Aging for Economic Growth," *Program on the Global*

Demography of Aging funded by National Institute on Aging. January 2011, PGDA working Paper No. 64, Grant No. 1 p. 30 AG024409-06

15 Partnership to Fight Chronic Disease, *The Growing Crisis of Chronic Disease in the United States*, 2008, accessed September 28, 2008, http://www.fightchronicdisease.org/

16 Centers for Disease Control and Prevention, *Complications Due to Diabetes*, accessed December 20, 2014, http://www.cdc.gov/diabetes/living/problems.html

17 Centers for Disease Control and Prevention, *National Diabetes Statistics Report 2014*, accessed October 5, 2014, http://www.cdc.gov/diabetes/pubs/statsreport14.htm

18 Nationwide Better Health, *Controlling the Cost and Impact of Absenteeism: Why Businesses Should Take a Closer Look at Outsourcing Absence Management*, 2010, accessed October 6, 2012, http://nwbetterhealth.com

19 Bruce Japsen, "U.S. Workforce Illness Costs $576B Annual From Sick Days to Workers Compensation, Forbes 9/12/2012, accessed 10/5/2014 http://www.forbes.com/sites/brucejapsen/2012/09/12/u-s-workforce-illness-costs-576b-annually-from-sick-days-to-workers-compensation/

20 Greg de Lissovoy, Feng Pan, Steve Siak, Valerie Hutchins and Bryan Luce, "The Burden of Disease: The Economic Case for Investment in Quality Improvement and Medical Progress," *Center for Health Economics and Science Policy*, United BioSource Corporation, Bethesda, MD 8/14/2009, accessed October 6, 2012 http://www.unitedbiosource.com

21 Nationwide Better Health, Controlling the Cost and Impact of Absenteeism: Why Businesses Should Take a Closer Look at Outsourcing Absence Management, 2010, accessed October 6, 2012, http://nationwide.com

22 Evercare Study in collaboration with the National Alliance for Caregiving, *Evercare Study of Family Caregivers: What They Spend,*

What They Sacrifice, Findings from a National Survey November 2007, accessed February 14, 2014 http://www.caregiving.org/pdf/research/Evercare_NAC_CaregiverCostStudyFINAL20111907.pdf

23 Tam E. Perry, Troy C. Andersen and Daniel B. Kaplan, "Relocation Remembered: Perspectives on Senior Transitions in the Living Environment," *The Gerontologist* 54, no.1, (2014) 75-81 doi:10:1093/geront/gnt070

24 Eugene Litwak and Charles Longino Jr., "*Migration Patterns Among the Elderly: A Developmental Perspective*," The Gerontologist 27, no. 3, (1987) 266-272 doi:10.1093/geront/27.3.266

25 *New York Times The New Old Age Blog;* "Another Month Another Home," blog entry by Mary Plummer, May 18, 2011, http://newoldage.blogs.nytimes.2011/05/18/another-month-another-home

26 "Read Faster, Reading Stats," Statistic Brain, April 28, 2013, www.statisticbrain.com

27 "The Adult Performance Level Study." Final Report, University of Texas (Austin), August 1977 Funding by the Office of Education of the Former Department of Health, Education, & Welfare.

28 Norvell Northcutt, "Functional Literacy for Adults: A Status Report of the Adult Performance Level Study," Paper presented at the 19th Annual Meeting of the International Reading Association, New Orleans, May 1-4, 1974.

29 Norvell Northcutt, "Adult Functional Competency: A Summary of the Adult Performance Level Project," University of Texas at Austin, 1975.

30 *The State of Aging and Health in America 2013*, Centers for Disease Control and Prevention, U.S. Department of Health and Human Services, 2013.

31 *The State of Aging and Health in America 2013*, Centers for Disease Control and Prevention, U.S. Department of Health and Human Services, 2013.

32 "Prescription and Illicit Drug Abuse," NIH Senior Health a service of the U.S. National Library of Medicine, http://nihseniorhealth. gov/drugabuse/effectsofmedicationabuse/01.html

33 Min Zhang, C. D'Arcy Holman, Sylvie Price, Frank Sanfilippo, David Preen and Max Bulsara, M.K. "Comorbidity and Repeat Admission to Hospital for Adverse Drug Reactions in Older Adults: Retrospective Cohort Study," *BMJ*, 338 (2009):a2752 doi:10.1136/ bmj.a2752.

34 "The Effect of Health Care Cost Growth on the U.S. Economy," final report for task order #HO-06-12 prepared for the Office of the Assistant Secretary for Planning and Evaluation United States Department of Health and Human Services, p.3.

35 *End of Life Care* (Lebanon, NH: The Trustees of Dartmouth College 2014) accessed http://www.dartmouthatlas.org/keyissues/issue. aspx?con=2944

36 C.I.A World Factbook: Afghanistan People and Society and Economy accessed December 20, 2014 http://www.cia.gov/library/ publications/the-world-factboog/geos/af.htum

37 Keith Melville, *The School Dropout Crises* (Richmond, VA: University of Richmond Pew Partnership for Civic Change, 2006).

38 "11 Facts About High School Dropout Rates," Do Something accessed March 22, 2014 https://www.dosomething.org/print/ tipsandtools/11-facts-about-high-school-dropout-rates

39 Keith Melville, *The School Dropout Crises* (Richmond, VA: University of Richmond Pew Partnership for Civic Change, 2006).

40 "Digital Set to Surpass TV in Time Spent with US Media". Daily Marketer Digital August 1, 2013, accessed October 10, 2014 http:/ www.emarketer.com

41 Reading Statistics, Statistic Brain July 14, 2014, http://www. statisticrain.com/reading-statistics/

42 *The Demand for Geriatric Care and the Evident Shortage of Geriatrics Healthcare Providers* (New York: The American Geriatrics Society,

2013) http://www.americangeriatrics.org/files/documents/Adv Resources/demand_for_geriatric_care.pdf

43 Christine Bishop, "High Performance Workplace Practices in Nursing Homes: An Economic Perspective," *The Gerontologist*, 54, no. 31 (2014): S46-52, doi 10.1093/gerontgnt163

44 "I Love Lucy's Famous Chocolate Scene," You Tube accessed October 10, 2014 http://www.youtube.com/watch?v=8NPzLBSBzPI

45 Michael Behrens, "How the Aged and Frail are Exploited in Washington's Adult Family Homes," *The Seattle Times Special Report Seniors For Sale*, January 30, 2010 accessed October 10, 2014 http://www. seattletimes.com/html/seniorsforsale/2010939195_seniors31. html

46 "Life and Death in Assisted Living," *PBS Online,* July 30,2013 accessed October 10,2014 http://www.pbs.org/wgbh/pages/frontline/life-and-death-in-assisted-living/

47 Sheryl Zimmerman, Victoria Shier and Debra Saliba, "Transforming Nursing Home Culture: Evidence for Practice and Policy," *The Gerontologist*, 54, no. 51, (2014): 51-55 doi:10.1093/geront/gnt161

48 Kristin Funderburg Mather and Tamilyn Bakas, "Nursing Assistants' Perceptions of Their Ability to Provide Continence Care," *Geriatric Nursing*, 23 (2002) 76-81, http://dx.doi.org/10.1067/mgn.2002.123788.

49 Dan R. Berlowitz, Gary J. Young, Elaine C. Hickey, Debra Saliba, Brian S. Mittman, Elaine Czarnowski, Barbara Simon, Jennifer J. Anderson, Arlene S. Ash, Lisa V. Rubenstein and Mark A. Moskowitz, "Quality Improvement Implementation in the Nursing Home," *Health Services Research*, 38, (2003) 65-83, http://dx.doi.org/10.1111/1475-6773.00105.

50 Eric Collier and Charlene Harrington, "Staffing Characteristics, Turnover Rates, and Quality of Resident Care in Nursing Facilities," *Research in Gerontological Nursing*, 1, (2008) 157-170. http://dx.doi.org/10.3928/00220124-20091301-03.

51 "Readmissions Reduction Program," *CMS: Centers for Medicare and Medicaid Services*, April 19, 2014, accessed October 10, 2014 http://www.cms.gov/Medicare?Medicare-Fee-for-Service-Payment/AcuteInpatientPPS/Readmissions-Reduction-Program.html

52 "30 Day Unplanned Readmission and Death Measures," Medicare.gov accessed October 10, 2014 http://www.http://www.medicare.gov/hospitalcompare/Data/30-day-measures.html?

53 Douglas Hershey and Kene Henkens, "Impact of Different Types of Retirement Transitions on Perceived Satisfaction With Life," *The Gerontologist*, 34, no. 2 (2013): 232-244 doi:10:1093/gerontgnt006

54 Lewis Carroll, *Alice's Adventures in Wonderland,* (New York: MacMillan 1865).

55 Richard Winton, Martha Groves and John Spano, "Trial in Market Crash Set to Begin," *Los Angeles Times*, 9/4/2006.

56 Richard Winton, Martha Groves and John Spano, "Case is Closed on Deadly Day at Market," *Los Angeles Times*, 5/22/2008.

57 Sara Honn Qualls, "What Social Relationships Can do for Health," *Generations: Journal of the American Society on Aging.* Spring 2014, p 8-13.

58 Megumi Tsubota-Utsugi, Rie Ito-Sato, Takayoshi Ohkubo, Masahiro Kikuya, Kei Asayama, Hirohito Metoki, Naomi Fukushima, Ayumi Kurioto, Yoshitaka Tsubono and Yutake Imai, "Health Behaviors as Predictors for Declines in Higher-Level Functional Capacity in Older Adults: The Ohasama Study, JAGS 59:1993-2000, (2011) doi:10.1111/j.1532-5415.2011.036333.x

59 "Social isolation may have a negative effect on intellectual abilities," *Medical News Today*, 30 Oct 2007. Retrieved from: http: www.medicalnewstoday.com/releases/87087.php

60 "Growing Older in America: Health and Retirement Study. *National Institute on Aging: National Institutes of Health: US Department of Health and Human Services.* NIH National Library of Medicine Publication No. 07-5757 March 2007.

61 Jonathan Vespa, Jamie M. Lewis, and Rose M. Kreider, "America's Families and Living Arrangements: 2012," *U.S. Department of Commerce Economics and Statistics Administration U.S. Census Bureau,* http://www.census.gov/prod/2013pubs/p20-570.pdf, p 3, 5.

62 "US Problems About More than Moral Values," April 12, 2014 accessed http://www.cnbc.com/id/100635460/print.

63 "Elderly Abuse Statistics 2013," Statistic Brain, June 18, 2013 accessed http://www.statisticbrain/com/elderly-aguse-statistics. Page 139.

64 U.S. Senate Judiciary Committee, August 29 and December 11, 1990, Senate Hearing 101-939, p.1, 12.

65 Andrew Klein, Terri Tobin, Amy Salomon and Janice Dubois, J. "A Statewide Profile of Abuse of Older Women and the Criminal Justice Response," (Sudbury MA, Advocates for Human Potential Inc., 12/26/2007).

66 Claire Matchwick, Rachel Domone, Iracema Leroi and Jane Simpson, "Perceptions of Cause and Control in People with Alzheimer's Disease," *The Gerontologist,* 54, no. 2, (2013): 268-276, doi: 10-1093/geront/gnt014

67 National Center for Health Statistics. National Vital Statistics System. Multiple cause-of-death files accessed http://www.cdc.gov/nchs/data_access/Vitalstatsonline.htm

68 John M. Grohol, "The Tragic Suicide Death of Junior Seau," *Psych Central Online (2012)* accessed http://psychcentral.com/blog/archives/2012/05/04/the-tragic-suicide-death-of-junior-seau

69 Jason Medina, "Muhammad Ali's Battle Against Parkinson's Syndrome: Is Boxing to Blame?" (2012) accessed http://voices.yahoo.com/shared/print.shtml?content_type=article&content_type_id=436969

70 Muhammad Ali Parkinson Center, http://www.thebarrow.org/Neurological_Services/Muhammad_Ali_Parkinson_Center/index.htm

71 John Hart, Jr., M.D. "Frontotemporal Dementia," accessed December 20, 2014 http://www.cdc.gov/nchs/ppt/icd9/attachment3.ppt

72 Landro, Laura. "The Informed Patient: The Importance of Trying to be a Good Patient," *The Wall Street Journal Online*, 4/29/2009 accessed http://www.online.wsj.com/article/SB124096023780965817 on 10/17/2012

73 Claire Matchwick, Rachel Domone, Iracema Leroi and Jane Simpson, "Perceptions of Cause and Control in People with Alzheimer's Disease," *The Gerontologist*, 54, no. 2, (2013): 268-276, doi: 10-1093/geront/gnt014

74 David Johnson, Michelle Niedens, Jessica Wilson, Lora Swartzendruber, Amy Yeager and Kelly Jones K. "Treatment Outcomes of a Crisis Intervention Program for Dementia with Severe Psychiatric Complications: The Kansas Bridge Project," *The Gerontologist* 53(1) (2013): 102-112, doi: 10.1093/geront/gns104

75 Becca Levy, Pil Chung, P.H., Talya Bedford and Kristina Navrazhina, "Facebook as a Site for Negative Age Stereotypes," *The Gerontologist*, 54, no. 2 (2013): 172-176, doi:10:1093,geront/gns194

76 "Badge of Honor or Recipe for Disaster? The Importance of Adequate Sleep for Nurses," The Free Library (2014) accessed June 14, 2014 http://www.thefreelibrary.com/Badge+of+honor+or+recipe+for+disaster%3f+The+Importance+of+adequate a0200506322

Index